The Censorship of British Drama 1900–1968

Volume Three: The Fifties

This is the third volume of Steve Nicholson's analysis of British theatre censorship from 1900 until 1968. The books are based on previously undocumented material in the Lord Chamberlain's Correspondence Archives.

The book charts the early struggles with Royal Court writers such as John Osborne and with Joan Littlewood and Theatre Workshop; the stand offs with Samuel Beckett and with leading American dramatists; the Lord Chamberlain's determination to keep homosexuality off the stage, which turned him into a laughing stock when he was unable to prevent a private theatre club in London's West End from staging a series of American plays he had banned, including Arthur Miller's *A View from the Bridge* and Tennessee Williams's *Cat on a Hot Tin Roof*; and the Lord Chamberlain's attempts to persuade the government to give him new powers and to rewrite the law.

This definitive survey has been expanded to four volumes: Volume Three covers 1953–1960; a fourth volume will cover the period 1960–1968.

Steve Nicholson is Reader in Twentieth-Century and Contemporary Theatre at the University of Sheffield and has published extensively in the areas of politics and theatre in Britain in the twentieth century, and of theatre censorship. He is the author of *British Theatre and the Red Peril: The Portrayal of Communism, 1917–1945* (UEP, 1999) and is a series editor of *Exeter Performance Studies*.

Exeter Performance Studies

Series editors: Peter Thomson, Professor of Drama at the University of Exeter; Graham Ley, Professor of Drama and Theory at the University of Exeter; Steve Nicholson, Reader in Twentieth-Century Contemporary Theatre at the University of Sheffield.

From Mimesis to Interculturalism: Readings of Theatrical Theory Before and After 'Modernism'
Graham Ley (1999)

British Theatre and the Red Peril: The Portrayal of Communism 1917–1945
Steve Nicholson (1999)

On Actors and Acting
Peter Thomson (2000)

Grand-Guignol: The French Theatre of Horror
Richard J. Hand and Michael Wilson (2002)

The Censorship of British Drama 1900–1968: Volume One 1900–1932
Steve Nicholson (2003)

The Censorship of British Drama 1900–1968: Volume Two 1933–1952
Steve Nicholson (2005)

Freedom's Pioneer: John McGrath's Work in Theatre, Film and Television
edited by David Bradby and Susanna Capon (2005)

John McGrath: Plays for England
selected and introduced by Nadine Holdsworth (2005)

Theatre Workshop: Joan Littlewood and the Making of Modern British Theatre
Robert Leach (2006)

Making Theatre in Northern Ireland: Through and Beyond the Troubles
Tom Maguire (2006)

"In Comes I": Performance, Memory and Landscape
Mike Pearson (2006)

London's Grand Guignol and the Theatre of Horror
Richard J Hand and Michael Wilson (2007)

Theatres of the Troubles: Theatre, Resistance and Liberation in Ireland
Bill McDonnell (2008)

Previous volumes in Steve Nicholson's survey of British theatre censorship

The Censorship of British Drama 1900–1968 Volume One, 1900–1932
2003 360 pp. ISBN: 978 0 85989 638 2

The Censorship of British Drama 1900–1968 Volume Two, 1933–1952
2005 440pp. ISBN: 978 0 85989 697 9

Forthcoming (2012)

The Censorship of British Drama 1900–1968 Volume Four, The Sixties
288pp approx. ISBN: 978 0 85989 846 1

From the reviews of Volumes One and Two:

"... offers a highly readable, intelligent, and good-humoured account of
the complex intersection of historical, political, social, and cultural forces
that influenced censorship during this period. The writing is lively,
authoritative, and full of wonderful detail acquired during Nicholson's
meticulous research into the Lord Chamberlain's theatre and correspondence
archives ..."   *Modern Drama*

"Nicholson is very readable. He tells a good story, both chronologically
and in the many accounts of particular wrangles, campaigns, negotiations,
paradoxes and outrages. ... he uses correspondence to give palpable life to
human agencies within institutional structures. ... this is also both a work of
reference—it efficiently points us to particular records—and a fine work of
synthesis and summary—Nicholson has done the legwork for a community
of scholars."   *Theatre Research International*

"Steve Nicholson's heroic archival work has resulted in the extraordinary
and consistently rich detail contained within these two volumes. ... Everyone
studying twentieth-century British theatre should have access to these
volumes, and Nicholson should be given an award for sifting so painstakingly
through the thousands of archive files which document the archaic process
of censorship which held such power over what the public were permitted to
see in the theatre until 1968."   *New Theatre Quarterly*

The Censorship of British Drama 1900–1968

Volume Three: The Fifties

Steve Nicholson

UNIVERSITY
of
EXETER
PRESS

First published in 2011 by
University of Exeter Press
Reed Hall, Streatham Drive
Exeter EX4 4QR
UK
www.exeterpress.co.uk

British Library Cataloguing in Publication Data
A catalogue record for this book is available
from the British Library

ISBN 978 0 85989 750 1

Typeset in Plantin by Carnegie Book Production, Lancaster
Printed in Great Britain by T. J. International, Padstow

Contents

Acknowledgements

I would like to thank the following for their support, assistance and contributions to the research and the writing of this book:

The Arts and Humanities Research Council, whose grants were crucial in allowing me time (and funds) to research and complete this book.

The Society for Theatre Research and the University of Sheffield, both of whom also made generous grants to assist the process of research and publication.

Kathryn Johnson, Curator of Modern Drama at the British Library and an expert at navigating the Lord Chamberlain's archives.

Staff in the Manuscript Room of the British Library and the Study Room of the Theatre Museum.

Queen Elizabeth II for granting me permission to read and make use of material in the Royal Archive at Windsor.

Staff in the Royal Archive, especially the Registrar, Miss Pamela Clark.

University of Exeter Press and its Editorial Board, especially Simon Baker, Peter Thomson and Graham Ley.

And to Heather, Katya, Vikka and Pushkin.

'That Happy State'

In 1959, an undergraduate student at Cambridge University wrote to the Lord Chamberlain's Office requesting information about theatre censorship for an article in a student magazine. He was particularly keen to know whether there was a clear policy specifying exactly what was allowed and what forbidden. In reply, Norman Gwatkin, the Assistant Comptroller at St James's Palace, told him that 'any written code of rules or precedents would be much too inflexible an instrument of control'. Gwatkin had no hesitation in revealing the principle of law through which the Office carried out its duties:

> The system followed by the Act is therefore to nominate as Censor someone who, by reason of the other duties of his Office, may reasonably be held to be experienced in the world, and to leave him to exercise his unfettered judgment as to what would be harmful.
> It is a personal censorship.[1]

While the Lord Chamberlain's detractors were not being completely fair when they claimed that his primary functions were organising Buckingham Palace garden parties and looking after the Queen's swans, it is still not immediately apparent how his 'other duties' necessarily equipped him to rule on what it was permissible to say and do on the public stage.

Of course, Gwatkin's statement did not reveal the whole truth. Certainly it was the Lord Chamberlain (at this time Roger Lumley, the eleventh Earl of Scarbrough) who signed the licences and took responsibility for all the decisions, and certainly his personal views—not to mention his tastes and whims—were a significant factor. Yet Lords Chamberlain through the twentieth century frequently sought advice from government ministers, civil servants, foreign ambassadors, religious leaders, the police, medical experts, members of the Royal Household, and anybody else whose opinion they considered worth having. They also paid attention to the views of their Examiners of Plays and other staff, and were never short of unsolicited opinions from members of the public, MPs, journalists, theatre critics, theatre managers, playwrights, or campaigning organisations such as the Public Morality Council.

It would also be slightly misleading to suggest that no written code existed. As far back as 1909, a Joint Select Committee set up by the government to consider whether to reform the system of theatre censorship had recommended that the Lord Chamberlain should be bound to approve a play unless it committed one of several categories of offence:

> It should be his duty to license any play submitted to him unless he considers that it may reasonably be held—
>
> To be indecent;
>
> To contain offensive personalities;
>
> To represent on the stage in an invidious manner a living person, or any person recently dead;
>
> To do violence to the sentiment of religious reverence;
>
> To be calculated to conduce to crime or vice;
>
> To be calculated to impair friendly relations with any foreign Power; or
>
> To be calculated to cause a breach of the peace.[2]

Inevitably, these terms were open to multiple—almost infinite—interpretations, and because no legislation was ever enacted the Lord Chamberlain remained technically free of any restraints on his powers. But in day-to-day practice, Lords Chamberlain would have claimed that these seven injunctions formed the basis of the policy on which they acted.

Another recommendation made by the 1909 Committee had been that a licence should be optional, and that theatre managers should have the right to present an unlicensed play if they wished, taking their chance over prosecution and possible conviction. While this proposal, too, had been officially ignored, the tacit consent given by successive Lords Chamberlain (and by the Director of Public Prosecutions) to the establishment of 'private clubs' presenting unlicensed plays to paying 'members' was in part an accommodation of this recommendation. And yet this principle of exception was built on the most dubious of foundations. The assiduous Cambridge student, not yet satisfied in his research by the reply he had received, wrote a second letter to St James's Palace to enquire specifically about the status of private performances. Again, Gwatkin's reply was almost disarmingly open: 'To say the least of it,' he explained, 'the alleged immunity of the so-called "private" theatre does not seem to stand upon a very firm legal footing.' The fact was that nobody really knew what freedom—if any—the law allowed, and the Assistant Comptroller told his correspondent that in order to resolve the issue one way or the other, 'a pronouncement of the High Court would seem to be required'; as he went on rather acidly to observe: 'so far this has not been forthcoming'.[3] What everyone interested in theatre and censorship did know was that a few years earlier the policy of discreetly allowing small clubs to put on usually obscure plays to minority audiences had been effectively blown out of the water when the Watergate Theatre Club combined with a major West End Theatre to present a series of plays by well-known American authors which the Lord Chamberlain had refused to license. This had raised a fundamental challenge and created a profound problem for the Censorship from which it would never fully recover. After all, what, now, was to stop any theatre from turning itself temporarily into a club, incorporating membership fees within the price of its tickets, and then performing anything it wanted to anyone who wanted to witness it?

Hostility towards and mockery of the Lord Chamberlain as Censor of Plays reached new heights during the 1950s. In particular, the Office came under concerted attack from some theatre managers and from a (relatively) liberal press, which was quite effectively—even cynically—manipulated by a new generation of playwrights and theatre directors. From the Lord Chamberlain's point of view, such people accepted neither the basic rules of the game nor the right of a social elite to referee it. Reading through some of the files now, the surprising thing is not that the system of theatre censorship should have been abolished in 1968, but rather that it managed to hang on so long. By the end of the fifties, its condition was clearly terminal.

This is the third of four volumes which set out to chart in greater detail than ever before a history of British theatre in relation to the control exerted by the Lord Chamberlain's Office between 1900 and 1968. The first volume covered the period up until 1933, and the second extended the story to 1952. That leaves only sixteen years before the system was finally dismantled with the passing of a new Theatres Act. Yet the various narratives of those sixteen years, and the richness of the details, are such that to tell their story requires the space offered by two further volumes. Not only are there the recurring and frequently bitter hand-to-hand struggles with upstart managements and authors over individual texts to consider—some of them now widely known and celebrated—but also the broader movements and campaigns, the advances and retreats, the surrenders and the shifts of position, the disputes over policy and strategy within the Lord Chamberlain's Office, the attempts to persuade governments to either amend their powers or else relieve them of the responsibility.

As with previous volumes, the bulk of the research for this book has taken place in three related archive collections. Every play submitted for licence (perhaps 1,000 per year) has a file devoted to it. Those files are now held in the Lord Chamberlain's Correspondence archive in the Manuscript Room of the British Library. Some files are thin, containing little more than the report, synopsis and comments supplied by the Lord Chamberlain's

Reader. Others are extensive and may contain a range of correspondence, memoranda, reports, letters, lists of amendments and cuts required, details of negotiations, and polite—or sometimes explicit—abuse. It has been my pleasure (well, sort of) to read through every file in the Correspondence archive. Furthermore, perhaps the great benefit of the system of censorship is that a copy of the script of every play licensed was retained at St James's Palace, and has survived for consultation. These scripts (the vast majority of them unpublished and unavailable elsewhere) are housed in a separate archive at the British Library—the Lord Chamberlain's Collection of Licensed Plays, 1900–1968.) The third source of which I have made extensive use is that section of the Royal Archive which is devoted to the Lord Chamberlain and theatre censorship, and which is currently held at Windsor Castle. The files here contain further and sometimes extensive correspondence, memoranda and materials relating to broader aspects of theatre censorship rather than to individual play titles.

In the earlier volumes, it seemed most useful to separate the material into sections by date, and then to divide each section into chapters focusing on different themes—moral, political, sexual, and so on. Although the period covered in this present volume is so much shorter, the combination of a chronological with a thematic approach still seems appropriate. So **Chapters One** and **Two** focus on the first couple of years of the new Elizabethan age, from 1953 until the end of 1955. One concentrates on a broad range of topics, Two on the single issue which recurred most frequently and provoked the most heated arguments—namely, homosexuality. Chapters **Three, Four, Five** and **Six** all take different perspectives on the years between 1956 and 1958; Three charts the undermining of the Lord Chamberlain's authority by the expansion of private Theatre Clubs into the West End, and his failed attempt to persuade the government to introduce new legislation; **Four** picks up from Chapter Two and looks at the continuing struggles and shifting ground over references to homosexuality, and the Lord Chamberlain's eventual capitulation and change of policy. **Chapter Five** then concentrates on a series of high-profile clashes with some of the more provocative and innovative theatre makers associated with the Royal Court and Theatre Workshop, and **Chapter Six** examines censorship practice in these same years in relation to Religion, International Politics and Sexuality. Finally, **Chapter Seven** discusses some of the key arguments and debates which arose in the final year of the decade.

A recent study focused on the moments in theatre censorship history when actual or potential legislation was discussed attributes the longevity of the system to 'inertia' on the part of the body politic.[4] There is a strong element of truth in this. Yet the term 'inertia' seems also to deny that governments had any reason—any motivation or self-interest—for maintaining the system, and I would question that assertion. (It is often valuable to a legislative authority to have outside and 'independent' bodies onto which it can deflect certain responsibilities, ensuring that those bodies must then absorb some of the abuse and unpopularity to which the authority itself might otherwise have been subjected.)The Government is not much bothered by criticisms of the Lord Chamberlain,' wrote Scarbrough, and 'it will very likely think it would be asking for trouble to change that happy state of insulation.'[5] Quite so.

In 1957, Scarbrough approached the Queen to seek approval for his efforts to persuade the government to put theatre censorship reform firmly on the political agenda. He also began a 'top secret' internal memorandum to his staff by stating that: 'The first question to consider is whether the censorship of stage plays should be abolished completely,' and went on to rehearse six justifications for abolition—and only four arguments for retention. It is worth quoting this document at length:

The arguments in favour appear to be—

a) That no other country has a system of censorship …

b) That any form of censorship is out of date, and out of tune with modern life. Those who hold this view are vocal and I would say quite numerous, and for them it is one of the fundamental requirements of a free society.

c) That with complete freedom of expression in the Press, and, with few exceptions, in books, it is difficult to justify the continuance of a censorship for plays.

d) That more plays about subjects at present forbidden will be written, some of them good plays, that more and more criticism will be heard if they are banned, and that this will eventually end in the abolition of the censorship.

e) That theatre clubs, unless controlled, will make the censorship a farce.

f) That a natural desire to avoid giving material to the critics will tend to make the censorship ineffective and its continuance therefore unjustified.

The arguments against complete abolition seem to be—

g) That to give complete freedom to those who want to exploit sex in its many forms will arouse a storm of protest and will be regarded as a surrender to unrestrained immorality.

h) That managers and producers would oppose abolition if it left them at the mercy of every local authority in this country.

j) That there are other subjects besides sex which need control, eg royalty, foreign heads of state, living persons, blasphemy.

k) That the tone of the British theatre which at present helps to place London in the first rank, as far as the stage is concerned, will be lowered.[6]

In the end, it was not the Lord Chamberlain who insisted on retaining theatre censorship into another decade, but government ministers who refused to bring the matter to parliament for debate.

This present volume begins just after the Earl of Scarbrough had taken up the staff of office, and with the inauguration of a promised golden age of peace and prosperity to be ushered in by the coronation of Queen Elizabeth II. It ends as the decade—or, perhaps, the decayed—of the 1960s supplanted it. In those seven years between 1953 and 1959, much shifted in Britain, not least in theatre and in theatre censorship. John Osborne arrived on the scene—a 'silly little man', as the Assistant Comptroller called him. So too Brecht ('the darling and standard-bearer of the left'), Beckett ('a conceited ass'), Pinter ('My God! How boring he is'), Ionesco ('a member of the Dustbin School of dramatists'), and Tennessee Williams ('Strindberg at his battiest'). Not to mention 'The unspeakable M. Genet'. There were bruising and bloody clashes between St James's Palace and Theatre Workshop ('The fingering of a woman's bottom is typical of this crowd, who preach intellectuality but introduce as much of the worst carnality as they dare'), including an embarrassing day in court ('they all lied'); also with George Devine and the Royal Court ('much too shrewd to take on the Lord Chamberlain, except on favourable ground'). There had been a reluctant capitulation by Scarbrough after years of striving to keep all references to homosexuality off the stage ('We will allow the word "pansy", but not the word "bugger"'). There had, too, been the refusal to allow the innovative theatre director Stephen Joseph to experiment with 'a more creative form of presentation' in which 'there will never be any fixed script'—a refusal which would surely be challenged again.[7]

Such examples are no more than the partially visible tip of a very large iceberg. Among the several thousand scripts submitted for licence between 1953 and 1959, only a few were banned outright and in their entirety. But, predictably, many others were approved only after cuts and amendments of all sorts had been imposed—of text, of action, of tone, of costume, of lighting, of casting; even of volume and the placing of pauses. The law required that the script of every new drama to be presented on any public stage—amateur or professional, in theatres, halls, schools or anywhere else—must first be approved and licensed by the Lord Chamberlain. He managed to evade taking responsibility for ice-skating shows ('a mode of entertainment not catered for by the Theatres Act'),[8] performances by puppets ('there is a considerable distinction between a "live" performance of a play and its representation by Marionettes')[9] and revues containing strip-teases but no sketches ('purely visual acts … are subject to no special censorship law').[10] Even so, that still left hundreds of scripts to rule on every year. Not to mention having to decide on such crucial matters as whether it was permissible for an artist to perform on stage naked beneath his kilt—('Any performer appearing in a stage play without underpants would ... have to do so with the knowledge that he would be held absolutely responsible for any act of exposure whether inadvertent or deliberate').[11]

Of course, the Lord Chamberlain still had his defenders. In November 1956—at the height of the Watergate rebellion—Horace Collins wrote an editorial for *Theatre Industry*, denying that censorship had ever had any significant impact or adverse effect on the stage:

> Having seen most of the plays presented during a period of over half a century ... I have no hesitation in testifying that the Lord Chamberlain's mild control has not prevented, in my opinion, any stage masterpiece from seeing the light of day. A play of merit may have been held in abeyance as not being suitable to the particular times or considered harmful to public morality but eventually as public opinion changed or, as some would have it, became more advanced the veto was removed ...
>
> I do not believe that the work of any author has suffered by the Censor's taboo because if the author is a skilful playwright and knows stage routine he can easily alter and adapt his script to suit official requirements—he need not be fettered by this slight Government supervision.[12]

On another occasion, the Secretary of the West End Managers Association, Chapman Mortimer, called at St James's with a draft version of an article he was writing for his organisation's journal, which was intended to refute accusations of repression, and reassert the value and indispensability of the Censor. Mortimer proposed that a 'just and accurate description' of 'the Lord Chamberlain's so called censorship' would be 'to say that the Lord Chamberlain and his staff relieve Dramatists and theatrical producers of the laborious and costly burden of undertaking themselves the task of ensuring that the play does not offend'. Again, he refuted any suggestion that censorship had 'a cramping effect' on the author's imagination:

> Having regard to the subject matter and dramatic action in some of the plays presented during the last 20 years the alleged inhibitions of unknown authors cannot be great and the number of 'excellent plays' stifled at birth almost certainly nil.

Surprisingly, Gwatkin seems not to have appreciated this act of sycophancy: 'The article was tedious,' he reported; 'He was more interested in the general moral decline of everything from Church and Parliament to stage and individuals.' By 1958 Mortimer's ringing endorsement of the status quo was no longer helpful: 'I think he was against any alteration in the Censorship except that we should tighten things up,' wrote the Assistant Comptroller; 'He struck me as quite the wrong chap in the right place.'[13] Though they would never say so publicly, most of the senior staff in the Lord Chamberlain's Office probably thought of themselves either as the right chaps in the wrong place, or possibly even the wrong chaps in the wrong place. As society and theatre shifted around them through the 1950s, they knew, perhaps better than anyone, that their situation was becoming truly absurd.

CHAPTER ONE

Censorship in a Golden Age

I am to say that his Lordship is surprised to find his ruling so blatantly evaded. Considerably more liberty can be allowed to those producers who can be trusted to comply with his Lordship's requirements than to those who cannot, and I am sure that you would not wish to be placed in that category for which inflexible administration of the letter of the Theatres Act is the only possibility.

Letter from the Assistant Comptroller in the
Lord Chamberlain's Office to theatre manager, June 1953[1]

Politics and the Coronation

By far the most spectacular performance event of 1953 took place at Westminster Abbey on 2 June, with Elizabeth Windsor appearing in the title role. The stage directions of the official script for her coronation indicate that the Queen processed 'through the choir, and so up the steps to the Theatre', accompanied by Psalm 122. Once there, she was required to 'turn and show herself unto the People at every of the four sides of the Theatre'.[2] As Head of the Royal Household, the Lord Chamberlain followed her in the 250-strong star-studded Procession, alongside such dignitaries as the Rouge Dragon Pursuivant, the Harbinger and the Gold-Stick-in-Waiting. Directed by the Duke of Norfolk, the performance was meant to impress. Indeed, it had been delayed for some sixteen months after Elizabeth's ascent, in order to allow sufficient time for preparations and rehearsals. Widely heralded as the inauguration of a new golden age for Britain, the Coronation was also a Lehrstück, designed to reinforce a set of ideological values, and to confirm that all was right with the world.

In his history of the fifties, Dominic Sandbrook cites claims confidently made in the *Daily Express* in 1955 that Britain was 'an essentially satisfied country', and by an American sociologist who referred to 'the contentment of British society', and declared that 'scarcely anyone here … seems any longer to feel there is anything fundamentally wrong'.[3] While this image of pre-Suez Britain as a nation complacently united and at ease with itself may be partially true, some of the arguments and tensions visible in the debates around the control of live performance remind us that things were not quite so straightforward.

The Earl of Scarbrough (KG, PC, GCSI, GCVO, former Governor of Bombay and Grand Master of the United Grand Lodge of Masons of England) had taken up the post of Lord Chamberlain the year before the Coronation. While awaiting his entrance in the wings on 2 June, he may perhaps have taken an opportunity to consult with George A. Titman, a former secretary in the Lord Chamberlain's Office who was now taking a break from inspecting the quantity and parameters of breasts at the Windmill Theatre, to appear at the Coronation in his role of Serjeant-at-Arms. Just a few days earlier, Scarbrough had received a letter addressed to the Queen from a Mr Hossain in Pakistan. Signing himself 'Your Majesty's loyal subject', Mr Hossain was the President of a minority Muslim sect, and the margins of his letter were adorned with quotations (printed, by coincidence, in the famous blue of the Lord Chamberlain's pencil) from a range of religious texts, including the Holy Quran and the sayings of the Buddha. The letter itself was motivated by newspaper accounts of recent clashes between the Lord Chamberlain and the Public Morality Council over the persistence and rise of stage nudity; its acceptance, said the report, had 'led to many second rate touring revues making this their box of lice [sic] attraction'. Mr Hossain drew a political link which perhaps neither the Lord Chamberlain or even the Council had previously noted:

> Surprised to read Reuters report (cutting enclosed) that female nudity is displayed in British theatre. From this it appears that a section of British people is devoid of human propriety and the principles of communal and social life. They are, to our estimation, in no-way better than communists. They are in the eyes of we religionists who believe in the Brother-hood of man and the Father-hood of God surely enemy to mankind.
>
> Your Majesty, communism is the greatest curse of the present age. Communism enters where religion banishes [sic]. Woman is the half of religion. Communism flourishes where nackededness [sic] and hoarding prevail. True religion is the first 'Defence Line' against communism.

Mr Hossain obsequiously pinned his faith on the new dawn: 'Your Majesty's cornation [sic] will be ever remembered if Your Majesty on the day of Your Majesty's coronation declare Your Majesty's PIOUS WISH for cessation of female nudity in British theatre and cinema.'[4] Scarbrough may well have sought the advice of the legendary Mr Titman as to how he might best respond.

The Abbey Procession also featured many visiting statesmen from within the Commonwealth—including the recently 'elected' Doctor the Hon. Daniel F. Malan from South Africa. Did Malan, perhaps, try to catch a word with the Earl of Scarbrough, or did they avoid each other's eyes? In the days before the Coronation, both had been embarrassed by the publicity surrounding an item in a West End revue. On 23 May, the *Daily Express* reported that

> With Dr Malan, South Africa's race-conscious PM arriving in London for the Coronation next week, South Africa House is bitterly indignant over the song 'A Plea' sung by coloured Marie Bryant in the new revue at the London Hippodrome.
>
> When I saw it the other night ('Don't malign Malan, he's doing the best he can') it produced some of the loudest applause of the whole evening. But says a South Africa House spokesman: 'This is a dirty rotten thing. It is hitting below the belt. What do these people think they are doing? Did the Lord Chamberlain really pass this offensive and disgraceful attack?
>
> 'Dr Malan is arriving in Britain in a few days time, and so the timing of this production could scarcely be more marked and more insulting to our PM.' [5]

Sandwiched between a gentle satire on Coronation preparations in Bognor Regis and a song about a soldier at Buckingham Palace fainting because his corset is too tight, *A Plea* seems mild enough. But it was a red rag to the South African government:

CHORUS:	Don't malign Malan!
	Because he dislikes our tan.
A:	We know that it's wrong to have skin that's all brown
B:	And wrong to be born on the wrong side of town.
C:	It's quite right that our filthy old homes be burned down.
TOGETHER:	Malan is a wonderful man!
	Don't malign Malan!
	He's doing the best he can!
B:	He's keeping us all out of white politics
C:	And from all that we've heard of political tricks
A:	We'd rather stay happy on straw without bricks!
TOGETHER:	Malan is a wonderful man!
	Don't malign Malan!
	For since his protection began
A:	Each Indian, Zulu and Kaffir boy cheers
B:	Whenever the lovable Doctor appears.
C:	What if we have gone back two hundred years?
TOGETHER:	Malan is a wonderful man!

And the sketch ends with a telling irony when a white man, who has been asleep on a bench, wakes up and declares forcefully:

> WHITE: Listen—if you don't like our country—why don't you go back where you came from?
>   BLACK OUT[6]

Recommending a licence for Edinburgh in March, the Lord Chamberlain's Office had failed to foresee any problem: 'At last a funny revue', had been the Reader's main comment.[7] But in Coronation London it was a different matter. The *Daily Express* deliberately stirred things up, contacting St James's Palace to inform them that South Africa House was 'extremely incensed' about the song, and 'that their indignation was deepened by the fact that Dr Malan was coming to the Coronation'. The Lord Chamberlain's secretary met this with the traditional English dead bat, carefully explaining that the Lord Chamberlain's licence 'was no indication of whether he approved or disapproved any sentiments expressed in it' but 'merely indicated that the play was not unfit for the public to see'.[8] St James's Palace was experienced enough to know that making an issue of something they had already licensed was generally counter-productive, and led to more publicity and public debate. That is why a system of pre-censorship was so important; the trick was to try and spot the contentious elements and suppress them in advance. Once missed, the best strategy was to avoid fanning the fire, and hope the affair would soon 'fizzle out'. When the danger of drawing more attention to the show was pointed out to the South Africans, the Embassy claimed to have been stung by the *Express*, and suggested the quotations published had been fabricated or distorted. As Scarbrough discreetly noted, they accepted his advice:

> I spoke to the High Commissioner on the telephone. He took the view that more publicity would be caused if I intervened and he preferred to ignore the matter. I pointed out that a 'spokesman from South Africa House' had already said a good deal and he was surprised and annoyed.

Nevertheless, Scarbrough was not impressed by the laxness of his own staff. He had signed a licence for the revue on the recommendation of his Reader, and without reading the script, so now he was inclined to apportion blame: 'I think,' he wrote in a memorandum, 'that attention might have been drawn when the play was submitted to the song.'[9] Such an evident ticking off was doubtless sufficient to ensure a tightening of policy and help ensure that any subsequent criticisms of the South African government would be more effectively silenced. Indeed, in an impassioned public debate on theatre censorship in 1956, the main apologist for the system, the theatre impresario Henry Sherek was asked 'whether the Lord Chamberlain would ban a play attacking apartheid in South Africa'. As the press reported: 'Mr Sherek thought he would, and a good thing, too.'[10] His assumption was almost certainly correct.

The Royal Protector

What could and could not be permitted on stage, then, was of as much importance at the start of Elizabeth II's reign as during that of her namesake, four hundred years earlier. Not the least important task was to preserve the sanctity of the monarchy itself. Thus in May 1953, Scarbrough had insisted on amending the libretto of Benjamin Britten's new opera *Gloriana*, which was to be staged at the Royal Opera House in honour of the Coronation. The difficulty was a scene in which 'a housewife empties a chamber pot from her window over one of the characters'. As the Reader pointed out, 'This is not, in any sense, germane to the plot', and the Queen must be protected from any possible embarrassment.

> I do not see why Her Majesty (who will be attending the premiere) should be confronted with an incident that we would not permit even the Crazy Gang to get away with. The pot can easily be changed for a basin or other less intimate vessel.[11]

Depicting the monarchy on stage was even more problematic. Few if any playwrights would have been ready to consider writing the current Queen into a list of characters, but what of her predecessors and her family? In July 1953, someone tentatively sent the Lord Chamberlain the synopsis of a hypothetical musical he planned to write: 'We should like to have the approval of your office before going ahead.' The plot would centre on 'a young and unmarried English princess ... in the not too distant future', but while it would have some contemporary reference points, the setting would be fantastical:

> The idea that we wish to convey is that of a modern Ruritanian romance taking place in London; allied to a satire on present day international politics. In no way is the Princess Caroline meant to ressemble [sic] Princess Margaret.
>   To ensure this we have:
>   a) Made the whole a fairy story ...
>   b) Omitted all other members of this mythical royal family from the cast.

Scarbrough quashed the idea at the outset:

The prospective authors might be thanked for consulting us in advance
and told that at the present time I would have some difficulty in granting
a licence for a play of this nature and that I suspect that it would be better
if they did not proceed with the idea.[12]

On the other hand, an absolute consistency was not feasible. A year
earlier, Tyrone Guthrie at the Old Vic had been advised that the Lord
Chamberlain was 'absolutely certain that no play about King Edward
VII, how ever seriously handled, would be passed'.[13] In September 1953,
however, a Mr. Lipscom submitted the synopsis of a proposed play which
included Edward among its cast. The Comptroller, Terence Nugent, recognised that the automatic ban created difficulties and might lay the Office
open to criticisms:

> We are, I feel, on not a very good wicket about this because plays about
> Queen Victoria were in fact allowed in 1937—i.e. thirty six years after
> her death, whereas King Edward VII has been dead for forty three years.
> Further, in 1937 there were still three of Queen Victoria's children alive ...
> but all King Edward VII's children have been dead these past fifteen years.

Yet he recognised that any vaguely accurate portrayal of Edward's life style
might be damaging:

> I think we shall have to be careful as to what reason we give for refusing
> Mr Lipscom. The real reason, of course, which we cannot very well put on
> paper, is that King Edward VII's life lends itself to much more indelicate
> representation than Queen Victoria's ever did.

While this particular script might be discreet and harmless, it risked
establishing a precedent:

> You may be very sure that there will very soon be plays in which
> Mrs George Keppel, Lilly Langtry, Lady Warwick and several of King
> Edward's more intimate friends flit through the gaming rooms of Tranby
> Croft! I am sure, therefore, that it would be too dangerous to encourage
> playwrights to use this theme yet a while.

Nugent concluded that the best way of dealing with the problem was 'to
be very vague' in their response. And so they were.

> Lord Scarbrough has read your synopsis, but although he sympathises
> with your desire to write a play on so interesting a subject, he regrets to

have to tell you that the time has not yet come for allowing plays about so recent a monarch.[14]

That should do it.

In November, the Office received the script for a 'rather tired revue' featuring 'a devastating parody' of Anna Neagle's portrayal of the Queen in *Victoria the Great*, a classic and hugely successful film which had been released in the previous coronation year of 1937. Heriot, the Lord Chamberlain's Reader, saw no objection, since the subject of the parody was not Victoria herself: 'I don't see why we shouldn't permit a caricature of a caricature—the impersonation ... is of Miss Neagle rather than the Queen.' But for Scarbrough this was too nice a distinction:

> Anything which brings Queen Victoria into ridicule does not come within the permission which can be granted. Although this sketch purports to take off Miss Neagle, in fact it ridicules Queen Victoria & must come out.[15]

Then there were re-enactments of royal ceremonials to worry about. In April 1953, the Home Office wrote to the Lord Chamberlain's Office:

> The Buckingham Palace people have sent us the enclosed letter from a schoolteacher who has submitted a script (also enclosed) for a pageant which involves the use of certain representations of regalia, and we wondered whether this was a matter about which you would wish to express any views?

The script also featured extracts from an actual speech by the Queen previously broadcast on the radio. It is doubtful whether the law was as clearcut as he suggested, but the Comptroller advised that they should steer carefully:

> As the pageant is to be produced at a School Open-Day, it is being performed in circumstances beyond the control of the Theatres Act, and we cannot intervene if we would. In any case the use of the Regalia is a legitimate one and we should not wish to interfere.
>
> As to the chorus repeating The Queen's Speech, I doubt whether you have the power to forbid, but it is, I think, up to the Private Secretary and to you to decide whether you suggest that it be not used, or whether you use that time honoured phrase 'permission can neither be granted nor withheld'.[16]

Slightly more problematic was a re-enactment of the Coronation at Blackpool within *The Ice Parade of 1953*. Ice shows were the latest craze,

'By far the greatest new factor in live entertainment outside the legitimate theatre', and the cuckoo in the nest of popular entertainment. The issue here was whether the original solemnity and dignity of Westminster Abbey would be damaged by

> a much magnified and accelerated pantomime on a 'stage' 200 feet by 100 feet which can play to an immense audience, the singers and speakers miming and mouthing on the ice while a shadow cast and chorus provide the words and music through microphones and loud-speakers.[17]

St James's Palace only became aware of this particular event when a member of the public who had witnessed it wrote to complain that the performance undermined the seriousness of the occasion and the authority of those involved:

> Mindful of the solemnity and reverence of the Coronation Service and the dignity of our beloved Queen, it seemed horrible to witness a supposed imitation, in a stage setting of the altar etc. of Westminster Abbey. The person of Her Majesty is most unsuitably represented ... Imagine Archbishops—Bishops—peers and Her Majesty etc skating to and from the altar and the throne.

Always reluctant to extend his remit, the question for the Lord Chamberlain was whether he could avoid taking responsibility for ice-shows. After all, his predecessors had managed to define such theatrical forms as music-hall, ballet and marionettes as outside their control. No script had been submitted for the *Ice Parade*, and the Comptroller helpfully assured his Master that such performances could indeed be categorised as beyond the Lord Chamberlain's authority. However, Scarbrough's secretary, the vigilant Ronald Hill, questioned the basis for such an exclusion:

> After looking through this programme, I am quite sure that it would be possible to prove that Ice Parade of 1953 is an entertainment of the stage within the meaning of the Theatres Act, 1843, and therefore subject to censorship. Most scenes are sketches telling a complete story, and from what our correspondent says there is added dialogue ...
>
> We do already license 'Ice' versions of Stage Plays—e.g. ... Ice Pantomimes; the question now arises whether we should extend our authority to the new type of entertainment evolved.

Hill pointed out that since ice shows were essentially commercial enter-prises targeted at large family audiences, 'we are unlikely to experience anything very bad'. But he was in two minds about the principle. 'If we do exert our authority,' he noted, 'There will be something of an outcry that we are attempting to censor where we have no right to.' But if they held back now, there was a risk that 'Unsuitable shows may be put before the public', and intervention would then be problematic: 'Immunity from control will lead to the acquisition of vested rights by custom, and it will become increasingly difficult to assume control if found necessary to do so.' Moreover, that might not be the end of it: 'Sooner or later the immunity of this type of Ice Show will be used to indicate that ordinary Revues and border-line Road Shows should not be subject to the Lord Chamberlain.'

Scarbrough decided to ask Blackpool's Chief Constable to inspect the performance and advise him of 'the extent of the verbal part'. On being assured that 'the speech is dignified and reverent' and that 'the whole scene was received extremely well by the audience', he decided that ice-skating was 'a mode of entertainment not catered for by the Theatres Act', and that he held no responsibility for it. However, it remained 'very much a borderline case', and the door was left carefully ajar:

> Had the items requiring histrionic as opposed to skating skill been more numerous, the Lord Chamberlain would have had no hesitation in deciding that the performance was an entertainment of the Stage.[18]

Crimes and Punishments

The Coronation has often been evoked as epitomising a time of national achievement (Everest ... the Ashes ... the four-minute mile) and harmony. The country did not necessarily look quite so unified at the time. Reporting on *Wide Boy* in January 1953, the Lord Chamberlain's Reader remarked that 'The current wave of juvenile delinquency has inevitably been reflected on the stage'.[19] A week later, he found *Squatter* 'a somewhat unconvincing dramatic plea that bad housing conditions are a main factor conducing to crime'.[20] *Wide Boy* was renamed *Vice in the Streets*, and its promotional posters provoked angry complaints to the Home Office, the London County Council and the Lord Chamberlain's Office: 'as if the exposure of one of the greatest of our National evils could be "exciting"' instead of something that should send us to our knees to cry to God for mercy and forgiveness.' The Office defended the decision to license the play on the grounds that it was simply the latest manifestation of a current fashion, represented by such titles as *The Worst Woman in London*, *Sins of London*, *Degenerates*, *Why Girls Leave Home*, and *The Streets of London*. This latest example, they insisted, dealt with the subject 'in a proper manner and not in one calculated to lead to immorality or crime'.[21] However, the Reader, St Vincent Troubridge was more disturbed by *Lady for Hire*:

> This play, frankly disguised as a melodrama, is an <u>exposé</u> ... of the 'vice-racket', that is to say that the degree to which alien souteneurs control the prostitutes of the West End of London. It is almost certainly suggested by the recent trial and conviction of the Massena Brothers.

While the theme itself was not necessarily beyond the pale—'The subject is repulsive, but ... the play might be considered as denunciatory of these vicious aspects of Metropolitan life'—some of the action went too far:

> The real offence in this play lies in the scene of the flogging of Queenie ... the woman is dragged off struggling into her bedroom, with the final adjuration to 'give it to her good and hard', after which her screams, (plus presumably the thuds of the cane, though these do not receive mention) are heard.

Troubridge concluded that 'Though this sort of thing is now a commonplace of films, it is clearly impossible on the stage', and recommended that a licence should be dependent 'upon the condition of the removal of the entire flagellation episode'. Scarbrough was more lenient and precise:

> I do not think the whole beating up episode should be deleted, but a very strong warning should be given about the sounds heard while it is supposed to be going on. The radio should be turned on loud and soon enough to drown everything but—as a maximum—one strike.[22]

In February, Troubridge reported on *Lady of the House*:

> The last play I know of that had for its theme the lady turned brothel-keeper was refused a licence; its name was *Mrs. Warren's Profession* ... but that was in 1902 and we have come a long way since then, so the theme itself will not debar this play.

On the other hand, there were specific elements requiring intervention:

> Plays with brothel scenes are, however, tricky, the natural lubricity of the audience being aroused by the setting, and there are some matters in these brothel scenes ... that may call for alteration ...

One of these was a 'more or less immediate post-coition scene', which Troubridge felt was 'always objectionable (except in *Romeo and Juliet*)'. The use of a lit cigarette to deliberately burn a woman's shoulder was 'beyond the permissible bounds of sadism', while the suggestion that the brothel was owned by the Archbishop of Canterbury was clearly unacceptable. Surprisingly, the Office allowed the substitution of Florence Nightingale.[23]

In March, Troubridge worried about 'another of the numerous plays on the now fashionable theme of the "vice racket"'; this was *Women are My Business*:

> the point for decision is simply the exact degree of violence of a semi-sadistic nature that is nowadays permissible on the stage, how many times a woman may be struck in the face—(I should say once was enough)—and the current attitude to razor-slashing, kicking those who have been knocked down and the new gambit, imported from American detective fiction, of hitting a man in the face with the barrel of a revolver.

Yet in the end, violence proved less disturbing than sexuality; the only endorsement on the licence in this case being that one of the characters 'will not be played as an effeminate type'.[24]

Generally, all such 'vice' plays ended with the police triumphing and the villains getting their just desserts, allowing managers and playwrights to claim that they were essentially reinforcing a moral lesson. In early 1954, three Labour MPs—probably under pressure from their constituents—complained about *Ladies for Hire*, and particularly the advertising. As Hill reported:

> The complaint is one of a series concerning plays using the device of pointing a moral as an excuse for depicting vicious or sadistic incidents on the stage, and they are generally allowed as 'just passable'. The producers then give disproportionate advertisement to the most unpleasant parts, and publish posters which many people think harmful, especially now that these 'Edwardian' gangs are rampant.

He suggested that the root of the problem was that managers were now competing desperately for dwindling audiences in a commercial world.

> There are a number of theatres in London and the provinces, all financially very rocky, that exist only by catering for the lowest tastes, and they are driven by economic necessity to be, or to pretend to be 'red hot'. Such theatres specialise in 'Nude shows' and the 'vicious' melodramas of the type of *Ladies For Hire*.

But Hill recommended that it would be wise to try and steer clear of censoring advertisements:

> Our Theatre conditions give us power to ban posters that are conducive to immorality, but practically I do not think it is of much use. I think it would be most difficult and dangerous, perhaps every week, to step

in and require posters all over South London say, to be stripped from the hoardings because the Lord Chamberlain thought them improper, especially when a case, even an ill-founded one, could be made out to show that they did describe the play.

Scarbrough took his advice and told the MPs that he had 'no jurisdiction over posters on the walls of theatres outside the area of my Theatre licensing authority'.[25]

Our Foreign Friends

Plays perceived as 'highbrow' and addressing major political issues generally caused little concern at St James's. In February 1953, Brecht's *Good Woman of Setzuan* was submitted by the Progress Theatre in Reading. Troubridge noted that 'Many of the usual Communist points and cracks are present, but agreeably disguised as phoney Chinese proverbs'. He had no sympathy for Brecht's politics, but could afford to be patronising about the script, since it was so evidently harmless:

> In this particular play he presents the unusual spectacle of a Communist in a tolerably good temper, even gay, and inclined to blame human nature ('man's inhumanity to man') rather than 'the system' for the evils of the world. It is too much of a strain for him to keep this up for more than two thirds of the way through, and at the end we have conventional sweat-shop and trial scenes, but I suppose this is inevitable.[26]

Heriot's attitude towards Ewan MaColl's 1954 version of *The Good Soldier Schweik* for Theatre Workshop was similar. 'The adaptation is, I think, better than Irwin Piscator's one,' he declared; 'But I should have thought that this kind of coarse satire on matters military with its obvious anti-militaristic angle, would attract small audiences in an age of bigger and better mysteries.'[27] In 1955, Troubridge again gave some credit to the script of *Mother Courage*, when it was submitted for the production in which Joan Littlewood would take the leading role: 'Bertolt Brecht is the leading Communist dramatist outside Soviet Russia, and he writes exceedingly well,' he acknowledged. Troubridge also recognised the ambiguity of the central character, describing her as 'virtually a personification of the brave, cynical, enduring, proletarian old woman'. Typically, his concerns centred not on the politics but on Brecht's vulgarity:

> In a generally acceptable denunciation of the horrors of war, he is able to slip in a good deal of the Communist Party line, indulging its religious

aspects, in a manner that would scarcely be censorable even in a country where the stage censorship was political in its nature ...

So we have just to consider the verbal coarsenesses, all appropriate to the 30 Years War, but less well admissible in Devonshire.

Among the phrases marked for exclusion were 'crap in the grass', 'wet my pants', 'smelling one's excrement', 'knock the shit out of you', and 'having it off'.[28]

The Threepenny Opera irritated and provoked the Reader rather more— but this seems to have been an issue of national pride rather than because of any ideological challenge in the text:

> About fifteen years ago a German Communist dramatist named Bert Brecht laid hands on the ballad opera and adapted it for continental consumption ... adding certain elements to the story, altering the former cynical and witty dialogue, coarsening the whole thing and providing fresh music ... This version has had considerable success abroad, but while there may be justification in varying so specifically English a piece for foreign consumption, there can be little or none in retranslating this hodge podge into English, when we have the original 'Beggar's Opera' itself ...

Again, the cuts were focused almost exclusively on toning down the 'sexual dirt', and the script was licensed without much difficulty. 'I hope it chokes them,' spat Troubridge.[29]

As we saw in the row over the 'Don't Malign Malan' song, there were still unwritten rules over how 'friendly' nations could be represented on the British stage. This was in part because a stamp of approval from the Lord Chamberlain was seen by some as tantamount to a positive endorsement from the very Top. In June 1953, Troubridge expressed concerns about 'a damning attack on the propaganda trials and similar proceedings of the East German Government'. He acknowledged that Peter Albery's *Sup with the Devil* contained 'no more than has been written in a hundred newspapers', but the theatre had a unique responsibility and status.

> I do not even know if we are in diplomatic relations with this Government, but the warning is relevant as the Lord Chamberlain's position is complicated by the knowledge of foreign representatives that there is a censorship of the stage in this country though none of newspapers.[30]

In this instance the Office ultimately decided that such references 'did not matter much' and issued a licence. However, they did intervene over *To See the Queen Pass By*, an intensely patriotic drama by Edward Barton, written to be performed in Chertsey as part of the summer celebrations, and containing parallel scenes depicting 16th and the 20th century Elizabethan coronations. In one 'a Catholic gentleman ... is approached by the Spanish envoy to assassinate Queen Elizabeth I', while in the other 'a modern gentleman is approached by a Russian envoy to print a libel about the new Queen'. The treacherous Spaniard is duly captured and hung up to watch the coronation of Elizabeth I, and the Russian envoy is similarly outwitted and tied up to watch Elizabeth II pass by in all her glory. Ironically, it was the honour of the Soviet Union (not Spain) which the Lord Chamberlain felt obliged to protect. 'We cannot have a real Soviet envoy suggesting such things. The country must be given some fictitious name.'[31]

Official attitudes towards the United States were perhaps surprisingly ambivalent; certainly, the Censorship was not always particularly careful to protect that nation from criticism. In January 1953, Heriot reported on *Stalag Seventeen*:

> If we are to believe the plays and novels about them, members of the United States armed forces are, without exception, brutal, hysterical, lachrymose, sentimental, panic-stricken, brave, sex obsessed and plain stupid. This effusion about American P.O.W.s is characteristic and makes its heroes—to British eyes—about as ape-like as their enemies.

Yet the only cuts imposed were on the physically explicit sequences:

> Warn that the beating up of Sefton must not be too stimulating ...
> Cut the scene where two soldiers dance together making suggestive remarks ...
> Cut the whole of the scene where a soldier has a bath on-stage and his companions remark on his virility ...
> A strong warning about not making the beating by the German officer too realistic or too long ...
> Cut the scene where yet another man tries to go into the lavatory ...[32]

In February, they approved *Here Comes April*, even though it consisted of 'a series of jibes at the United States Air Force'. Troubridge's comments are revealing:

> It is certainly (to quote the words of para (f) of the recommendations of the Royal Commission on Stage Plays (Censorship) 1909) 'calculated to impair friendly relations with any Foreign Power'. It is, therefore, galling for an Examiner to recommend it for licence, knowing well that the United States are so massive that they do not give one little God-damn about what we may say of them on our stage, though if the Allies criticized were, for instance, the French, there would be diplomatic repercussions the day after production.[33]

There was no hesitation, either, in licensing *Thirty Pieces of Silver* by the American playwright Howard Fast, even though it was an overt attack on repressive elements in contemporary America

> Howard Fast is an American Left-wing writer ... who has served a term of imprisonment for Contempt of Congress, presumably by refusing to testify before some Committee.
>
> He has here (in a work dating from 1948) written a technically quite brilliant and extremely moving play about the moral dangers of the kind of witch-hunting associated with McCarthyism, in the days before the advent of Senator McCarthy himself ... this is quite a notable play that heralded a danger to the American people that has actually occurred much as prophecied [sic].

Troubridge recommended licensing, even though 'It has been produced as anti-American propaganda in various Iron Curtain and other countries'.[34]

Real People, Real Lives

Another strand of censorship which sometimes carried political overtones was the reluctance to allow 'real' people to be represented. Reporting in January 1953 on *What The Stars Foretell* 'a gay farcical comedy about a Beaverbrook type press lord', Troubridge noted that 'the real danger point of this play ... would arise if Lord Inchgarvie were made up to resemble Lord Beaverbrook'. The Office issued 'A confidential warning that no attempt to make the part resemble a living personality should be attempted'.[35] In February, Troubridge, who claimed to trace his own ancestry back to Lord Nelson, was contemptuous of *The Woman's Way* as

> one of those large and (to me) extremely tiresome class of plays in which the social and amatory lives of impossible and fantastic Dukes and Duchesses are glibly handled by authors who may once have shaken hands with a Knight's widow.

He insisted that 'As Lord Falmouth is an existing title, the name should be changed'.[36] The following year, reporting on *The Real News*—'A highly improbable and pretty silly play about Fleet Street, Politics and Moral Rearmament'—he recommended that the 'Foreign Secretary who resigns on a point of principle over foreign policy ... should not be made up to resemble Sir Anthony Eden'.[37]

In 1954 a licence was issued for Ludovic Kennedy's *Murder Story*, 'an emotional plea against the death sentence'. The play was inspired by the recent and well-known case of Derek Bentley, who had been hanged for his part in a robbery in which a police officer had been killed, though Bentley had neither fired the shot or carried a gun. The Bentley figure in Kennedy's text is Jim—a nineteen-year-old who has been sacked from his job in a warehouse because he can't read the instructions, and who is then persuaded to take part in the robbery so he can pursue his hobby of buying toy soldiers. As Jim awaits his execution, a humane prison officer teaches him to read and write; and when this officer is admonished by his superior for showing friendliness towards a murderer, his powerful reply probably voices the author's perspective:

> Murder! Don't make me laugh. Do you think he'd have been near the place if it weren't for that bastard next door? Murder indeed! He's not capable of killing a dog. But this is murder, if you like. Nothing hot-blooded about it either. Oh no! We put the bloke in here for a minimum of three weeks, and we don't even tell him whether he's going to die or not. We give him a special hospital diet and let the doctor see him every day, so as to keep him in good physical trim. You and I have to stay here so he doesn't come to no harm. The padre sets about putting his soul in order. And then when everything is nicely tidied up, we get two strong men to truss him up like a chicken, take him in there, and launch him into eternity. If that's not murder, then I'd like to know what the hell is.[38]

More hesitation might have been expected over licensing a play which was so overtly critical of both the law and a recent court decision. The Reader noted that 'the argument is too one-sided'; but he hesitantly recommended it: 'I feel myself, without sharing the author's views on capital punishment, that if you are to have propaganda plays on a subject you might as well permit this one.' Gwatkin, the Assistant Comptroller in the Office agreed: 'The only reason we could have for disallowing this play is that it is propaganda against an existing law—and I don't think that's a very sound reason.' Although some modifications were required to distance the play from its source, Scarbrough's position laid down a significant and surely commendable principle: 'It is a legitimate function of the theatre to discuss the controversial issues of the day,' he insisted, 'and I see no good ground for refusing a licence.'[39]

One play which did provoke heated feelings on political grounds was Oliver Martin's *Guilty and Proud of It*, a dramatisation of events which had occurred in London's East End in the 1920s. 'This is submitted for production by the Poplar Civic Theatre,' reported Troubridge in the autumn of 1953, 'and in Poplar they like their politics and their political drama hot and strong.' He would, he said, have raised 'no objection to the strongest possible dramatic pleading that the conviction and imprisonment of George

Lansbury and the other Poplar Guardians in 1921 was wrong, or to the frothy general denunciation of the "idle rich"'. But there were other aspects which reduced the Reader to near apoplexy:

> Where this playlet puts itself entirely beyond any entitlement to licence, is that in twenty-two foolscap pages, it appears to me to include blasphemy, incitement to murder, accusations of murder, and such utter disregard of the rules against the stage representation of living or recently dead persons that this aspect can only with difficulty be disentangled.

He listed some specific objections:

> Blasphemy
> To me it is blasphemous to say that the purely political symbol of the Red Flag represents Christ's blood shed for mankind ... It must give deep offence to a majority of any audience, even in Poplar ...

> Incitement to Murder
> The 'bosses' should be 'chased and finished off' like dirty, stinking rats.

> Accusation of collective murder
> 'Our own government sends troops to murder men and women of different nations and different colours.'[40]

Troubridge, who already had a bee in his bonnet about theatre subsidy, particularly objected to the fact that th production was supported by the local authority. In December 1952, he had drawn Heriot's attention to an article in *The Times* stating that the Arts Council was prepared 'to allocate funds for the production of individual new plays without any suggestion that such plays should be licensed before a financial allocation is made'. This, warned Troubridge, could lead to some awkward confrontations; 'I wonder whether either Sir Terence or Sir Norman has perceived the danger that seems to me inherent,' he mused, and Troubridge went on to spell out his concerns:

> Surely nothing can be more deplorable for the institution of the stage censorship ... than the danger that any conflict that may arise from his Lordship's decisions, instead of being with the individual theatrical managements, might in future be with official bodies, especially those supported by public funds. Public funds ... involve a Minister responsible to Parliament, and the occurrence of such a conflict would lead to the Lord Chamberlain's decision being open properly to discussion in Parliament in a manner not at present possible ...

What happens when a play selected for subsidization by the Art Council is not considered suitable for licence by the Lord Chamberlain? Are there not then big wigs on the green?

Troubridge wanted a restriction to be placed on the Arts Council, requiring them to consider for support only plays which had been officially approved by the Lord Chamberlain. But any such move would have stirred up controversy, and the Reader's fears had been largely dismissed: 'I think VT is an alarmist, don't you?' wrote Heriot to Gwatkin.[41] Now, reporting on *Guilty and Proud of It*, Troubridge returned to the issue of subsidy:

Our legislators can hardly have foreseen when they passed a Bill a few years ago permitting local authorities to spend up to a sixpenny rate for the encouragement of drama, that the result would be 'civic', rate-endowed enterprises like this.

He drew the attention of the Assistant Comptroller

to the fact that as public (i.e. ratepayers) money would be concerned in the production of this play, this might possibly render the Lord Chamberlain's decision upon it open to question in parliament in a way not otherwise permissible.

Gwatkin agreed that this was a 'nice point', and one which raised serious issues. But Scarbrough, keen to avoid exposing the Censorship to public debates, refused to go down that road:

The fact that a theatre in which a play is to be presented is supported by the rates should not affect my decision. There cannot be one practice for rate-supported theatres and a different one for the rest. This play, therefore, must be considered for censorship purposes by the same standards as any other play. It is for the Legislature or the Ratepayers, not the censor of plays to deal with the issue of public money for party purposes.

Scarbrough did endorse many of Troubridge's specific complaints about this play, and insisted on some significant exclusions:

The references connecting the Red Flag with Christ's blood to be omitted
...
   Omit 'when our government sends troops to murder men and women of different nations and different colours' ...
   Omit 'and then they put the horses in and smashed us up with their capes and batons' and 'smashing up respectable people'.

But he over-ruled his Reader's recommendation to turn down the licence. That would surely have been too contentious: 'the general theme, which is political party propaganda—must pass as we do not make a practice of excluding such plays.'[42]

Divine Visitations

The Poplar play was by no means the only occasion when Troubridge's gung-ho wish to reject outright was over-ruled by superiors who were keener than he was to avoid confrontations. The Reader was all for banning Hugh Evans's *Five Philadelphia Physicians*—'a curious and deplorable play' from America about reincarnation:

> the contention is that a or the messiah is born every fifteen years or so, but most do not attain maturity owing to the action of modern King Herods. The last three were a youth in China, who was shot as a revolutionary, a baby in Philadelphia, born dead through the refusal of doctors to attend at night, and the negro boy in this play.

To Troubridge, these ideas were 'blasphemous', and 'doubly dangerous for production at the Embassy Theatre, where the audience is eighty percent Jewish with strong Messianic views of their own'. But it was the political and racial dimension which clinched it:

> I am afraid I cannot claim to be a deeply religious man, but if, sitting in a theatre, I was told in a play that Christ's Second Coming had been inaugurated by His reincarnation as a negro boy, now aged 10, I would certainly join early in the inevitable riot by tearing up my stall and throwing it at the stage.

Scarbrough did not share his anxieties: 'This may be rubbish,' he observed of the text, 'but I do not think it can be held to be blasphemous or offensive to a degree which would call for a refusal of a licence.'[43]

The following month, Troubridge was equally keen to suppress a foreign language production of *Les Gueux au Paradis* by Gaston-Marie Martens and André Obey:

> The appearance of the Virgin Mary as a speaking character ... is contrary to anything which has hitherto been permitted in view of the Lord Chamberlain's established veto upon the presentation of Divine personages on the stage.

He acknowledged that 'One individual performance in a foreign language in the East End of London is not likely to cause trouble', but maintained there was 'not only the question of the principle involved, but also of the precedent should this play be translated and submitted for licence in English'. Scarbrough checked with his staff and then licensed the play without delay, directly contradicting the Reader's assertion: 'There have, I understand, been a number of precedents for talking parts for the Virgin Mary.'[44]

Brecht's Gods descending to earth to negotiate with a prostitute had gone unremarked, but the story of an angel who marries a Conservative MP was a different matter. *Straight From Heaven*—Royce Ryton's curious if somewhat clumsy domestic satire from 1954—juxtaposed politics with religion, as the angel (Angela) embarrasses her husband and his colleagues at dinner parties by exposing their arms-race profiteering:

> SIR PERCY: I supplied England with the tools to defeat the aggressor.
> ANGELA: You supplied the tools to blow off young men's arms and legs.
> SIR PERCY: That's what munitions are for ...
> ANGELA: Earth could easily be mistaken for Hell to my mind. People spending millions perfecting devices to maim each other when they carp about half-a-million for cancer research funds. Perpetual and cacophonous noise driving anybody left into mental houses. Sunday newspapers full of cheap scandal and sex crimes and everybody lying ... Tell me is this conduct world-wide?
> GEORGE: I wouldn't say that but it's British and we're much better behaved than other races.
> ANGELA: According to our percentage intake into heaven you're way down the list.
> GEORGE: Oh. Who's at the top?
> ANGELA: The Australian Aborigines.[45]

Troubridge, recommended that *Straight From Heaven* should be not be licensed:

> Angels are not ... per se objectionable, but as their theatrical treatment inevitably causes offence to a number of devout persons, each case must be considered with careful regard to the point at which a line must be drawn. I draw it without hesitation at this play.

He found the discussion of 'the sexual potentialities of female Angels' to be particularly distasteful, and the fact that the relationship with the MP was 'gloatingly affirmed to be carnal, consummated, and resulting in frequent marital intercourse' was 'grossly offensive'. Though Troubridge professed himself a non-believer, he studiously supported his case with ecclesiastical references:

> Perhaps I may be permitted to summarize the teaching of the Church of England on Angels (Archbishop's Commission of 1922 'Doctrine in the Church of England ...) This is that while it is legitimate for a Christian to interpret the Scripture with regard to angels in a purely symbolic sense, 'most Christians' accept the view of the New Testament writers that angels are 'ministering spirits sent forth to do service for the sake of them that shall inherit salvation'. Such services can surely not include those of a wife to her husband.

Again, his colleagues thought he was being over-sensitive and too extreme:

> in its present state it might give offence to certain religious people. I should, however, have thought that a little judicious alteration would make it all right. Could the author not change the heroine from an angel into a fairy, or Genie and have a sort of 'Brass Bottle'?

The Lord Chamberlain agreed:

> To my mind the point is not that it does not conform to the C. of E. teaching about angels but whether it will scandalise the Church-going public. I doubt if it will, provided a few lines on the sexual aspect were omitted.

To be on the safe side, Scarbrough had the script sent to the Dean of Windsor—'Inspired by your sermon on Sunday, the Lord Chamberlain bids me send you this play'—and he proved even more relaxed about it: 'I doubt whether anyone could take such a bogus angel seriously enough to be shocked,' wrote the Dean, adding that 'if the angel was exchanged for a fairy the play would fall to pieces.'[46] The licence was issued with only minimal changes.

Good Nudes, Bad Nudes

The BBC's coverage of the Coronation famously led to a massive increase in the ownership of televisions in the UK, and the advent of commercial broadcasting soon afterwards meant that the amount of 'at home' entertainment available effectively doubled. This was almost bound to have a significant impact on audiences for live performance, and the impact was particularly severe in the arena of 'variety'. In an article written in 1954 tracing the decline of the music hall, the *Guardian* suggested that for those few which had managed to survive, it had been a case of 'Nudity to the Rescue'.[47] Although music halls were generally outside the Lord Chamberlain's authority, a report by his secretary suggests that the problem was not confined to such venues. Moreover, not all managements were keeping to the rules:

> Amongst the theatres that the Lord Chamberlain licences [sic] are a number which are situated in comparatively low class neighbourhoods, and which can presumably only find the money to engage the poorest type of 'revue' and 'roadshow'. The appeal of these shows is so small that hardly any patrons would be attracted to the theatres were it not for the nude posing acts that are made the culminating point of the programme. Every one of these shows, therefore, has a posing act at the request of the managements, and when official visits are made to them it is nearly always found that there are unauthorised poses included.[48]

The Lord Chamberlain received regular complaints about such performances:

> HERES ANOTHER PROGRAMME FOR YOU. HAVE A GOOD LOOK AT IT ... YOUR GOING TO GET A EMPIRE PROGRAMME UNTIL THEY GET CLEAN SHOWS DOWN THERE [sic].[49]

Hill listed five venues which regularly generated such complaints, and which had recently required reprimands, and he recommended putting pressure on licensees to make sure that only poses and images expressly approved by the Lord Chamberlain should be presented. The problem, he said, was that while there was 'no difficulty in securing a conviction where nude posing is introduced into a show where none of it is permitted', it was much harder to persuade courts to accept the validity of distinctions between what was artistic (and therefore legitimate) and what was merely erotic (and therefore not).

> It is, unfortunately most difficult to secure either a conviction or an adequate penalty for the inclusion of unlicensed poses amongst licensed ones, since Magistrates will not differentiate between them. For this reason we are losing some measure of control over nude posing.

He therefore concluded that 'a threat of action may be more effective than the action itself', and a stern and private warning was duly issued to all managements involved:

> I am to tell you that his Lordship is perturbed to find that on almost every occasion upon which his representatives see these 'nude' acts, it is discovered that one or more of them has never been submitted

for licensing, and even on occasion that disallowed poses have been reintroduced.

An attempt has been made to deal with this situation by warning, but it is becoming evident that warning alone is insufficient, and that resort to prosecution or other means must be considered ...

I have to tell you that the current situation requires that a closer watch be kept upon the type of performance in question, and to make it plain that his Lordship relies upon you to cooperate with him in this matter.[50]

In reality, of course, the Office had insufficient staff and no effective way of instituting regular checks. They could only hope that their bluff would not be called.

Stage nudity (or at least, female stage nudity) was indeed on the increase, and it came in different shapes and sizes. 'Those who imagine that nudity is an absolute state,' wrote the *Guardian*, 'can easily learn otherwise in the cheaper variety shows—and even in some of the most expensive in Central London.'[51] Reporting on a revue featuring 'an alleged comedian called Benny Hill', Charles Heriot, noted that the nudes had become 'part of the "décor", so much so that eventually one forgets they are there'.[52] Certainly, the boundary between Art and Obscenity became increasingly problematic when live performers were used to embody classical paintings. In 1954, Heriot described 'a vulgar revue' at the Woolwich Empire as 'a display of nudes as travesties of famous pictures'. He confidently declared that 'this certainly isn't art'.[53] But in a five-page briefing paper on the history of stage nudity, intended to help Scarbrough prepare for a meeting with the Public Morality Council, Hill recognised that the system and definitions by which the Office claimed to operate would hardly stand up to scrutiny:

As originally conceived 'nudes' were to be used sparingly, to be still, artistic, suitably posed in a non-erotic fashion and dimly lit.

In fact, having accepted the principle of 'nudity', control is to a considerable extent lost in the following ways:-

a There would be great difficulty in prosecuting an actress for moving a leg say two inches one way, although this made her pose most objectionable.

b A similar disability would apply to a charge for having material coverings slighter, smaller or thinner than those allowed.

c And the same applies to a producer who, charged to produce in a dim light, introduces spotlights.

d Some attempts are made here to limit poses to the actresses depicted in the submitted photographs. Such attempts to distinguish between performers would be hard to justify in Court.

The approach of managements had changed since the war:

> Special models are no longer employed. The chorus girls strip—often all
> of them. In consequence the 'living statues' of 1939 have gone. The nudes
> are no longer remote, artistic models, but participating actresses appearing
> on the stage sometimes clothed, at other times nude.
>
> In 1939 a wisp of voile or something was generally cast round the
> middle of posing actresses (except at the Windmill), and lighting was dim.
> Today lighting is full, even spot-lights are used. Nothing is worn, there are
> even cases it would seem of models posing without cache-sexes.

Indeed, as managements and producers competed desperately to attract
the punters, even the Office's most basic rule forbidding movement was
under threat:

> Efforts are being made to circumvent this by putting them on a roundabout,
> or making them walk with hands folded over chest. These attempts are
> repressed, but indicate that promoters feel a new advance is necessary.
> This is confirmed by the introduction of coloured and Chinese girls into
> posing groups.[54]

There were even venues where audiences could enjoy 'Strip-tease ... fan
dancing ... Nude posing with out even a cache-sexe, and naked mimes'.
Such monstrosities were officially banned in performances controlled
by the Lord Chamberlain, but it frequently had to be explained to
journalists and the public—and also to ministers and members of parliament—that much of the nudity they complained about was beyond his
control:

> I am to explain first of all that the majority of these performances are
> 'variety' shows over which his Lordship has no control whatever. The only
> people who are capable of dealing with Variety shows are the police ...
>
> It is quite true that the Lord Chamberlain does license some poses
> in the 'nude' or 'semi-nude'. There are reasons why his Lordship is
> constrained to do this, which are too involved to be argued here, but he
> does endeavour to mitigate any bad effect by doing what he can to ensure
> that the poses are free from eroticism.
>
> I am to assure you that this whole subject is one that is continuously
> under review.

Regrettably, the Assistant Comptroller explained,

> Until the Civil authorities, however, find it practicable and necessary

to take action against the Variety shows it will remain impossible for the Lord Chamberlain, on his own, to place a total ban on this type of show.[55]

Meanwhile, although the Public Morality Council was perhaps a less potent force than during the inter-war years, it continued to make female undress the focus of its complaints against the stage, as its annual report on the year 1953 shows:

> The chief ground of criticism again is the continual exploitation of nudity. The development which the Committee has considered inevitable, following the toleration of nudity on the stage by the Lord Chamberlain has, in fact, taken place, and the country has been inundated with a spate of revues, mostly appearing in the second-rate music halls, the chief feature of which has been blatantly advertised nudity.[56]

The Council's sub-committee on Stage Plays (now with an expanded remit to cover television and radio) met nine times a year to discuss performances at major London theatres, on which members had taken detailed notes. They then compiled an official list dividing performances between the three categories of 'commended', 'unobjectionable' and 'criticized'. Though the Council tried hard to pressurise the Lord Chamberlain into shifting his stance, and thus usher in the era of 'wholesome entertainment which the public at large sincerely desire', it also acknowledged that 'the remedy for the evil of Stage nudity lies in the hands of the public'. Indeed, 'By a refusal to patronize such harmful entertainments it could terminate them almost overnight'.[57]

In March 1954, the Home Office sent the Lord Chamberlain cuttings culled from a *Daily Sketch* campaign against stage nudity. He acknowledged that the articles contained 'much truth', but insisted 'that public standards of what is decent and indecent in literature, the Daily Press and the Stage have considerably deteriorated since the war'. Because of this, police were disinclined to prosecute, and producers were 'getting bolder' in what they dared to present. Furthermore, the refusal to clamp down could be justified on practical grounds:

> So far as the Lord Chamberlain is concerned, he allows 'nude' still poses to a limited degree really for two reasons:-
> a) Because he feels it better to allow a very controlled version of this sort of thing as an alternative to driving it underground and
> b) Because, whatever his views, whilst places of entertainment not subject to him can stage 'nude' shows, and others refuse to book shows without 'nudes', he does not feel justified in being responsible for companies

playing under his licence being refused work, or operating at too great a disadvantage compared with the rivals of the variety stage.[58]

As the Lord Chamberlain's Comptroller neatly explained to someone declaring himself 'horrified that such a thing should be allowed in a Christian country', it seemed reasonable to assume that 'as no one goes to a casino unless he wishes to gamble, so no one goes to the Windmill Theatre unless he desires to witness a performance such as is given there.'[59]

It would be frivolous to suggest that the occasional theatre trip to check up on female nudity may have been considered one of the perks of working for the Lord Chamberlain, but there was certainly an art to carrying out these inspections effectively. Titman had been a master at it, and Hill had probably picked up quite a lot from him. But for those less experienced, and having their first experience of such an occasion, the exercise could be fraught with difficulties, as a report by the LCC on *Bon Soir Cocks* demonstrates:

> Through the loud-speaker system it was announced that reproductions would be given of famous works of art ... the curtain then rose on the right-hand aperture announced as 'Bathsheba's Toilet'.
>
> From my position I could see nothing at all, the artiste being too far back, and in common with many others who had viewing angles similar to mine I hastily slid along the row towards the centre where I just had time to see a girl sitting full right on a pedestal. From the momentary glimpse, just as the aperture curtain was closing, it appeared that breasts were bare with legs well together making no exposure of middle parts.
>
> The next pose was announced as 'The Source Of Life' ... This time I saw absolutely nothing ...
>
> From the right came 'Leda and the Swan', but impatient men on my left were pushing past and I saw nothing of this.

For future reference, the inspector helpfully recommended that 'the most satisfactory place to view this set of poses would be from the Circle'.[60]

Yet for all the official handwringing and straight-faced professions of concern, it was common knowledge—at least within St James's—that the policy on nudity was not operated consistently and that the Office had its favourites. Most notably, the Windmill Theatre had traditionally been allowed a degree of freedom not granted elsewhere. As Heriot observed with some cynicism in February 1953: 'Nowhere else in the British Isles do we permit a fan-dancer, but she has always been at the Windmill for the only reason that she has always been there.' He added, with a broad hint, that, 'I would, of course, like to cut her altogether, but this would appear to be too much against the favourable policy of this office towards Miss Mitelle'.[61]

Everyone knew, too, that it was common practice for dancers at the Windmill to 'accidentally' expose more than was allowed; if caught out, the manager would apologise and blame it on the costume-makers. In November 1953, the Public Morality Council complained to Scarbrough that in the current show 'The number of breast exposures which occurs is far too great to be accidental'. Titman was duly dispatched to check, but the management probably saw him coming: 'even from my privileged position it was quite impossible to see any detail whatsoever,' he reported. However, he added that, 'The number of "breast exposures" was no more than usual, but too many to pass unnoticed', and a mild reprimand was issued to the manager, Miss Mitelle, who 'promised to see about it at once'.[62] This seems to have had little effect, for the Windmill's next script contained 'The mixture as before, with nudes—which we must see'. Heriot knew such checks were actually meaningless; 'not that it will make any difference,' he observed; 'breasts will continue to pop out and fan dancers move to the apparent contempt of the Lord Chamberlain and his office.'[63] For its part, the Public Morality Council complained that 'a new technique has been developed whereby the dancer makes no bones about breast exposure during the dance'. Once again, they objected that 'inadvertent breast exposures by the dancers in chorus numbers are now made too frequently to be accidental'. Titman informed the management 'that more care must be taken by the girls in fixing the costumes and that there should be constant supervision'. They apologised, and told him that the problem arose as a result of 'the wearing of costumes by girls of different sizes'.[64]

The historical arrangement with the Windmill may have been distastefully cosy, but other managers, including a young Paul Raymond, were beginning to go much further. In 1954, the Office noticed that *Folies Parisiennes*, for which they had issued a licence, was being advertised by Raymond as offering not only a 'strip-tease spectacle', but also 'the only moving nudes in Europe'. Hill's inspection revealed that Item 14 on the programme—'The Queen of Glamour'—was the centre of the claim, since it featured 'Four nudes standing on a turntable that goes round and round.' This was indeed a worrying innovation which demanded action:

I think serious note must be taken of the turntable, since although in the present instance its use was unobjectionable this is only the beginning. There is absolutely no control of the pose, especially where no triangles are worn, and when going round and round has ceased to titivate the public, then nudes will go over and over. The time to stop this is now.

Raymond was also practising a deception which offers evidence of the practical value managements attached to the Lord Chamberlain's licence as a protection against prosecution. Hill discovered that, although the performance was being presented under a title which had been approved, in practice 'the show had been so altered that practically nothing of that licensed by the Lord Chamberlain remained'. Moreover, he insisted, 'the current version, consisting of nothing but cross talk, dancing and clowns is not a stage play'.[65] The Lord Chamberlain could presumably have tried to instigate legal action on the grounds that the company was deviating from the script as licensed to them. But this might have proved problematic since the show actually being presented was of a kind which did not fall under his remit.

When *Folies Parisiennes* reached Oldham, the ever zealous authorities there complained to the Lord Chamberlain. Gwatkin told the Chief Constable that he knew the licensed script had been effectively jettisoned, and that if the police could prove that the performance was 'being represented as a Stage Play', it would be possible to institute a prosecution against the producer. He also wrote to Raymond, asking how he wished the performance to be categorized. When Raymond assured him it was 'purely a Music and Dancing show', Gwatkin dryly replied that he was glad to know there were 'no sketches or other dramatic material that would bring it within the Lord Chamberlain's control'. Raymond sought clarification:

> So that I can be perfectly clear when you state that I have no sketches or other dramatic material in this show, would you please be kind enough to inform me of your interpretation of a sketch and also dramatic material.

The Office had its definition ready—one which they would cite on numerous occasions, even though it had no legal status: 'By dramatic material is meant any sequence which has some consecutive train of thought running through it and which requires the exercise of histrionic skill.' St James's Palace had no authority over performances which lacked these key components:

> If it consists of nothing but dancing, singing, music, acrobatics, disconnected patter, then it is a Music and Dancing show which is not subject to the Lord Chamberlain. But, if to the show you add any item or items such as sketches 'two or more handed gags' or other items involving continuity of action and thought, then the entire entertainment becomes one 'of the stage' and subject to the Lord Chamberlain.[66]

In effect, a management could insert a couple of such sketches simply to obtain a licence from the Lord Chamberlain, which generally (though not in legal fact) was seen to guarantee safety from prosecution. Once they had the licence, the management might quietly discard the sketches, knowing they would be very unlucky to be found out.

Louder than Words

In January 1953, the Colonial Office contacted Scarbrough on behalf of the government of Kenya to ask for advice on how to control performances. With the Mau Mau struggle at its height, and Kenyatta and other activists about to be arrested and imprisoned, this was an issue of some importance. The government and the Colonial Office had evidently assumed that censorship could be applied only to the spoken word, but it was quickly explained to them that this was not at all how the Lord Chamberlain interpreted his role:

> He has always enforced his view that a copy of the play means a statement of the entire action of a play, as opposed to 'the book of the play' which would be the phrase for use where the dialogue only was concerned. In pursuance of his opinion the Lord Chamberlain requires the mss submitted to him to contain brief descriptions of the scenes, of dances if they are not routine ones, of any 'business' or stage action affecting the character of the play, and in fact the submission of sufficient material for him not only to know what is to be said, but in what surroundings and circumstances, so that he may assess the actual impression given by the performance.

The Office cited an instance where the addition of a red lamp to a scene ostensibly set in a café had led to a successful prosecution. Interestingly, they also advised against inspecting rehearsals, because of the shifting of accountability this implied:

> The Lord Chamberlain has always maintained that it is the duty of the theatre manager who submits a play to acquaint him with everything connected with the play which will materially affect the impression which it will make upon the audience. His Lordship is most careful never to detract from this responsibility, and for this reason he very seldom allows his officers to attend rehearsals: he requires all relevant matter to be included in the submitted ms.[67]

Whether such an approach was equally applicable in a society facing violent rebellion is, perhaps, another matter.

With a few notable exceptions, it is obviously inconceivable for 'everything connected with the play' to be included in a written script. Nevertheless, there were plenty of occasions when costumes, movements or gestures had been the subject of censorship. In the autumn of 1953 a successful prosecution was brought against the manager and producer of Sartre's *The Respectable Prostitute* for interpolating a piece of business which had not appeared in the licensed text. The production had been on tour some three years, and there had been fairly regular complaints about it on a variety of grounds. In November 1953, an anxious Inspector Hegg wrote to the Lord Chamberlain:

> I would point out that much of the dialogue when read, is not so offensive as when played on the stage accompanied by actions and inflections of voice. It is certainly not a play suitable for young persons, and is billed as for 'Adults only', neither do I think that decent men would care to let their womenfolk see it.
>
> A further aspect, and one which requires careful consideration, is the possible effect on the coloured population. The theme of the play is the American 'colour bar'; and the action is fairly strong.

However, the successful legal proceedings were instituted after a performance at Liverpool, when the curtain fell just as the character played by the actor-manager was apparently about to lie on top of a woman on a bed. It could hardly be argued in court that the action was of itself an obscene one, but the charge was that because it had not been included in the script, the Company was presenting unlicensed material. The Lord Chamberlain was vindicated in court for his insistence that dialogue was 'but an ingredient of a play' and that 'the necessity to describe business is well known in the Theatrical Profession'. Better still from his point of view, the trial and its outcome were reported favourably in the newspapers, and the Office was able to bask in its triumph: 'For once we seem to have got a good press.' 'Yes, what a change.'[68]

The ruling proved a useful deterrent. When the Office inspected a performance of *Ladies for Hire*, they discovered that 'stage business, some of it obscene, has been added to the performance', and threatened the management with legal action: 'the Lord Chamberlain has little doubt that the evidence now in his possession is sufficient to sustain a charge under the Theatres Act, 1843 since "business" is an integral part of the play and must be specifically allowed.' The management promised to delete all such additions, and escaped with a warning.[69] But with no effective method of policing, and more managers tempted to flout their rulings, it was not easy for the Office to keep control of what was actually happening on stage. Except for productions reviewed in the national press, they usually only heard about things if a member of the public wrote in to complain. Then they could either fire a warning shot across the theatre's bows (taking care to make no definite accusations since there was no formal evidence) or set about gathering proof. In January 1954, Scarbrough received a letter objecting to *Wish You Were Here*, a musical set in 'Camp Karefree', an American Holiday Camp, in which 'boys and girls lie around in the woods' with 'the men on top of the girls in what can only be described as "the last stages of cohabitation"'. Hill saw the show and was appalled; 'the entire theme is promiscuity, euphemized as "having fun",' he reported, and he described a dance in which a man

> comes from behind and puts his right hand not on her thigh, which would be bad enough, but distinctly within an inch of her groin. His hands then go down to her knee and he makes to put them up her skirt, is rebuffed and 'butterflies' his fingers up the sides of her legs and thighs to her hips.

In another, 'a sort of Tarzan, clad in the briefest and the most revealing trunks' leant over a woman from behind, to instruct her on how to hold her baseball bat, while she 'rolls her bottom as seductively as possible'. For the Lord Chamberlain's secretary, this was beyond the call of duty. 'From the front row of course I was very near, and saw more than the majority of the audience,' he perspired; 'and what I saw wasn't nice.' If this was American culture, Hill wanted none of it: 'After seeing this show,' he declared, 'I feel that if anything could reconcile me to a life in Moscow, it would be the prospect of an alternative of a life at Camp Karefree.'[70]

Equally shocking was *La Venexiana*, a 'bawdy little Venetian erotic comedy' from the sixteenth century, to be staged at Leeds University. 'The sex life of patrician Venice in 1510 was no kindergarten,' acknowledged Troubridge; but he drew particular attention to 'A most questionable semi-Lesbian scene in which an amorous woman makes her maid pretend to be the desired male lover, kissing the girl with her tongue, lying on top of her, and finally going to sleep with the girl in her arms'. The Reader conceded that 'As translated by the clever professor of Italian, it would probably delight rather than harm the Italian society of the University of Leeds'; the danger was that 'a play once licensed may be transferred to less sophisticated surroundings', and this particular play would be 'very strong meat indeed for the public stage'. This time Scarbrough agreed: 'You could not of course pass this play if it was written today,' he noted; 'It is entirely about copulation and as far as I can see it jolly nearly happens on the stage!' Played in its original Italian, of course, no licence would have been required; but 'to us it is a play written in 1954 about something that might have happened in 1510 and must be treated as such'.[71] A string of cuts was therefore imposed.

The Queen's English

Sexual language was also important. In 1955, Troubridge reported on two plays by David Horne. Horne, explained the Reader, had been 'a very good friend of mind for about thirty years' and, through his military background, was also known to both the Comptroller and Assistant Comptroller. With friends like Troubridge, Horne hardly needed enemies. 'He has many fine qualities of heart and mind,' noted the Reader, 'but, alas, cherishes the illusion that he can write plays, whereas this gift has, in fact been denied him.' Yet, as Troubridge explained, 'his father recently left him 800,000 pounds, so his plays continue to get produced'. The only specific objection to *Uncertain Destiny* was 'a very infelicitous reference to a young seduced girl having "opened her casket of jewels"'; a second Reader agreed that this was going a little too far: 'Alter—the author is not Shakespeare, but an ex-Grenadier Officer.' However, they were persuaded by Horne to change their minds, since the phrase had already been approved in a previous version of the text: 'I do think that it would be rather bad luck to ask you to remove this.'[72] More problematic was the same author's *Legacy*, which focused on the Old Bailey trial of two doctors charged with conspiring to procure an abortion. The main problem lay in the detail of what they were obliged to explain. 'Such questions and answers would no doubt be given at the Old Bailey,' wrote Troubridge, 'but those attending an abortion trial there know what to expect, which is not the case with the audience in a theatre.' The endorsement on the licence included the stipulations:

> For 'an early miscarriage and a violent menstruation', substitute 'an operation and the violent re-assertion of nature' ...
> Omit 'she was behind hand with her dates' and substitute 'and was probably still upset on that account' ...
> Omit 'bring on her period' and substitute 'cure her condition'.

The original lines, said Gwatkin, 'would be intolerable even at his Guards Club', and were 'impossible in a theatre'.[73]

Equally distasteful was *Vile Inheritance*—'A mildly pornographic offering, probably written by an elderly bachelor'—which centred on a grandfather—blinded through venereal disease—and his two grand-daughters, one of whom he eventually murders. The script was licensed only after extensive cuts, including

> All over-emphasised sexual passages ... all reference to the debauching of children and perverse sexual techniques ... the reference to Chinese sex ... the reference to sexual intercourse ... the emphasis on the girl's enjoyment ... the old man's enjoyment ... the blasphemous misquotation of one of the Seven Words.[74]

Comedians were known to be particularly prone to lapses in taste. 'A general warning should be given that no players must indulge in any business indicative of an urgent desire to leave the room during this sketch,' advised Heriot in his report on 'an otherwise clean show' in which Ted Ray was 'the nigger in the wood pile'.[75] On one occasion, the Office insisted that 'There must be no pause between "he's wet his trousers" and "in the rain"', and on another they deleted an 'unnecessary reference to the purgative effects of liquorice' in a gag about Liquorice Allsorts giving you 'a good run for your money'.[76] References to nappies were always cut, and actresses were not to be made to look pregnant. When 'a mammary inference' was identified in one sketch, they stipulated that 'there must be no suggestion that the sugar or biscuits are taken from the lady's corsage'.[77]

The Queen's Theatre in Poplar, found itself in trouble over *The Naughtiest Night of Your Life* when an undercover inspection discovered that they were including a line which had specifically been disallowed:

> In scene 15—a cafe in France—Pauline Penny wobbled her buttocks and rolled her r's as she read the menu. You then commented 'don't you roll your r's when you talk'.

The manager, who had already been prosecuted for similar offences, claimed that the accusation against Penny was unfair since 'in her normal walk she "wobbles" slightly, as frankly I think most females do'. He was informed that the Lord Chamberlain always disallowed 'buttock wobbling', and that the action 'has not been sufficiently restrained'.[78] Even Arthur Miller's *The Crucible* received its first British performances only after 'arse' had been changed to 'sitting-down place', and 'A fart on Thomas Putnam' to 'Damn Thomas Putnam'. As someone in the Office pointed out: 'Fart was OK in Ben Jonson's days but it isn't now.'[79] The sound itself was even more problematic. In December 1953, the Chairman of Rutherglen Repertory Theatre was asked to give 'an undertaking that on page 28 "Johnnie" will not blow a "raspberry"', as suggested in the script. He replied:

> Presumably I have no option if the show is to go on. At the same time I can't but voice protest. As a Director of the theatre I have to read scores of plays to consider their suitability for presentation. When I think of the fornication and blasphemy passed by the censor in many of our modern plays this restriction seems petty and more worthy of Mrs. Grundy than a responsible public authority like the LC's Office.

The Office admitted their objection might appear trivial, but that there were 'so to speak, raspberries and raspberries'. Specifically: 'A good loud blast on a trumpet is one thing, while a noise described by Mr Partridge as "an anal escape of wind" is another, and would be offensive.' The Lord Chamberlain solemnly indicated that he was prepared to withdraw his objections in return for a guarantee 'that this raspberry on page 28 is, and always will be, of the blast variety'.[80]

From *Fanny Get Your Gun*, Heriot insisted that 'all references to the machete' should be removed, since it was 'an obvious synonym for the male organ'.[81] Troubridge found 'references to male sperm very distasteful in the theatre', and in *Facts of Life*, a line about 'The forty-million sperm which have carried half our nation's heredity' was changed to 'The masculine factors'. Also deleted was a mention of 'the descent of the testes', and the word 'evidence' from a question put to a servant by a father in relation to his son: 'Have you ever noticed ... any evidence that he is precocious?'; Troubridge observed that 'To my mind the only evidence of sexual precocity available to an elderly housemaid would be traces of nocturnal emissions, an unsuitable subject for the stage'. The Lord Chamberlain also required that the words 'the opposite' should be inserted before 'sex' in the question 'Have you seen any sign of interest in sex?'[82]

The Young Ones

One of the justifications often invoked by Scarbrough for his more heavy-handed interventions was that his licence allowed for no qualifications or caveats. Any play which he approved became available to any audience and any age, including (unlikely though it may seem) the child who wandered in from the street. By contrast, in 1951 the British Board of Film Censorship had added a third category of licensing; an 'A' now required that anyone under the age of 16 must be accompanied by an adult.[83] Through the fifties and sixties, it would frequently be suggested that theatre should follow cinema's route, thus giving the Lord Chamberlain more flexibility. When the idea was first put to him in 1954, by the producer and impresario Henry Sherek, Scarbrough's initial response was positive. 'This is interesting I think,' he wrote in an internal memorandum.[84] However, the obstacle—which would prove insurmountable—was that no such system could be introduced without legislation. And that would have required opening the whole system and principle of theatre censorship up to parliamentary and public debate.

There were always voices demanding that young people needed greater protection than the Censorship was willing to provide. Take this letter sent to the Office in January 1954 by a teacher who had taken a party of adolescent girls from the commerce department of Hendon Technical College to the London Coliseum:

> I write to express my horror at the type of play which you are placing before the public ... In my opinion the show at the Coliseum is a disgrace, and should be withdrawn as speedily as possible, so that the public—and

young people in particular—shall not have their Christian, their moral, or their ethical foundations undermined by witnessing such a spectacle.[85]

The show they had seen was the musical *Guys and Dolls*. The Public Morality Council, too, frequently expressed concern about 'the harm caused to youth by shows that are undoubtedly suggestive and sexually provocative', and their division of plays into categories of suitability was primarily intended as guidance for youth leaders and parish priests. In 1954 they demanded that the Lord Chamberlain should withdraw the licence he had issued for *I Am a Camera*, John Van Druten's adaptation of Isherwood's pre-war Berlin stories.

> as the entire theme of the play is fornication, treated in such a way as to have a most damaging effect on all who see it and especially the younger element in every audience, it has no redeeming feature. I remind your Lordship that the girl in the play (Sally Bowles) was not forced by any tragic compulsion or material need to live the life of a harlot, but only did it because she liked it.

It is striking to see the power which the Council still attributed to theatre to influence behaviour:

> what seems to be particularly regrettable is that at a time when all are agreed that there is the greatest possible need for a tightening up of the moral fibre in the whole country, that a play such as this which cannot but have the most deplorable effect on public morals, should have been licensed.

Gwatkin suggested the play would act as a warning, not an incitement, but the Council would have none of it:

> No young person could possibly be expected to see through the thick layer of glamour to the horrifying reality ... to say that this way of life is shown in an unpleasant light is a travesty of the truth: it appears almost infinitely rewarding.

Scarbrough backed his Assistant Comptroller and refused to concede, insisting immorality was 'not represented in any attractive light', and that he had 'no doubt that it would act as a deterrent rather than as an encouragement to vice'.[86]

When a deputation from the Public Morality Council visited James's Palace in January 1955, its members reminded Scarbrough that they 'greatly deplored the licensing of certain plays in recent years depicting depravity and vice, holding up to contempt fidelity in marriage and encouraging sexual promiscuity'.[87] Actually, it was not just the effect on an audience but also on performers which they took it upon themselves to worry about. In December 1955 they told the Lord Chamberlain they had received 'Numerous complaints' about an American comedy called *Anniversary Waltz*: 'the theme of this play, premarital intercourse suggested as a normal thing, is most unwholesome and cannot but be very damaging to young people and especially to the two young people taking part,' they declared. Scarbrough had already received other protests about this play, including one from an 'anxious British subject' and another from the London Housewives Association for the Protection of Family Life, which was 'at a loss to understand how such a play could be passed by Your Lordship to be staged in the United Kingdom.' No-one from the Association had actually seen a performance, but 'The press report indicates that the play is one which could be appreciated only by a degenerate public'. Again, the Lord Chamberlain remained firm: 'to ban all plays of an equivocal or doubtful nature would be wrong,' he insisted, and concerns about the impact on the performers were naïve:

> As for the young people taking part it is pointed out that the youngest is rising sixteen years old. Bearing in mind what young people can see in the cinemas, the press and in contemporary publications, not to mention the impression that they must get when they walk about the streets, the Lord Chamberlain feels that young actors of that age are sufficiently sophisticated to take part in the play.[88]

Obscene but not Heard

At first sight it may seem surprising that the Office should have been ready to license a stage version of *Lady Chatterley's Lover* in the early 1950s. But the script submitted was a tame and largely innocuous affair, in which even Troubridge could find little to object to:

> The point is that in the novel D. H. Lawrence (a tubercular weakling) repeatedly and gloatingly used four or five of the simple words that the Law and decency regard as obscene. These have been removed by the very expert Hungaro-American adapter ... so that the play becomes an ordinary if sexy story of the wife of a war-paralysed baronet who has an affair with her husband's gamekeeper.

Heriot agreed that the text was 'not more scabrous than dozens of other sexual discussions disguised as dramas that the Lord Chamberlain has already passed'. Nevertheless, one or two delicate and subtle changes were imposed; the lines 'It <u>was</u> ... wonderful' and '<u>was</u> it for you?' were amended to 'It <u>is</u> ... wonderful' and '<u>is</u> it for you?'—the change of tense immediately transforming the 'it' from sexual intercourse to anything from their relationship to the weather. Moreover, on Heriot's suggestion the title was amended to the more discreet *Lady Chatterley*.[89]

The reason there was so little to trouble the Lord Chamberlain's Office in the submitted script of *Lady Chatterley's Lover* was—as Troubridge pointed out—that the necessary censorship had already been applied in the process of making the adaptation. It is no coincidence that many of the most awkward and prolonged confrontations between theatre managements and St James's Palace should have occurred over plays by foreign playwrights, who had not written with the Lord Chamberlain peering over their shoulder. In 1954, Ernst Toller's *Hinkemann*—'an ugly and pretentious piece of work' which would assuredly 'cause much embarrassment to both sexes'—was turned down again, as it had been in 1935 and again in 1947. The Office considered this an act of generosity which would help safeguard Toller's reputation and 'help to relegate it to the limbo of repulsive errors'.[90]

Another foreign playwright for whom the Censorship displayed particular antipathy was Tennessee Williams. *A Streetcar Named Desire* had stirred up considerable animosity in the late forties and early fifties, and *The Rose Tattoo* in 1953 was similarly problematic.

> The play is most outspoken, as *Streetcar* was, and as the speech of such people must be portrayed more or less as it is or not at all, the anomaly arises that the Examiner is almost forced to apply a rather lower standard than he would in a cleaner play.

Troubridge recommended 'with distaste' that the script should be licensed, but drew attention to details which he considered dubious:

> Little buggers
> The ascertainment of the sex of a parrot
> (*She glances below his belt*)
> It should be explained that dependenti is the usual Italian word for the male genital organs ...
> ... the audience will know that the noises marked on these three pages are being made by a woman during intercourse, and as such they should be cut.
> '... clad only in a sheer white slip ...' According to the dictionary, 'sheer' means diaphanous, but perhaps feminine advice is needed.

However, even his eagle eye missed some things, as his second report 'on this grimy play' admitted:

I am most obliged to the anonymous correspondent from the Hyde Park Hotel, who has saved me from repeating a serious mistake. It is true as he says that 'In this play a French Letter is dropped and the object commented on'. It is also true that I did not detect this on my first reading. This is on page 114, and is a good example of the difference between seeing and reading a play, however trained may be the powers of visualization. The object is disingenuously described as a disk. I did not associate the passage with the possibility of a French letter, thinking the object some Sicilian love talisman or the like. None the less I am humiliated, and offer my apologies.[91]

Enter Godot

If foreign dramatists were less prone to instinctive self-censorship than most British playwrights and managers, they were also often less inclined to accede so willingly to official demands. In the spring of 1954, *Waiting for Godot* marked the first arrival of Samuel Beckett at St James's Palace, with Peter Hall as his champion. Troubridge was ready for him, having read about recent European productions of *Godot*, but even he was puzzled:

> With many years on the Council of the old Stage Society, I have had much experience of 'advanced', 'expressionist', and similar imaginative kinds of plays, but I find this one extremely baffling ... It is written by a former secretary of James Joyce, the Irish author who finding it necessary to invent virtually a new language to express himself, left his message to the world far from clear in consequence ... I can describe the simple happenings on the stage, and indicate for elimination the words and lines of Joycean grossness, but I can only offer the merest glimmer of a suggestion of what the author intends it all to mean.

In fact, the interpretation he 'tentatively' offered was not without perception:

> The play is a modern cry of despair, and Godot, for whom we human tramps are always waiting in expectation, is Death. Pozzo and Lucky are allegorical figures passing before our eyes of how men treat one another, by acts of enslavement that lead to blindness for the enslaver and dumbness for the slave. The best way out is a piece of rope—what Shakespeare called 'the charity of a penny cord'.

Overall, though, the Reader was not impressed: 'Why the shrewdest of our young managers should contemplate the production of so bitter, dark, obscure an allegory is almost as mysterious as much of the play.'

A dozen cuts were demanded in Beckett's text. These included reference to flies being undone ('You might button it up all the same'), and a brief discussion about the chances of obtaining an erection ('The lines ... about a known secondary effect of hanging'). Other objections included 'Estragon comparing himself to Christ', 'You piss better', 'Fartov', 'Gonococcus! Spirochet', and 'Who farted?'. Estragon's trousers were only permitted to fall down 'provided he is well covered', and the 'mockery of religion' in Lucky's speech was to be altered, along with a 'foetal posture', and the threat to kick him 'in the privates'. Beckett seems to have been willing to concede most of these points, as he told his London producer, Donald Albery:

> I am prepared to try and give satisfaction on ten of the twelve points raised. This for me is a big concession and I make it with the greatest reluctance. Were it not for my desire to be agreeable to Mr Glenville and yourself, I should simply call the whole thing off without further discussion.

But there were a couple of sticking points:

> two of the passages condemned ... are vital to the play and can neither be suppressed nor changed. I cannot conceive in what they give offence and I consider their interdiction wholly unreasonable. I am afraid this is quite final.
>
> Until these two passages are reinstated as they stand, there is no point in my submitting amendments of the others.

The two passages in question had both been rejected because of their religious references: the lines in Lucky's speech from 'Given the existence' to 'fire the firmament', and the section comparing the suffering of Estragon and Vladimir to those who had 'crucified quick'.

Unusually, Heriot attended a private reading of the play on behalf of the Lord Chamberlain, and the Office withdrew their objections to these passages. There was a brief further quibble over whether 'who did that?' was an acceptable substitution for 'who farted?'—('There is no need for this. The Lord Chamberlain should stand firm about any business of breaking wind')—before the compromise of 'who belched?' was accepted. The script was officially licensed in August 1955 (some seventeen months after it had been submitted), with ten endorsements, and the private performance at the Arts Club transferred to the Criterion Theatre.

Not everyone was satisfied with Scarbrough's leniency. In November, an outraged Lady Howitt wrote to inform him of her displeasure and disbelief. It is hard to believe that *Waiting for Godot*, of all plays, should have provoked such indignation;

Lady Howitt presents her compliments to the Lord Chamberlain. She wishes to inform him that she visited the Criterion Theatre with her husband and that both were completely disgusted by the play *Waiting for Godot*. They cannot understand how such a production can possibly get through the British procedure of censorship.

The play itself is sordid, bestial and brutal to an extent which cannot be justified by any desire to point a moral, whatever it may be.

The toilet humour was one aspect which particularly roused her ire:

one of the main themes running through the play is the desire of two old tramps continually to relieve themselves. Such a dramatisation of lavatory necessities is offensive and against all sense of British decency. In this particular it is a disgraceful production for a West End theatre to which young and old people may go, having little or no idea of what they are going to see, and much misled by the placards outside quoting from the Press which have the effrontery to eulogise the play as being a moral one which all should see.

And Lady Howitt let it be known that she expected something to be done:

It is useless to write to the Press on this subject as it might result in increased box office demands; the only remedy is to appeal to the Censor to withdraw the play, or at any rate to omit all the lavatory references— actions as well as words—which could be done, without appreciably affecting the actions of the play.

Lady Howitt hopes very much that the Lord Chamberlain will find it possible to take some action in the matter.

Scarbrough forwarded the letter to Gwatkin: 'This reads rather convincingly to me,' he wrote; 'I think someone ought to go and see it. I dare say they are doing all sorts of filthy things by now. There are plenty of opportunities in the script.' Heriot was duly dispatched. He would probably have enjoyed himself more at the Windmill, though his report (if it can be believed) is instructive in terms of documenting the response of at least one audience to what would come to be seen as perhaps the pivotal play of the twentieth century:

I visited this play last night and endured two hours of angry boredom. Peter Hall's production seems to emphasise the slapstick elements, while the entire cast act like mad to inject drama and meaning into a piece quite without drama and with very little meaning ...

There is only one interval. At the fall of the first curtain, the man

next to me cried 'Brother, let me out of this!' and fled, never to return.
He was not alone: many empty seats gaped during the second act. In the
bar, several women were apologising to their escorts for having suggested
a visit to such a piece. The general feeling seemed, like mine, to be one
of acute boredom—except for a sprinkling of young persons in slacks and
Marlon Brando pullovers with (according to sex) horsetails or fringes, who
applauded pointedly. There was no laughter—only the merest titter at the
convulsive efforts of the actors to be funny. I may add that I overheard
a nice Italian girl, gloomily imbibing gin, observe to her companion: 'e
molto symbolico, ma—!'

For all his disapproval, Heriot was not able to support the complaint:

> Lady Hewitt's [sic] case is not proved. There are lavatory references, of
> course, but where the whole text is more or less offensive and in doubtful
> taste, no useful purpose could be served by pruning—and the Lord
> Chamberlain might endanger the dignity of his office if he rescinded his
> licence at this point in the play's run. Having passed this carbon copy
> of 'Ulysses', he has, it seems to me, satisfied the demands of those who
> claim it to be Literature with a capital L. Let him leave it at that (with
> a non-commital answer to Lady Hewitt) and allow public opinion quietly
> to disperse this ugly little jet of marsh gas.

Gwatkin thanked him: 'You will now no doubt write one of your most
non-commital and tactful letters to Lady H!'

Indeed, the confidential letter, which went out under Gwatkin's name,
was almost unctuous in tone. It is also a nice demonstration of the ability
of the Censorship to point in different directions at once, and to tailor
observations to what the listener wants to hear. This, surely, was what
the art of diplomacy was all about. So, having apprised Lady Howitt of
Beckett's connections with Joyce, and of the play's success in Paris, the
letter offered a less than completely honest version of its journey through
St James's Palace, before expressing deep regret that it was simply not
possible to do as she had asked, even though the Lord Chamberlain agreed
with her views:

> It was submitted to this Office early this year clearly with some trepidation:
> and quite rightly, because the original was appalling, and some of the more
> outrageous passages were deleted, much to the author's rage. What is left is
> unpleasant enough but the Lord Chamberlain felt that to cut more would
> be tantamount to banning the whole production.
>
> You may well think that course should have been taken. On the other
> hand it is not an immoral play and as the Lord Chamberlain's authority

does not cover matters of taste, frequently he finds that he has to pass plays which, from that angle, he would far sooner ban.

The letter finished by reassuring Lady Howitt that 'It is a great help to the Lord Chamberlain to have the opinion of intelligent playgoers, and I am to say how grateful he is that you should have troubled to write'.

However, Lady Howitt was not quite ready to surrender the field to the French. She took issue with the Assistant Comptroller's attempts to distance himself:

> I realise that the play may not be considered immoral but as regards the Censorship Department not being concerned with matters of taste, I would have thought, but perhaps I am wrong, that they were concerned with obscenity.

From a historical point of view, what perhaps now seems the most interesting aspect of Lady Howitt's letter is its political take on Pozzo—not least because the point is made in passing, as though self-evident:

> I am perturbed to think what may follow if a play such as this is allowed and I do wish that two of the incidents could yet be omitted. The first is when one of the tramps goes into the wing and the other tramp and the big capitalist (I forget his name) both watch the man in the wings making remarks about what he is doing. This I thought extremely objectionable. The second incident was when one of the tramps ran along the stage until he reached the tree in the centre of the stage when he evidently pretended to do what I never expected to see on any English stage, although a French audience might find it amusing.

Heriot added a comment on the bottom of the letter: 'Lady Howitt saw what *I* didn't see', and the file was closed.[92]

The event staged at Westminster Abbey in June 1953 was probably more the sort of performance at which both Lady Howitt and the Earl of Scarbrough would have felt at home; there is certainly no evidence in the files that he ever visited the theatre himself to see any of the plays he had passed. While the Coronation was the most public of performances, it required no licence from him—though, ironically, censorship did rear its head, with television being banned from showing either the anointing of the Queen or the Communion. And if the official script for the occasion had been sent to St Vincent Troubridge, one suspects he might have been extremely anxious about the wording of a stage direction which stipulated that the Dean of Westminster would draw a sword from its scabbard and 'carry it naked before her Majesty'.

This sword, taken from the altar and delivered to the Queen partway through the Coronation ceremony, was hers to use 'for the terror and punishment of evildoers'. Specifically, it was to help her

> stop the growth of iniquity ...
> restore the things that are gone to decay,
> maintain the things that are restored,
> punish and reform what is amiss,
> and confirm what is in good order.[93]

Some people thought the Lord Chamberlain had a similar responsibility with regard to the public stage, and were aggrieved by his willingness to give ground. There was, however, one particular iniquity against which Scarbrough did take up the sword—or at least the shield—and it is on this that the next chapter will focus.

CHAPTER TWO

'Packed with Nancies'

Homosexuality and the Stage (I)

> The Lord Chamberlain is frequently urged to pass plays on homosexuality on the plea that the airing of that particular vice and its usual attendant disasters would have a cathartic affect. The majority of his advisers, however, advise against the licensing of such plays and, undoubtedly, those who wish to produce them have their eyes more on the box-office than on moral uplift.[1]

As with Beckett, so with Genet. On 1 January 1953, Troubridge reported on the script of *The Maids*.

> Nobody had ever heard of Jean Genet until Jean Paul Sartre, founder of Existentialism, wrote a short book saying that he was a blackguard, a ruffian and a pervert, but a writer of genius. He then became popular in Paris, where his one novel ... and his plays, notably this one, created a minor morbid vogue.

The Royal Court had already staged *Les Bonnes* in its original French. According to Troubridge, 'The more responsible dramatic critics deplored it as decadent, and also hinted that Sartre had been sold a pup as to Genet's genius'. Nevertheless, the same theatre now wanted to perform an English version. But there were elements in the translation which aroused the Reader's worst suspicions:

> '*the twin beds where two sisters fell asleep dreaming of one another.*'
> Might be harmless, but not in this play, I think ...
> '*You don't want us to ... to organize things in the dark.*'
> I suspect this, though I do not understand it fully.

Troubridge was not oblivious to the play's theatrical potential, but he saw it as his duty to protect audiences from unpleasant ideas and spectacle.

Even if he wasn't always sure of where boundaries should be set, Genet's play could not be allowed to invade them:

> Though written with a certain hysterical power, this is a horrible, deeply decadent and morbid play, quite unsuited, I should have thought, to public performance before mixed audiences. But as the point at which mere decadence in itself is sufficient to incur the refusal of a licence is a difficult and delicate matter to determine, I am cowardly enough to welcome the definite indications of Lesbianism which simplify my task.

Scarbrough agreed:

> this play appears unwholesome and macabre, and no doubt on the stage, if it were effectively acted, those characteristics would be more pronounced. I would not, however, think it would be justifiable to refuse a licence if that were all that should be said about it: but running through the whole Play is a suggestion of Lesbianism, not easy to follow, not directly described and in the main left to be inferred: none the less it appears to be the essential background to the plot.
>
> In my opinion that invests those other characteristics with a depravity which makes the play unsuitable for public performance before mixed audiences.

The Royal Court took up the gauntlet, and Genet's translator, Bernard Frechtman, professed what was perhaps a slightly disingenuous innocence: 'We have reflected upon the possible reason for your refusal to grant a licence,' he protested 'and in the absence of any explanation from your office, have been unable to imagine what the reason might be.' Aware that the Lord Chamberlain might have been influenced by reviews of the Court's French language production, Frechtman queried the fairness of these. *The Maids*, he insisted, was just 'a play about two simple-minded girls' of 'infantile mentality', and he contested the accuracy—and competence—of the press reports:

> I do recognize the fact that the London production of the play, in the original French text, did give rise to misunderstanding. Various critical articles in the press contained serious errors of interpretation. Some critics, for example, referred to Madame and Monsieur as a prostitute and a procurer. I submit that there is absolutely nothing in the text to justify this interpretation. Such errors can be attributed only to an imperfect knowledge of French.

While the drama appears to be melodramatic, explained Frechtman, this was 'only the instrument of the author's dramatic irony'. He insisted it was a deeply serious and philosophical work which 'transcends the trivial plot and evolves into a metaphysical drama of appearance and reality and a quest for the truth of the self'. The translator also played the status and sympathy cards: 'M. Genet and I are professional writers who live by our pen': the refusal of a licence was therefore 'a cause of hardship to each of us', and 'a stain upon our professional reputation'. Meanwhile, the playwright himself was currently in London and prepared to delay his departure until this matter had been resolved. They were willing to compromise:

> M. Genet and I should welcome an opportunity to talk with you in order to learn the reasons for your rejection and, if possible, to make such modifications as would enable the play to meet the requirements of the British stage.

But Frechtman's letter did not go down particularly well: 'I expected something like this,' wrote someone at St James's; 'But not such a triumph of understatement of which any Englishman would be proud.' The slant offered on the sisters did not persuade them: 'Heaven save me from such "simple-minded girls".'

The following month, a revised script was submitted. 'I have to report that all the indications of Lesbian relations between the mistress and her two maids have been removed,' noted Troubridge; 'also all other lines objected to in my first report, except for three which, under the changed circumstances, I agree are no longer suggestive.' Though he still considered Genet's play to be inherently 'horrible, deeply decadent and morbid', the crucial change had been made and the revised text could be licensed.[2]

Public fear of homosexuality was rife during the early 1950s, in part because of its deep associations with international political treachery and betrayal. De Jongh tells us that the homosexual was widely identified as a 'potential traitor and spy', and that 'witch hunts' were by no means limited to America. In Britain, too, the homosexual was 'demonised, cast as the archetype of danger, the epitome of the decadent and corrupt'.[3] Shellard agrees that the 1950s represented 'a period of persecution for the gay man in Britain', and suggests that the defection of two British homosexual spies (Guy Burgess and Donald MacLean) to the Soviet Union in 1951 'provided a scarcely needed pretext for a clampdown'.[4] For some, the rapid decline of the British Empire was all too easily linked to sexual degradation and perversity:

> commentators described the prospect of British imperial eclipse in terms of immorality, corruption and perversion. Manly virtues had, it was

supposed, built British power, and its decline was therefore explained as the degeneration of aristocratic manhood into sexual deviance and political radicalism. 'Perversion is very largely a practice of the too idle and the too rich,' wrote the popular *Sunday Express* columnist John Gordon, 'It does not flourish in lands where men work hard and brows sweat with honest labour.'[5]

According to Shellard, pressure from the FBI resulted in 'a full-scale persecution' in which the British government was expected to identify and remove homosexuals holding public office. Alan Turing, the mathematician who had cracked the war-time Enigma code, was one of many who underwent enforced hormone therapy, and an article from a medical journal published in April 1954 asserted that 'in over 100 cases of castration' carried out on homosexuals, all but one had led to 'gratifying results'.[6]

The sheer number of arrests and prosecutions rose hugely, and Shellard contrasts the remarkable 1,686 of 1952 and 2,034 of 1954 with the total of 299 for the whole of the second half of the nineteen thirties. In a not untypical case of the early fifties, a judge imprisoning the members of a 'gang of homosexuality', expressed his shock and distaste at finding 'the criminal calendars packed full of cases of indecent assault and gross indecency between males'. When the actor John Gielgud was famously and successfully prosecuted for 'persistently importuning male persons for an immoral purpose', the judge warned him that his behaviour was 'dangerous to other men' and 'a scourge in this neighbourhood', advising him to 'see your doctor the moment you leave here'.[7]

In terms of public profile, previous cases were eclipsed by the prosecution and conviction in early 1954 of Lord Montagu, Michael Pitt-Rivers and Peter Wildeblood on indecency charges also involving two members of the R.A.F., who were given guarantees of non-prosecution in return for the evidence they gave. Shellard describes the case as 'a show trial', and 'the UK's closest experience to McCarthyism'.[8] Yet some have drawn attention to the 'surprising wave of sympathy', widely felt and expressed towards the defendants in this case, and Alan Sinfield detects a major shift in which homosexuality came to be seen not as a sin, but as a clinical condition and a social problem. Nonetheless, Sandbrook points out that 'Surveys in the mid-fifties ... suggested that at least half the population considered homosexuality "disgusting"'.[9] Be that as it may, a significant event with long-term ramifications took place in April 1954, when the government established a committee of fifteen men and one woman under John Wolfenden to consider and report on the laws relating to homosexual offences and to prostitution. This, then, was the context in which the Lord Chamberlain continued to restrict stage references to homosexuality.

In the spring of 1955, the Assistant Comptroller, Norman Gwatkin, sent an 'off the record' letter to W. P. Roberts at the Home Office, requesting some information and advice:

1 Is there any indication that male homosexuality is on the increase?
2 If so, a) within what age group? b) in what particular professions?
3 Is the number of prostitutes increasing?
4 Is there any indication that any of the above owe their waywardness to plays or cinemas?

Gwatkin explained that, following private consultations carried out in 1946 and 1951 on 'the advisability or otherwise of passing plays on male and female sex abnormalities', the Lord Chamberlain's current policy was to ban such plays:

We try to keep more or less abreast of the times, but so far we have not licensed more than two or three plays in which unnatural vice is mentioned. We have never passed a play about Lesbianism and, as I say, very very rarely one in which homosexuality is mentioned.

However, he added: 'We have had a great many plays on the latter theme and a number on the former.' Pressures were therefore mounting, and the Office knew that the principle of whether to license was going to resurface sooner rather than later. As Gwatkin told Roberts:

It would help Lord Scarbrough, when he is thinking of this matter again, if he had some concrete facts to range alongside the opinions and theories which he has already learned.
    It occurs to me that you may have acquired just such statistics as His Lordship requires, and that it may be possible for you to let me have them for his official use.

In reply, Roberts sent a series of statistical tables showing the annual figures for 'unnatural offences' which had come to court in the past twenty-five years, and the age and profession of those involved. While acknowledging that the figures were incomplete and flawed, he suggested that the Home Office had 'no doubt that the increase, which is between four- and five-fold over pre-war figures, reflects a pretty substantial increase in the prevalence of such activities'. He pointed out that the rise appeared to be 'evenly spread over the various groups' and that there was also 'nothing to suggest that the increase is particularly noticeable in certain professions'. Indeed, the evidence suggested that 'homosexuality is not a phenomenon peculiar to any profession or social stratum, but manifests itself among all callings and at all levels'. Gwatkin expressed surprise at this last point: 'It is instructive to see that homosexuality is manifested at all social levels,' he wrote; 'one had rather the impression that this irregularity was more prevalent in the "stalls" rather than in the "gallery".' Interestingly, he suspected that the figures given for homosexuality amongst the upper classes were too low, and speculated that some offenders were astute and wealthy enough to escape the attentions of the police.

Roberts also disparaged the 'general laxity of public opinion on these matters which did not prevail (say) fifty years ago', and here the Assistant Comptroller agreed:

> I well remember in my youth that homosexuals were met with very rarely in comparison with today; and they received very short shrift. Now they walk the streets with their sisters. Similarly, one meets socially in the 'stalls' class, people who are well-known homosexuals and whose presence would not have been tolerated a few years ago. Equally, the subject is quite openly discussed by the young of both sexes as, it seems, nothing more than an interesting phenomenon.

In response to Gwatkin's question about theatre's possible influence on the growth of homosexuality, Roberts said he would 'hesitate to venture any opinion on whether the present state of affairs is due in any way to the influence of plays or cinemas'. On balance, he thought it more likely that these media were reflecting rather than creating public attitudes. Perhaps more interestingly, his reply undermines the claim that references to homosexuality had been entirely absent from the stage:

> I have seen three or four revues at west end theatres since the war (and very good they were, too!) which have convulsed the house with homosexual innuendos conveyed by a skilful use of gesture and double entendre. If, in fact, the stage has had any adverse influence on the position (which I, personally, doubt), then I would think that it would be by way of shows such as this, which treat the whole thing as a laughing matter, rather than by way of the straight plays which treat the subjects seriously. But this is just a personal view.

Roberts also quoted someone recently convicted of a homosexual offence, who had claimed that:

> The popularity in Britain since the war of frankly homosexual entertainments such as the *Soldiers In Skirts* revues suggests that such men (i.e. homosexuals) are now regarded by middle- and working-class audiences with tolerant amusement instead of with scorn.

Defensively, the Assistant Comptroller replied: 'We do try to cut all homosexual jokes, whether by gesture or double-entendre.' But he conceded that 'we are not always successful'. The problem, said Gwatkin, was that such gags 'always raise a laugh'.[10]

There were indeed many occasions when the Office cut overt gags from the scripts of comic routines: 'Shakespeare not to be played as a homosexual', they insisted in relation to a sketch which required Shakespeare to enter 'rather pansy'.[11] More than once, they required that 'the word "peculiar" should be changed to something that cannot be interpreted as meaning homosexual'.[12] Other typical stipulations included 'there must be no homo-sexual business accompanying the line by Arthur: "Oh, Vicar!"';[13] 'Cut the business of the two male ballet dancers. It's bound to be effeminate';[14] 'Omit "the place is packed with Nancies"';[15] 'Omit "I thought you were a gentleman's gentleman?" "No fear, too many women about".'[16] From a William Douglas Home play, they removed lines about Cousin Alec going to Algeria to practise his painting: 'Well he does'; 'Yes on his face'.[17] Troubridge was even worried there was 'some vulgar and possibly homosexual connotation' in a reference within a naval farce to a guided missile which was nicknamed The Creeper 'because it attacks its target from the rear'.[18]

Stand-up comedians who more usually appeared in shows and venues outside the Lord Chamberlain's control frequently encountered problems when they found themselves in situations where they were subject to his licence. Frank Randle, and especially his co-performer Gus Aubrey, hit trouble with *Randle's Scandals of 1953*:

> The strongest objection is taken to Gus Aubrey's imitation of a pervert ... and I am to request that all such business be deleted at once. So that there may be no misunderstanding I detail the objectionable features of his Act:–
>   The mincing walk and effeminate hand gestures.
>   The making of an obscene gesture with the index and middle finger of the right-hand.
>   The feminine pose with one knee slightly touching the other.
>   The ogling of other male characters.
> His Lordship wishes to make it quite plain that he takes the most serious view of this sort of thing, and that instructions have been issued for immediate action to be taken in any case where 'pansy', 'nancy', or other perverted characterisation is introduced on the stage.[19]

Bud Flanagan and the Crazy Gang also clashed with the Censorship at the start of 1955, following an inspection of *Jokers Wild*. Hill reported that 'The pansies were not the worst examples of their type', and might be adjudged 'merely "precious" young men', but changes were demanded:

the Lord Chamberlain feels that he must use the powers given to him by S. 14 of the Theatres Act and forbid the use of the line 'We've hardly had time to put our things together', together with the accompanying business of the Gang sticking brooms through each other's legs at this juncture. As regards the young man, it is obvious that a stage Varsity accent can convey more than one implication, and I am to do no more than to ask that you will do your best to ensure that no false impression is conveyed.

They also insisted that 'Mr Chester Wheezy must not act in an effeminate manner' and eliminated the lines 'I bet I know what he is', 'I bet you don't'. (The Assistant Comptroller helpfully pointing out that 'The same objection would not exist to "I bet I know who he is"').[20]

Yet the policy was not always consistent, and some contraventions were discreetly overlooked. On one occasion, the Lord Chamberlain was persuaded to give permission for a punch line in a revue sketch in which a tough looking cowboy shoots his way into a saloon, terrorises the occupants, and strides across the bar in silence before asking in 'a small mincing voice' for a 'Small port and lemon'.[21] Presumably the fact that the revue was to be performed by GCHQ staff in Cheltenham made Scarbrough more prepared to turn a blind eye. Anyway, it was more or less common knowledge that even as the Lord Chamberlain banned some gags, much cruder and more explicit ones were being presented up and down the country, in shows outside his control.

On the whole, playwrights were probably easier to control than live comedians. As with *The Maids*, *The White Terror* was licensed in January 1953 only after it had been 'de-Lesbianized', with 'Daphne's jealous Lesbian friend' replaced by 'a spiv-type young man'.[22] In April, a play in which a father 'suddenly wakes up to the knowledge that his 19-year-old son Charles ("Lolo") is a pansy' was submitted by H.M. Tennent for production at the Lyric, Hammersmith. The original French text of *Les Oeufs de l'autruche* had been refused two years earlier, and the Reader found the English version equally provoking and unacceptable: 'though most amusing, it belongs to its country and will not travel.' 'What a pity,' remarked Gwatkin in the margin. By October, the management had removed or sufficiently disguised the character, and a licence was approved.[23]

In the autumn of 1953, Sophia De Crespigny enquired whether it would be worth while submitting her script, *The Jewel in the Lotus*. The dramatis personae included Plato, Socrates and Alcibiades, and the author claimed that 'four fifths of the lines are verbatim translations from the classical Greek'. But she explained that although her project had the support of several practitioners—including Peter Brook and Norman Marshall—

they 'all agreed that it would not pass the Censor except in a version so bowdlerised that half the charm and merit of the play would vanish'. De Crespigny offered a number of reasons why her script deserved a licence:

> the classical Athenians were bi-sexual and to portray them in any other way would be ridiculous, and impossible, but the actual plot of my play is simply the adventures (authentic) of Alcibiades (and his page boy, Myiscus,) from the time he betrayed the Athenians, till his murder by the Persian Satrap's hirelings. And this exact story has already been done in a recent film in which Dirk Bogarde is a fugitive from justice, together with a little eight year old boy. The more danger and adversity they share the greater becomes their spiritual affection for each other, so gradually this affection is the one ennobling factor in their lives. In fact my play is AGAINST homosexuality, and endeavours to show that only platonic love between men is admissible, whilst physical love is the reverse ...

She also attached a lengthy statement by Professor Hans Licht supporting her claims for platonic homosexuality and the authenticity of her portrait:

> The Greek love for boys is a peculiarity of character based upon religious and aesthetic foundations. It was not hostile to marriage, but supplemented it as an important factor in education. We may speak of a definite bi-sexuality amongst Greeks, and to portray them in any other manner is to juggle with history, and to misrepresent this great people.

None of this cut much ice at St James's Palace. Gwatkin explained that the script could only be considered when it was submitted, but warned her it was unlikely to be approved. As so often, he tried to suggest that this had less to do with the Lord Chamberlain's own views than with public attitudes and expectations:

> In fairness I should make it plain that, however exalted the sentiments in which it has been expressed, the Lord Chamberlain has not hitherto accepted that a theme of homo-sexuality or of bi-sexuality is one that can be properly appreciated by contemporary audiences.

De Crespigny's script seems never to have been submitted.[24]

Heriot was also uneasy about a scene in Enid Bagnold's *Little Idiot*, in which a young woman complains about finding herself at a party 'where all the men were pansies'. Heriot agonised about how seriously to take this. 'It's inoffensive enough—and God knows, realistic enough, too,' he reported; 'I don't quite know what to suggest.' Gwatkin was clearer: 'If we are consistent we must still emulate the ostrich!' 'Pansies' was cut, and a reference to 'a young man out of the British Museum who can't think of anything but a young man out of the Victoria & Albert' was altered to 'a young man out of the National Gallery who can't think of anything but beansprouts and Chinese cookery'.[25] Yet it would be naïve to think that changes such as these would have removed all suggestions of homosexuality from the performance. As Dan Rebellato has observed, there were languages, of greater or lesser degrees of subtlety, which pointed audiences towards reading homosexuality into a play, 'through indirection, encoding, irony, ambiguity and *double entendre*'.[26] The fact is that even with regard to homosexuality, the Lord Chamberlain's Office sometimes seems to have been going through the motions and covering its collective back, rather than seeking to root out the subject entirely.

In September 1953, Binkie Beaumont telephoned the Lord Chamberlain's Office to ask if they would read Julian Green's American civil war play *Sud* in its original French, to test its chances of receiving a licence in some form. 'If the report is satisfactory, they will then proceed with an English adaptation, but they don't want to go to the expense of this if the theme is unacceptable,' explained Titman. Troubridge reported on the French text, and considered the implications: 'This play raises once again the question of the degree and extent to which the perversion of homosexuality may be dealt with on the public stage, which is a matter of high policy for the Lord Chamberlain alone.' The narrative centred on a lieutenant in the army who, on the eve of war, suffers a 'revelation of the depths of his nature and of a most imperious love' for a young man whom he encounters. Though he tries to suppress his feelings and to proceed with a marriage, he is unable to do so, and ends up sacrificing his life in a duel with the man he loves. Troubridge said the narrative was based on 'a conception that is new in my theatrical experience, that of platonic homosexuality'. He was not convinced that this was much better than the other sort. 'How grave and noble is platonic homosexuality?' he asked. 'In my eyes not very.' He noted that there was 'no concealment' of the 'homosexual passion', and drew attention to 'a certain suppressed flagellomania' in the form of 'gloating and unnecessary references to various whippings'. As things stood, there was only one possible recommendation. But Troubridge seemed to think that perhaps a change in policy might be on the cards—and that *South* might even lead the way:

> As this is an altogether morbid play about an aspect of homosexuality, I am not in doubt that I must pronounce against it, but with the proviso that, if the Lord Chamberlain should have in mind any possible relaxation of the present attitude, this would provide the occasion, as *Sud* is not exactly scabrous in the manner of other plays on the subject, and the author may

be said to have succeeded in effecting the limited degree of sublimation of which the nature of the theme allows.

The Comptroller added his pennyworth: 'I do not pretend to have read this play in French,' he told Scarbrough, 'although I have stumbled through a bit of it.' But he was clear that 'The question is one of principle and for you alone to decide'. He warned that, while it might not be physicalised, there was 'nothing ambiguous in the relationship between the two men'. Scarbrough duly ruled that 'The theme is unacceptable, and a licence would not be granted', and the Office wrote to Beaumont to warn him against bothering to have the text translated.

In the spring of 1955, an English version of *South*, was presented by the Arts Theatre Club, which then sought a licence for public performance. On the request of H. M. Tennent, Scarbrough went to see it, and invited his Comptroller and Assistant Comptroller to accompany him. 'I suggest that we all three go and compare notes afterwards.' It is clear that he was beginning to look for a way to relax his policy a degree or two. 'Let no one think that I am going to give the green light to plays about homosexuality,' he wrote; 'The point which arises here is precisely where to draw the line and it must be a line which is defensible and not one which can be breached and let the flood through.' It had been suggested to him— probably by Beaumont—that the core of *South* was 'a David and Jonathan friendship and that this is very different from carnal homosexuality'. The question was whether Scarbrough could accept the distinction. 'Can a line be drawn between the two?' he asked. 'I think it might be: but ... I would like the collective wisdom of the office on this point.' Reading the English script as submitted, Gwatkin found only 'the very remotest suggestion of homosexuality—in this translation at any rate', and suggested he had 'had to try very hard to find any illegitimate suggestion'. Reviewing the private production, the Press had taken a similar attitude; 'even *Punch* I gather, thought we were being a bit spinsterish,' noted Gwatkin; 'Admittedly the author in his avant-propos talks about homosexuality as a "grave and noble subject" but then he's French!' However, after watching it in performance, Scarbrough decided that Green's play was not quite so innocent as he had been led to believe: 'I was wrong in thinking this was about a David or Jonathan kind of friendship,' he wrote; 'Its line is more accurately described by the author.' The ban on *South* remained in place until 1959.[27]

Yet even as he imposed this ban in the autumn of 1953, the Lord Chamberlain was licensing Philip King's *Serious Charge*—a drama in which the 'bachelor vicar of a small village is slandered with charges of homosexual assault by a young ruffian whose own vices he has found out'.[28] It was a decision which a later Comptroller of the Office would call 'a minor landmark',[29] and the fact that the Lord Chamberlain and his staff knew even at the time that they had made a big call is best demonstrated by the title they assigned to the relevant file in the Lord Chamberlain's Archive: 'REPORT ON *SERIOUS CHARGE*—FIRST PLAY LICENSED WITH ANY ASSOCIATION WITH A PERVERSION THEME'.

Heriot had a clear justification for his recommendation: 'We are in no doubt at any time that the vicar is innocent of the "serious charge",' he wrote; 'Therefore, though the forbidden topic of homosexuality shadows this play, it does so in an inoffensive manner.'[30] Indeed, the accusation against the vicar is trumped up in front of our eyes by Larry, an unpleasant and unscrupulous 'wide boy', in order to further his own ends. It is not hard to see why King's play was more acceptable than some of the banned plays; just enough had been left out to make it seem safe, and the Public Morality Council even placed it in their 'Recommended' category. On the other hand, Kenneth Tynan's review suggested that a better dramatist 'would have given the hero suppressed homosexual tendencies of which he is made suddenly and poignantly aware', and conjectured that 'Perhaps the idea occurred to him; and with it the certain knowledge that the Lord Chamberlain would have crushed it on sight'.[31] This, as Tynan was implying, is actually censorship at its most effective. Writing about it much more recently, Nicholas de Jongh has charged King with 'exploiting the period attraction of homosexuality and titillating prominent audiences'.[32]

But only at the most obvious level is it possible to maintain that the accusations of homosexuality against the vicar are intended to be read as complete fabrications. Early in the play we are given a clue, with the information that the newly arrived vicar has no wife, and we also observe that he is not attracted to the woman who is making a play for him. Then we learn that he is personally responsible for the tasteful décor of the room—in itself to be read as unusual—which, moreover, is described as 'a real woman's room'. Furthermore, while Larry may be unpleasant, he is far from stupid, and there are overt hints that he recognises something in the vicar which others have missed: 'p'raps I'm not so dumb as they are. P'raps I can see a bit further in front of my nose than they can.' We also discover that Howard has thrown Larry out of the choir because he 'overheard him pouring absolute filth into the ears of two of the youngest lads in the choir',[33] and when he sarcastically compliments Larry on his convincing courtroom behaviour, it is hard to miss what King wants us to gather from the boy's response:

> HOWARD: Yes, Larry, you made quite an impression with your soft voice; your golden hair; your angelic face …
> LARRY: That's sissy talk. (*After a long curious look at Howard*) Isn't it?[34]

Again, Scarbrough hesitated over his decision. 'This is where we want the

Solomon touch,' wrote Gwatkin, who was only too aware that other texts had been refused or cut 'for less obvious homosexuality'. But the licence was issued. 'The judgement of Solomon has been given!' wrote Gwatkin; 'And may God have mercy on your soul.'[35]

Rebellato suggests that *Serious Charge* 'is structured around hints, semi-disclosure, a possible queerness beneath the apparently false charge',[36] and Sinfield agrees that it 'teases the audience, challenging it to ponder whether there can be so much smoke without the glimmer of a fire'.[37] In truth, there is not much ambiguity about the message. Certainly a member of the public who wrote to complain to the Lord Chamberlain (signing herself 'a mother') had no doubts what the play was about:

> In view of the number of grave cases of this nature which have recently engaged public attention, does the Lord Chamberlain consider this is the moment for public performance on a play of this theme? ... plays on the subject of inversion are attended in the main by those who are themselves perverts or near perverts. The writer of the play is himself a well-known homosexual whose life is spent amongst men of the same type ...
>
> The theme should be left to the Royal Commission, to the psychiatrist, to the police and to social workers.

The issue also dominated discussions about the making and licensing of a film version of the play, with examiners from the British Board of Film Censorship observing that if they were to license this, 'It will make it very nearly impossible to reject other films of a melodramatic kind which flirt with the topic of homosexuality'. In fact, the first version of the film script shrewdly changed Larry into Dora, so that the vicar stands accused of the presumably less heinous offence of interfering with a girl.[38]

Reviewing the stage production, press reviews drew an obvious connection between King's play and *The Children's Hour*, the plot of which centres on similarly unproven accusations against two school teachers.[39] First rejected by the Lord Chamberlain's Office in 1935, Lillian Hellman's play had been submitted down the years by a number of managements. It had been largely well received by theatre critics when staged privately in London in 1950 ('uplifting and cleansing' ... 'Beautifully and intelligently handled' ... 'never in the least salacious');[40] and the author herself had visited St James's Palace in the early summer of 1953 ('a nice woman, and not quite what we expected'), when she even offered to change the ending:

> She said that she was disappointed and surprised that it was not allowed on the English stage, as it was a moral play in that it ventilated an evil and its dreadful results.
>
> The Lord Chamberlain agreed that it did all that, but he was not

prepared to pass plays of this kind: moreover he was encouraged not to do so by strong support from a very wide field of advisers.[41]

Gwatkin could not help but wonder whether the Reader's recommendation to license *Serious Charge* was out of step with this. Heriot insisted: 'But I am being consistent. Here there is no suggestion of real homosexuality—it is all lies.' It is possible that if *The Children's Hour* had been submitted for the first time after *Serious Charge* had been approved, it too might have been accepted. Certainly the Office was much more reluctant to take the decisive action of overturning a ban they had previously imposed, since this signalled either that the original decision had been mistaken, or that there was a definite change in policy.

Yet doubts about the wisdom of having licensed King's play remained. When the Comptroller went to see it, he was singularly unimpressed: 'It is melodramatic twaddle,' he wrote; 'The dialogue is quite appallingly unrealistic, and the situations bear no relation to what would happen in real life.' He admitted, though, that the play appealed to audiences:

> In spite of the very bad weather the theatre was quite full, and the audience seemed to enjoy the two hours of sheer melodramatic nonsense. I noticed one small girl, aged about nine or ten, in the audience. What her parents could have been thinking of to take her I do not know.

In his view, the 'forbidden theme' was impossible to miss: 'the whole point of the play is blackmail,' and since 'the only possible offence for which the young man could blackmail the clergyman is homosexuality,' he concluded, 'so there could be no play without the theme of homosexuality.' In licensing the play, then, Scarbrough was surely trying to shift the boundaries and establish a new dividing line. As Nugent knew, it would be hard both to maintain and to justify:

> I would suggest, therefore, that the answer to any application from authors who have written rather similar plays is that the Lord Chamberlain, after very careful consideration, could not see his way to refusing a licence for this play on the grounds that it was about homosexuality because the theme is not that but blackmail, and that the homosexuality is brought in only because it is the one offence that could produce the situations in the play.[42]

The Lord Chamberlain had taken a cautious step in licensing *Serious Charge*, but he was not about to cave in.

The early months of 1954 saw the rejection of two scripts focused on Oscar

Wilde. *The King of Life* was 'a wholly unnecessary play' which had been 'infelicitously translated from the French'. In Heriot's view, 'If the Lord Chamberlain should at any time permit the Wilde Case to be the subject for a play, there are several better works waiting in the files'.[43] The second was Maurice Rostand's *The Trial of Oscar Wilde*, which had been due for a private production twenty years earlier, before being cancelled because of protests by Lord Alfred Douglas. Heriot thought there would still be objections from Wilde's descendants, and that what he called 'the general atmosphere of sodomy' precluded a licence.[44] In the paranoid atmosphere of the early 1950s, it is unthinkable that the Lord Chamberlain could have permitted the debate which takes place between Wilde and Harris:

> WILDE: Do you suppose that I should have been condemned for my relations with a few disreputable boys, who lived by selling themselves? England is full of men who are doing what I did ... No, no, England has no objection to that; there is no vice she will not tolerate so long as hypocrisy can mask it skilfully enough; but she will rise up in all her wrath against love ... That a love, pure, capable of the utmost sacrifice, can burn in one man for another—that is what the middle-class dare not admit. That is why I'm here ...
> HARRIS: Can't you understand at all why the whole of humanity, from the mysterious depths of its very being, turns instinctively against your kind of love? It's because life itself revolts against it. ...
> WILDE: Prejudice, only prejudices ... It shines in the sonnets of Shakespeare, lights up the marbles of Michelangelo and throbs in the wisdom of Socrates.[45]

Also thrown out in February was *The Wicked and the Weak*, another of the 'currently fashionable "vice racket" plays' set in a near brothel. 'THIS WILL NOT DO AT ALL,' insisted Troubridge.

> where it would seem to me to be out of the question for public performance is that the hotel-brothel concerned has for inmates four female prostitutes, one male prostitute and one male homosexual amateur. The male prostitute displays on the stage lace panties he is proposing to wear professionally, and is found also to be wearing beneath his shirt a pair of silk cami-knickers stolen from one of the tarts.

As the Reader explained: 'I do not consider matters in the least improved by the paltry device of stating on a Dramatis Personae page that neither of the homosexuals must be played in the least effeminately.'[46]

By contrast, Terence Rattigan's *Table Number Seven* could be licensed without objection because it sufficiently concealed its subject. Set among the elderly residents of a hotel in Bournemouth, it centres on a Major who is convicted for pestering a woman in a cinema. As Shellard shows, there was a 'discreet coded meaning', and the story may well have been intended to allude specifically to the recent arrest and conviction of Rattigan's friend, John Gielgud. Certainly the Major's crime was not taken at face value by critics, while Rattigan himself asked the producer of the American production to alter the woman to a man, stating that this had been his original intention, abandoned because of his (doubtless accurate) assumptions about how the Lord Chamberlain would react.[47]

In the autumn of 1954, a licence was refused for *The Immoralist*—an adaptation of Gide's novel which had recently been staged on Broadway. Heriot described the play as 'riddled with its subject'—something which was 'not to be wondered at, when one considers that Gide himself was a homosexual'. Heriot suggested that the theme was 'not treated detachedly enough', but Tynan used his review of the private production at the Arts Theatre to launch a coruscating attack on the Lord Chamberlain for having 'overstepped his brief', describing *The Immoralist* as 'the most detached play about homosexuality our theatre has yet seen'.[48] Four years later, it would be one of the first beneficiaries when the Lord Chamberlain retreated from the trench into which he had dug himself: 'Having re-read this play on our change of policy I have no doubt that it can rightly be termed a serious play on the theme of homosexuality and can now receive a licence.'[49]

Perhaps the most undisguised attempt to address the subject directly in the first half of the decade was Winifred Comstock's *The Golden Mask*, a play which, as Troubridge explained, 'concerns itself entirely with homosexuality, past, present and future'. His summary of the plot makes clear why it had no chance of receiving a licence:

> A charming widow of forty named Caroline certainly has very bad luck with her men. Her husband Charles was in the RAF, and shot himself at the end of the War, the reason being, though Caroline does not learn this till late in the play, that he was to be court-martialled for homosexual offences. Their son Julian, who is extremely good-looking and does not like girls, is in the army with another six months still to serve. He has inherited his father's taint.[50]

Caroline duly falls in love with an archaeologist, and from his first entry there is no missing the signals:

> Ivor Williams enters, gently propelled by Caroline. He is slender, dark, good-looking: the eyes are large and expressive, the mouth and nose thin and ascetic: his smile is charming and shallow. His movements are quick

and graceful. He is well-tanned though it is winter, and wears his town clothes with ease, though his suede shoes are caked with mud.

In case any doubt remains, we quickly learn that he is a proficient pianist, and that 'he likes gardening, the tidying bit especially … and flowers'.[51] As Troubridge tells us, Ivor marries Caroline 'in a sort of last attempt to grasp at normality'; but when Caroline's son arrives home unexpectedly on the day of their wedding, having being mysteriously discharged from the army, all is lost: 'The meeting with Julian proves too much for Ivor's not very strong heterosexual impulses.' Meanwhile, he has unearthed a Mycenean golden mask of indeterminate sex, which had originally been used 'in ancient and perverted sex rites'. Ivor shows it to Julian, and 'the emenations of this object at once bring together the handsome, talented youth and the perverted man'. The mask then 'runs through the play as an evil symbol of homosexual desires', with Ivor himself referring to it as 'the golden mask that we all wear, the guilty ones'. His marriage with Caroline remains unconsummated, and the two men go away together to Greece 'on a holiday of unhealthy male friendship'.[52]

Back in England, Ivor retreats into denial, too scared to name his feelings. Believing himself spurned, Julian falls in love with a young American girl, and in desperation, Ivor is driven to reveal the truth:

> IVOR: What can she give you compared to me?
> JULIAN: Let me go, you're hurting me.
> IVOR: Answer me! Do you think she can match my love, my affection, my companionship?
> JULIAN: You're an old man … She's young and pretty, and she kissed me.
> IVOR: Have you forgotten it all? The days on the beach, the sun … The mask? (*he snatches up the mask*) The mask I found the day we met! (*he thrusts it against Julian's face*) Look, look at yourself … How beautiful you are. You know what sort of a mask this is now, don't you?[53]

But Julian runs away, and the distraught Ivor—perhaps in a reference to the real life Wildeblood prosecution—'picks up a young airman returning to a camp, and indecently assaults him'.[54] The following morning, a police sergeant arrives at the house to arrest Ivor: 'To my mind your kind are among the worst criminals in the country, because you corrupt the young. If I had my way, you'd be given the cat and locked up for the rest of your life.'[55] Having tried and failed to shoot himself, Ivor is led away to prison, leaving Caroline in tears. While the play's sympathies and views about homosexuality may have been ambiguous, its blatant depiction of the subject placed it well beyond any possibility of amendment, or of public performance.

In February 1955, another unsuccessful attempt was made to persuade the Office to license *Huis Clos*. Sartre's play was staged privately as *Vicious Circle*, and Scarbrough received a letter from Curtis Brown Ltd, the author's representatives, inviting him to attend a performance and reconsider his ruling. The letter pointed out that 'The play has been broadcast four times in the Third Programme', and claimed that 'as a result of the present revival, the subject matter has been discussed widely in the National press without any suggestion of offence.' While acknowledging that 'the Lord Chamberlain's office performs an essential service in protecting the public from crude and tasteless displays', Sartre's play was neither 'degrading or designed to corrupt', and it was 'difficult to defend' the maintenance of a total ban from the British stage:

> *Vicious Circle* has been acted all over the Continent and in America and is universally acknowledged as the finest work of one of the best modern French authors; it has now been filmed and is showing to packed houses in Paris.

However, the reply from the Office was cool, and hardly encouraging:

> If you particularly desire it, the Lord Chamberlain will of course send a representative to see this play, but I think it only fair to point out to you that the chances of his Lordship being able to reconsider his decision at the present time are remote ...

Sartre's play had always been rejected because of its references to lesbianism: 'I do not suppose that this has been eliminated in the present edition of the play.' St James's Palace also maintained—as they were bound to do—that a live stage performance was unique in terms of its potential impact:

> The fact that the play has been broadcast in the Third Programme and has been discussed in the Press does not really affect the situation. You, I am sure, will be the first to understand that there is a difference between words coming over the air and the same words spoken in the more personal atmosphere of a theatre by visible characters. It is interesting to note that certainly when this play was listened to on the air in 1947 many people who listened to the broadcast of the play did not notice the perversion ... whereas it is quite apparent when produced in the theatre.

A representative from the Office did attend a private performance, but simply confirmed that the ban should remain:

> Although Miss Faith Brook, who plays Inez, the Lesbian does not go out

of her way to be erotic, she has to 'make passes' at the girl in a most unpleasant manner during the play. The dialogue may appear innocuous, but the action necessary to the play and the way she speaks certain of her lines leave no doubt as to Inez's 'appetites'. For this reason alone, so long as the ban on perversion exists, it would not seem possible for the Lord Chamberlain to grant a licence for this play.[56]

Personal Enemy, co-written by John Osborne, did at least receive a licence in 1955, but only after some significant alterations had been imposed. Set in America in 1953, just after the end of the war in Korea, the play shows two brothers—Don and Arnie—falling under the influence of an older man. The influence appears to be both political and sexual. Don, unseen in the play, defects and stays in Korea, while the seventeen-year-old Arnie—whose hands are 'long and delicate' and who has long hair and dubious hobbies ('I've never seen a man handle flowers the way he does') is eventually driven to suicide and a possibly false admission that he is a 'pervert'.[57] Troubridge commented:

there is a strong and repeated suggestion that Communism, in connection with those young male characters supposed to believe in it, is associated with sexual perversity. This is, in the final Act, more or less denied, but by that time the strands have got so twisted, and the whole thing so dubious that it needs slow and careful rather than hurried consideration ... It would just be another anti-witch-hunt play, were it not that, at least to my mind, the way the play is written leaves it in most considerable doubt whether the relations between Ward and the two young brothers were in fact innocent.

Gwatkin agreed that 'The perverted element seems to be a gratuitous addition' and proposed 'that the producer should be telegraphed to remove all traces of this from the play'. A series of unspecified compromises was agreed at a private meeting, and the play was licensed 'on the understanding that the alterations agreed ... between Mr Osborne, the Comptroller, Lord Chamberlain's Office are adhered to'.[58]

In recommending that Gide's *The Immoralist* should be turned down, the Reader had warned that it was liable to 'have a corrupting effect on any person not very conversant with the subject'. Scarbrough agreed that 'However skilfully and powerfully it may be written, it will arouse curiosity in the theme'.[59] The key factor which underlay the general ban on references to homosexuality was supposedly to avoid the risk of making people aware of something which they did not know existed—and thus encouraging them to try it. But by the mid-fifties the issue was being so widely discussed in the press and elsewhere, that this argument was becoming less tenable. It only required a couple of plays capable of generating public interest, and a management ready to confront or circumvent the Censorship, and clashes were inevitable.

Robert Anderson's *Tea and Sympathy* had already been a success on Broadway when Binkie Beaumont sent the script to the Lord Chamberlain's Office in November 1953, along with a review of the American production. As so often, Beaumont was testing the water and trying to sound out the likely response before committing himself. Nugent's reply suggested it was hardly worth the cost of having it read:

> I return herewith the script of *Tea and Sympathy*, which both Norman Gwatkin and I have read. We both came independently to the same conclusion—namely, that it would be a waste of your time to submit this play for licence, for the reasons which I gave you on the telephone this afternoon.

It may just have been politeness, but Nugent's letter also contained a hint that perhaps he did not fully support the policy he was bound to enact: 'I read the play with the greatest interest and am only so sorry that I have no alternative but to give you this advice.'

The following year, Donald Albery formally submitted the script. He drew attention to the play's success in America, and probably hoped to win some favour at St James's Palace by promising to keep the setting remote: 'I don't think the locale should be changed from America,' he wrote, 'and I feel that the play should be done, when done in London, exactly as it is done here.' However, the emphasis in Heriot's précis of the plot made a licence seem unlikely:

> A schoolboy at an American college is accused of being a homosexual. To vindicate his manhood he tries to sleep with the local bad girl, but cannot function. The ex-actress wife of his house master has been sorry for him all along—to the extent of alienating her husband's affections, because he has sub-conscious homosexual desires himself. Cut off from him, she comforts the boy (who is to be expelled, since the escapade with the local bad girl has been discovered) by giving herself to him as the final curtain falls.

Surprisingly, he suggested that even if they were somehow to excise the most obvious problem, the tone would still be unacceptable:

> The atmosphere of adolescent sex is common to all boarding schools, I suppose; but the American kind, with its unusually adult swear words and its furtive slavering after desire is too different from the English brand to be acceptable, even if there were no homosexual element.

The Reader dutifully marked specific lines and words which would require amendment if the play were to be licensed; 'I do'nt [sic] however think,' he added, 'that this will arise.' Scarbrough confirmed this judgement, and turned the play down.

Then, in late 1954, Beaumont contacted the Office again to say that the American owners of the copyright were pressing him to submit the script for licence. 'I appreciate that the play may cause certain difficulties,' he acknowledged, 'but I wondered whether—if deletions were made—the basis of the play would be acceptable.' Once again, Nugent's response was far from encouraging: 'I wish I could be more optimistic, but honestly I do not think you would serve any good purpose by submitting this play again. I really have nothing to add to what I told you when we discussed the play about a year ago.' He also advised Beaumont that the script had recently been submitted by another management and been turned down by the Lord Chamberlain: 'I do not think there is any possibility at all that he will change his mind.'

Over the next six months, Beaumont and the American owner of the rights to the play, Mrs Frank, did their very best to persuade the Censorship to reconsider. Given its commercial success in New York, they were not ready to settle for a few nights in a small private club in London. Mrs Frank questioned 'if there is any way to discover what aspects of the play make it objectionable so far as English audiences are concerned', and whether 'a certain amount of re-writing and editing' might solve the problem. Then in February 1955, she and Beaumont visited Nugent, who repeated his view that he 'did not think it at all likely that the Lord Chamberlain would be able to see his way to granting a licence for this play in anything like its present form'. The problem was 'that I did not see how its main subject—viz. homosexuality—could be eliminated from it'. Again, Nugent seemed to hint that perhaps Scarbrough's stance was not fully endorsed by all his staff:

> I told Mrs Frank that both the Assistant Comptroller and I had read the play with the greatest interest and had liked it very much, but the basic principle now in force—whereby the Lord Chamberlain does not allow any plays about perversion—really effectively prevented any question of a licence.

Mrs Frank's response was to dangle a tempting carrot in front of the Comptroller. She offered to pay all expenses for him to travel to Chicago and watch the production there, so he could see for himself that the play was not a danger. She repeated the suggestion in writing, in a letter sent from her hotel in Geneva: 'We are most anxious to have you, or someone you may designate, see the production in America,' she wrote; 'I will be happy to make all arrangements for any time which may be convenient to you, with all costs for our account.' She also sought to reassure him about the play's message: 'I am quite sure you will see that as the script plays homosexuality is at no point condoned and that the theme of the play is loving-kindness.'

Nugent later admitted that he had been 'sorely tempted to accept' the offer, but had reluctantly decided that he 'could not conscientiously accept such lavish hospitality, knowing as I did how very remote were the chances of the ban on her play being withdrawn'. He therefore wrote to Mrs Frank, thanking her for 'the honour of visiting me last week', and explaining that the decision was not in his hands:

> I am overwhelmed by the generosity of your suggestion that I should come out to Chicago to see *Tea and Sympathy*, but I really could not feel justified in putting you to this trouble and expense for a project that I know could not benefit you in any way. As I tried to explain when we met, the objection to *Tea and Sympathy* is the fundamental one that at present the Lord Chamberlain does not allow plays on the subject of homosexuality, whether it is condoned or not, and however tactfully and sympathetically it is treated—and I am quite sure that with Miss Deborah Kerr and your cast it is played quite beautifully and most tastefully—the Lord Chamberlain could not see his way to granting a licence for this particular play.

The Comptroller had actually sounded out Scarbrough about the proposal, and realised he was not going to back down:

> I have spoken to the Lord Chamberlain since we met, have reported the gist of our interview and have now shown him your kind and generous letter but he agrees with me that no good purpose could possibly accrue if I, or any other representative he might choose, saw the play.
>
> I am extremely sorry to give you such a disappointing reply but I would never forgive myself if I took advantage of your kindness, well knowing that all your trouble and expense was bound to be wasted.
>
> Again thanking you so much, and hoping that we may meet again on one of your future visits to London.

Embarrassingly, the story of the offer became public knowledge in May 1955, when a newspaper reported it under the headline 'A Free Flip for the Lord Chamberlain'. Mrs Franks was not mentioned, but the report described Anderson himself as 'a young man more than anxious to write out a cheque to the Earl of Scarbrough'. Quoting the playwright directly, and noting that Scarbrough had 'refused outright' to license this 'fine play', the newspaper shockingly announced that 'so determined is Anderson to persuade him to change his mind, he has made a sensational and unprecedented offer—to fly the censor over to New York *to see the play performed'*. Following this sensational publication, Anderson immediately wrote to apologise to Nugent, claiming that the interviewer had 'blown up a passing remark' and insisting that he would consider it 'the height of bad taste for a visitor in a country to criticise the authority of that country'. While the article certainly caused some discomfiture at St James's Palace, Nugent had little choice other than to accept the apology:

> Items of this sort seldom have much relation to the truth of the interview and, as you can well imagine, we are very used here to misrepresentation. Indeed, when one realises that in some papers nothing is news unless it is a little nasty and in all probability false, one becomes quite hardened to anything that is said. The press are always having a tilt at the Lord Chamberlain, as they tilt at all authority, but that does not worry him at all.

It is impossible to know how fulsome Anderson's apology really was, and how unplanned the press announcement. Certainly, he remained 'unhappy a play which I have always hoped would be considered a highly moral play had been branded as objectionable'. But there, for the time being, *Tea and Sympathy* rested.[60]

A few months later, the script of *Cat on a Hot Tin Roof* arrived at St James's. It sent Heriot into a near frenzy of disgust:

> Once again Mr. Williams vomits up the recurring theme of his not-too-subconscious. This is the fourth play (and there are sure to be others) where we are confronted by the gentlewoman debased, sunk in her private dreams as a remedy for her sexual frustration, and over all the author's horror, disgust and rage against the sexual act ...
>
> The whole thing is pretentious, over-strained, over-emphasised and hysterical. The author obviously believes that he is writing Literature with a big L ... The language is repetitively coarse.

The Reader recommended extensive cuts and 'a careful consideration of the homosexual element'. Only then might it be possible to grant a licence for 'this bogus play'. Williams declined to make any alterations, the licence was withheld, and this play, like Anderson's, remained in abeyance.[61]

Then a third American play added to the pile up. One might not have expected that Arthur Miller's *A View from the Bridge* would have proved especially contentious, but it quickly became the focus of a major confrontation which would damage—perhaps fatally—the Lord Chamberlain's authority. Once more, Binkie Beaumont sent the script to the Office unofficially in January 1956: 'I am naturally very anxious to have your personal views as to whether you think the theme would be acceptable.' This time, he must have had a more encouraging response, because five days later he forwarded the fee so that the play could be formally considered. Heriot reacted quite positively:

Mr Miller may be regarded as one of the few American writers for the stage today whose work has any quality likely to be lasting. Unlike Mr. Tennessee Williams, whose neuroses grin through everything he writes, Mr. Miller's work is always objective.

However, he did identify one possible area of difficulty: 'The implication of homosexuality is clear though it is always oblique,' he noted. Yet he was confident that 'the love-scenes between the young people disprove the charge on every count', and Beaumont was advised that the script could be licensed once four alterations had been made. These included the brief on-stage kiss between two men, and a similarly brief reference to it in the dialogue:

Act Two, page 58, omit the stage direction 'suddenly kisses him'.
Page 59, omit 'You kissed him, he didn't kiss you'.

Given the extent of amendments so frequently demanded, such require-ments must have seemed trivial to the Lord Chamberlain's Office. But the tide was turning, and more dramatists—especially, it seems, foreign ones—were becoming reluctant to accept the basic principle of the Lord Chamberlain deciding what they could and couldn't include. Unusually, Beaumont neither agreed or contested the changes demanded, and his refusal to play ball greatly irritated and discomforted the Lord Chamberlain, as the story entered the public realm with an emphasis and accusation which he did not accept. The Office tried to face down all queries or protests by insisting that 'although it is good publicity to say so', so far as they were concerned Miller's play had not actually been forbidden:

I should like to make it clear that the Lord Chamberlain has not banned this play. When it was submitted for censorship the agents were informed that the Lord Chamberlain was prepared to issue a licence for the Play on receipt of an undertaking that four alterations would be made. These alterations consisted of the omission of a few lines, the alteration of one word, and the omission of a stage direction and a phrase relevant to the stage direction. The stage direction referred to the small action where Eddie kisses the boy. The deletion was required on the grounds that it was too forceful a homosexual implication. It has been the practice for some time not to allow homosexuality on the stage, and the Lord Chamberlain is of the opinion that that view would be supported by a considerable cross-section of public opinion.

It would not appear that the requested omissions would prejudice the general theme and action of the Play. Nevertheless, no reply has ever been received to the Lord Chamberlain's letter referred to above, and no application for a licence for an amended version has been received.[62]

Yet whichever way you looked at it, three American plays by established writers (four if we include *The Children's Hour*), which had all enjoyed success at home, were not being allowed on the London stage. Some of them, at least, had considerable potential to gain not just critical but also commercial success for their owners and managements. The playwrights were unwilling to change the scripts, the owners were reluctant to let them play to limited audiences in small clubs. It seemed like an impasse. Then, in 1956, an alternative presented itself. Namely, to stage the plays privately, but to do so in a large West End theatre, turned into a private venue. It was a strategy which would, as we shall see, challenge and greatly embarrass the Lord Chamberlain, and fundamentally undermine his authority.

CHAPTER THREE

Breaking the Rules,
Breaking the Lord Chamberlain

Unlicensed Plays in the West End

It may well be thought that in the second half on the twentieth century, the censorship of plays should pass from the Lord Chamberlain to a Government department, to some other body, or that it should be abolished altogether.[1]

In April 1956, *Picture Post* printed an article about *Cat on a Hot Tin Roof* under the headline 'THE PLAY YOU MAY NEVER SEE'. In it, Robert Muller explained that the play had been performed on Broadway for 55 weeks 'to standing room only', and that the critics and the public agreed this was Williams's best play. But would it come to England?

A wall of secrecy has been built around the play's possible London production. With the continuing dearth of new British plays, West End theatres are desperate for a sensational 'pre-sold' Broadway success such as this. Yet no commercial management will admit to having obtained the British rights, and none will confess either to having submitted the play to the stage censor, the Lord Chamberlain, or to having it rejected ...

Yet there is strong evidence that the play has been submitted—and been refused a licence. Is it likely that the new Williams play will be treated more leniently by the Lord Chamberlain than Robert Anderson's *Tea and Sympathy*, Julien Green's *South*, Andre Gide's *The Immoralist*, Jean Genet's *The Maids*, or Lillian Hellmann's *The Children's Hour*, all plays of absolute integrity, which have been banned for offending his qualms about dramatised homosexuality?

Muller anticipated that the Arts Theatre—'a private membership club theatre famous for its excellent salvage work'—might come to the rescue, but he pleaded for the Lord Chamberlain to think again:

The problem of homosexuality is at this very moment being discussed by a Royal Commission. Numerous books on the subject are freely available. *Cat on a Hot Tin Roof* is published in this country in book form, and has been widely reviewed. It is, even now, not too late to hope that the Lord Chamberlain will agree to let you see on the stage what, for less trouble and money, you can see in print.[2]

Recalling the events of fifty years ago in a recent interview, Anthony Field, whose decision it was to turn the thousand seater Comedy Theatre in the heart of the West End into a private venue in order to stage unlicensed plays, insisted that it was taken in innocence and with no intention of bringing down the Lord Chamberlain: 'we didn't set out to break the censorship laws, we set out to produce three plays we had great faith in.'[3] Nevertheless, setting up the New Watergate club in Panton Street, just off the Haymarket, was recognised immediately by both sides in the censorship battle as probably the biggest threat the system had ever faced. It led to the Lord Chamberlain himself petitioning the Home Secretary to change the law, asking the Queen to sanction an enquiry into the very existence of theatre censorship, and recommending its possible abolition. It is true that, on a superficial level, the Censorship would survive the crisis intact, apparently seeing off the challenge; the Comedy Theatre and the Watergate would abandon their experiment in 1958, with the former reverting to its public status under the control of the Lord Chamberlain, and he would continue to act as censor, with no official change in his powers. But the events would leave his authority dented. It would be another ten years before legislation was finally enacted, but the strategy of instantly redesignating public theatres as private clubs in order to evade censorship would not be forgotten, and would prove to be a weapon which other directors and managers would wield very effectively.

An irony underlying the whole confrontation was that the very principle of exempting private clubs from the Lord Chamberlain's authority had no established legal basis. No-one knew better than St James's Palace that, if asked to do so in court, it was extremely doubtful whether any distinction could possibly be drawn in law between 'public' and 'private' theatres. What had happened was that successive Lords Chamberlain had turned blind eyes and permitted small clubs to perform unlicensed (usually obscure and/or 'highbrow') plays, seeing this as a harmless and useful safety valve which made it easier for them to maintain their control elsewhere. It was a policy which Scarbrough had no wish to abandon. But the new provocation of a large theatre club presenting extended runs of major plays to a thousand people a night put him in a difficult situation. If he responded by revealing in a court of law that the performance of unlicensed plays in any theatre was almost certainly illegal, and that a private club status afforded no protection against this, he would be accused of instituting a more draconian censorship than ever. Worse, the practical effect would almost inevitably be the stirring up of a level of hostility which might well bring the whole system of theatre censorship crashing down. It might even damage not only the authority of the Lord Chamberlain, but that of his Royal masters and mistresses, in whose household he served. The principle behind the Watergate's innovation was therefore much more dangerous to the Censorship than any of the individual plays—however radical or provocative those seemed—staged there or elsewhere.

The affair kicked off in late August 1956, when the Lord Chamberlain's Office received a request for a meeting from a firm of solicitors representing both Binkie Beaumont, of H.M. Tennent Ltd, and the New Watergate Theatre Club. The latter had recently lost its premises and now proposed to take over the Comedy Theatre, which would duly surrender its licence for public performance and operate as a private club 'for the production of plays, of recognised merit, which have, however, not received your licence'. It may well have been more than coincidence that the letter from the solicitors arrived when most of the staff at St James's were away on annual leave. Scarbrough was shooting pheasants on the Yorkshire moors, Nugent, the Comptroller, was absent, and Gwatkin—his assistant—was about to head off for his holidays to Dunbeath Castle in Scotland. The significance of the letter was obvious, and Gwatkin broke off from his packing to write an internal memorandum.

> It is pleasurable, and usually profitable, to discover a way in which the law can be legally evaded (viz. income tax, motor cars, houses etc.). Provided the evasion is of reasonably small proportions action is usually not taken but when it becomes something really big, and almost a public scandal, the interested government authority puts the necessary stopper on by testing the law, or procuring a new Act.

Gwatkin pointed out that whatever the practice—connived at by successive Lords Chamberlain—may have been, there was no legal distinction between public and private theatres, and no basis for separate treatment:

> The Private Theatre which is at least an evasion of the current Act, if not an actual illegality, has existed since before 1918 and has acquired vested rights, as well as performing a useful function to the Censor in permitting aggravated authors to ventilate their claims.
> The Law Officers have been consulted on this problem from time to time and they have always advised a cautious policy, suggesting that a very strong case be awaited before action is taken. They have, however,

gone so far as to say that in their opinion a performance would not be a
genuinely private one if admission was so general ... that the performance
should be considered a public one.

Beaumont's proposal was different from previous practice not in principle, but in degree. 'The situation is now to be pursued to its logical
consequences by establishing a large commercial theatre as a "Private"
theatre.' Gwatkin wondered whether grounds might be found for barring
this particular step without challenging the overall principle. Perhaps the
Comedy's need to attract large audiences in order to remain financially
viable would lead to club rules being 'laxly administered', giving opportunities for prosecution. Or perhaps the Law Officers could be asked 'as to size
being a factor in determining what is public'. In the meantime, however,
any reply to Beaumont must be carefully worded:

> In view of what we have been told by the Law Officers in the past, even
> tacit approval seems dangerous, and it does not seem to me to be right
> that the Lord Chamberlain should go out of his way to give advice on
> how the law he administers can be evaded—or, indeed, to bind himself
> to any agreement as to action he might or might not take in the future.[4]

It fell to the Lord Chamberlain's secretary (and general dogsbody),
Ronald Hill, to hold the fort at St James's while everyone else was *en
vacances*. Conscious that Hill actually knew more about the history and
practice of theatre censorship than anyone else at St James's, Gwatkin
asked him to 'do a paper on the subject'. Hill was an inveterate writer of
lengthy papers, and probably relished the task more than having a couple
of weeks in the fresh air. His junior position meant that he had to avoid
criticising his superiors, but Hill—himself no liberal when it came to
cutting plays—suggested that the Office had rather brought the problem
on its own head by seeking to impose a rigid policy in relation to homosexuality. Historically, he suggested there had always been 'an upsurge'
in the private theatre movement when a Lord Chamberlain had 'departed
from his policy of judging each play on its merits, and has banned plays on
principle'. Citing previous instances in relation to prostitution and venereal
disease, he observed that the current ban on homosexuality and lesbianism
had again provided 'a focal point' for opponents of censorship. Scarbrough
had trapped himself into a situation where he was now forbidding plays
which were neither pornographic nor obscure, but acclaimed works of art
and potential vehicles for financial exploitation. The Watergate's proposal
for expansion 'into one of the Regular Theatres', supported by Stanley
Rubinstein, 'a very sharp solicitor specialising in theatrical matters', would
be just the start of it:

Not unnaturally the commercial competitors of the Watergate are also going to avail themselves of this opportunity of making money out of the number of homosexual plays at present banned and Mr. Campbell Williams of the Arts Theatre urgently wishes to see the Lord Chamberlain to establish his attitude toward an Arts Theatre Annexe.

Others will follow.

The very act of banning increased the market value:

Many of the plays around which these schemes revolve are American, and they are dramatically good ... The owners are men of substance and they are not willing to lose the chance of making large sums by allowing the plays to be given before tiny audiences in Private Theatres. We may assume, therefore, that they will in general not allow their plays to be produced except in a big theatre and with the prospect of a run of 2 or 3 months.

Hill calculated that over such a period, some 72,000 people might watch a play. Perhaps he had private conversations with those involved, or perhaps he worked it out for himself, but he confidently predicted what would be the next stage:

I can, unless the Lord Chamberlain takes steps to enforce the law, see no reason why the procedure should not be still further enlarged as follows:–

i. An impresario has a first-class play on which he can make much money banned by the Lord Chamberlain

ii. He leases any available West End Theatre in the ordinary way.

iii. He negotiates with each of the established Theatre Clubs to act as his agents in turn and to

(a) Adopt the theatre as its annexe

(b) Use its mailing lists.

He thus has at his disposal a very large allegedly private audience sufficient for any purpose.

iv. If the play fails, or when the run peters out, the theatre merely re-opens under the Lord Chamberlain's public licence.

v. The impresario has run no greater risks than usual. The Private Theatre Clubs have run no risks but made money. The Censor has been completely evaded.

Indeed, the original letter of enquiry had made it clear that the only thing holding back the Watergate and the Comedy was the concern of the solicitors to make sure that they were not burning their boats behind them. As Hill explained, 'completion of the deal only awaits the Lord Chamberlain's

assurance that the establishment of a private theatre on the premises will
not militate against the renewal of the Lord Chamberlain's licence when it
is required'. Hill did not think the Lord Chamberlain would be reasonably
able to refuse to restore a licence subsequently, unless there were specific
grounds for doing so. 'A theatre, for example, which, owing to the type of
performance had become a meeting ground for pederasts, could be refused
a licence.' Otherwise the Lord Chamberlain 'would have to re-grant his
licence on demand'. Nor did Hill pin much hope on Gwatkin's strategy of
hoping the theatre would leave itself open to prosecution for minor breaches
in club or safety rules:

> it will be difficult to obtain all the evidence required to bring them to
> book—Police would have to be introduced as members, etc. ...
>
> The pin-pricking prosecution where a member of this Office gets in
> on one night and the Theatre is fined £5 would be worse than useless.
>
> There will be vast adverse publicity, and the Lord Chamberlain's
> motives will be mis-represented to the limit.

As for whether to blow open the whole issue of 'private theatres' by bringing
a test prosecution against the Watergate/Comedy for presenting an unlicensed script, Hill pointed out that there was no absolute guarantee that
the Office would win the case, since terms used in the Theatres Act such
as 'Places of Public Resort' and 'Plays produced "for hire"' had never been
effectively defined in law. A failed prosecution would be disastrous: 'If we
lose it means that there is little point in the Censor banning anything at
all, since this will only give the piece a cachet and not prevent its being
seen publicly.'

Hill concluded by listing the alternative positions Scarbrough might
adopt in his meeting with the Comedy's solicitors:

> (a) Benevolent neutrality—the Lord Chamberlain will do nothing
> unless he is forced to.
>
> (b) An attempt to prevent these objects coming to anything by
>
> (i) Pointing out the legal difficulties and saying that the Lord
> Chamberlain in defence of the Censorship is bound to test the law.
>
> (ii) That he is bound to maintain stringent watch over the practice
> at such Annexes and prosecute for every irregularity.
>
> (iii) Point out that eventually these proceedings will not rebound to
> the benefit of Private Theatre Clubs, but only to that of the big impresario
> (inapplicable to Mr Beaumont).
>
> (c) A non-committal attitude now, followed by a rigorous check up
> of each project and the institution of proceedings if evidence can be
> found.[5]

Hill sent his lengthy paper, and Gwatkin's original memorandum, to the Comptroller:

> I am sorry to bother you with this, but we are under the necessity of replying ... I have stalled both parties, but have promised replies early next week, and I shall be grateful for your instructions.
>
>   I do apologise for breaking in on your leave.[6]

Nugent favoured brinkmanship, and proposed warning the managers that if they went ahead the Lord Chamberlain would 'test the law and ascertain its limits and defects'. Such a threat might cause them to have second thoughts about proceeding. Scarbrough agreed:

> they should be told that large scale developments of theatre clubs would be found to lead to a test of the law—and might also attract the tax authorities; that therefore my advice to them would be not to take these risks—for they might lead to a tightening of the existing law on Clubs and even to the Govt. taking over the Censorship.[7]

On 4 September, Scarbrough met with Beaumont, two directors from the Watergate Theatre Club, and Mr Rubenstein, the solicitor.[8] He guaranteed that he would not withhold a licence from a venue just because it had previously operated as a private theatre, but warned them that it was 'by no means certain' that a private theatre had the legal right to perform an unlicensed play. He had, he said, chosen not to test this while such clubs were 'serving a useful purpose' and catering 'only for specialized and small audiences', as had traditionally been the case.

> However, the Lord Chamberlain made it quite clear that if the procedure of producing unlicensed play [sic] at public theatres under the auspice of theatre clubs, became so widespread as to make the censorship of plays and, indeed, the whole of the Theatres' Act, ridiculous, it would be his duty as custodian of the Act to take steps to test the law.

Scarbrough also warned them that if a prosecution against one private club were successful then 'the death knell could be sounded for them all'. According to Nugent's account of the meeting, 'All present fully appreciated what the Lord Chamberlain had said', and indicated in response that 'they would naturally not wish to do anything to embarrass the Lord Chamberlain'.

But, as Hill had predicted, the idea was already spreading. Two days later, Scarbrough met the owner of the Arts Theatre Club, Mr Campbell Williams, who was planning a production of *The Children's Hour*, and was 'considering negotiating with a theatre normally open to the public, with a view to forming an annex to his Theatre Club'. It would be, he explained, 'a great boon if he could have an arrangement with another theatre nearby' so that he could transfer plays capable of attracting larger audiences, and he cited St Martin's Theatre as a possibility. Scarbrough repeated the arguments he had made to the Watergate directors, and also pointed out that whereas the Watergate, having lost its original theatre, genuinely needed a new venue, the Arts Club would be creating an additional space.

> Mr Campbell Williams, very much supported by Mr Roberts, his lawyer, then said that he quite saw the position and he, personally, thought it would be the greatest mistake for him to jeopardise his present position by launching forth into his new plan. He thanked the Lord Chamberlain very much for his explanation and the impression he left was that he would take no further action at all.

The following day, a letter from one of the Watergate directors seemed to confirm that Scarbrough's tactics might be working:

> One thing I do want to say to you, and I know that I am speaking for my other Directors. The last thing we want to do is to cause any embarrassment to the Lord Chamberlain, and if it was brought to our notice that we were tending to bring the law into disrepute, we should want to close down whatever the cost might be.

Nugent was quick to thank him for the 'very kind letter' which he promised to send on to the Lord Chamberlain. 'I know he will be very pleased to see it.' Nugent did indeed forward it:

> You will be most interested to see the enclosed letter from Jimmie Smith which arrived yesterday afternoon, and must therefore have been written very shortly after his interview with you. His assurance on page 2 makes it a very valuable document although I think it might be difficult to insist on keeping him to this assertion! Anyhow, it shows that they took to heart what was said to them and are, at least at the moment, anxious to please you.

So significant did Smith's letter seem that the Comptroller asked Scarbrough to send it back 'as we must keep it safely under lock and key'.

Perhaps in the past, some of Scarbrough's staff thought he had not always given theatre matters as high a priority as he should have done: 'I am so glad [the] LC has taken an interest,' wrote Gwatkin, 'as I do think he is vitally affected.' But now Nugent paid tribute to Scarbrough, telling

Gwatkin he had 'thoroughly mastered' his brief, and played his hand like the diplomat and politician he was: 'The Lord Chamberlain was quite excellent and I know that his hearers were much impressed because they came up to my room afterwards and had a further talk.' Nugent was convinced that they had been genuinely concerned about where things might end up if they went ahead:

> One rather interesting thing was said by Binkie to me after the interview. The Lord Chamberlain had very properly explained that if the law was made to look too ridiculous, some action would have to be taken to test it, and if it was ruled that the censorship could be got round so easily it might end in the Theatres' Act being repealed. Binkie said to me, very seriously, and I am quite sure, sincerely, that he wanted to make it quite clear that the very last thing that he, or indeed any London manager, would wish, would be for the Lord Chamberlain to stop being the censor.

Yet the matter was far from concluded; 'we shall see what we shall see,' wrote Nugent; 'The Watergate are determined, I think, to go on with it and obviously ... we can't stop them trying it on if they wish.'[9]

Nugent's prediction proved accurate. The Watergate went public with its plans almost immediately, and the project caught the headlines. Even though the Arts Theatre did not follow the same route, choosing to remain as it was, it also became part of the same news story. 'FOUR FRANK PLAYS GO ON DESPITE THE CENSOR', announced the *Daily Mail*, and a slightly premature sub-heading reported that 'Rush To See Them Brings Boom For Theatre Clubs'. The report described *The Children's Hour* as 'the first of four frank, hard-hitting plays that will be seen in the West End although they have never been passed by the censor', and drew attention to the fact that they had all been banned 'because they deal with homosexuality'.[10] The article also explained that clubs were exploiting 'a legal loophole' in order to present 'good plays which deal with difficult subjects', and it claimed that applications for membership of the New Watergate were 'pouring in at the rate of 3,500 a week'.[11] Tynan had also used his column in *The Observer* to announce the plans, under the heading 'Dodging the Ban'. He described the venture as 'welcome and surprising', though he also expressed cynicism at the motives of some of those involved, suggesting that commercial rather than libertarian instincts were the inspiration. Tynan never missed an opportunity to deride and needle the Lord Chamberlain, but he also expressed regret that the Watergate's challenge had not been more courageous and aggressive:

> The new directors insist that their purpose is not to circumvent the law but merely to offer interesting plays to minority audiences. All the same, I am

in little doubt that the true creator of the new venture, the catalyst to whom our thanks are due, is that anachronistic bogy, the Lord Chamberlain.

Forbear, if you can, to smile at the mighty machinery of evasion that had to be constructed before London might see, properly produced, three plays which have been staged with no difficulty at all on Broadway and almost everywhere else in Western Europe. Do not mistake me: I applaud the new enterprise: but I wish it had taken a firmer stand against the mischievous anomaly of a censorship which ... is implicitly to blame for the fact that the whole panorama of British theatre contains only a rheumatic handful of plays dealing at all controversially with sex, politics, the law, the Church, the Armed Forces and the Crown.

Tynan wanted not an accommodation and compromise, but a direct challenge and an end to a system which, he insisted, had the potential to become far more repressive than its current bumbling revealed:

a Russian company visiting England would stand a good chance of having its entire repertoire banned if a really conscientious Lord Chamberlain held office. It is to the earl of Scarbrough's credit that he has been slacker and less conscientious than the law he upholds.

Clubs, said Tynan, could not be the solution: 'The new venture has tacitly accepted the censor's gag,' he complained; 'It may one day wish that it had taken the harder course, and sought to gag the censor.' Worst of all, most theatre managers still wore the gag with pride:

The obstacle to reform can be simply stated: most theatre managers approve of the Lord Chamberlain. He is their guarantee of safety: once blessed with his licence, they are immune from legal action. This attitude is likely to persist as long as our theatre skulks inside the nursery, irresponsibly refusing to claim the right which, long ago, the film industry demanded and won: that of censoring itself.[12]

A further headache for Scarbrough emerged in September 1956, when the British Board of Film Censors committed a *volte-face*, and issued a licence (albeit with an 'X' certificate) for one of the Watergate plays, *Tea and Sympathy*. They explained to him that their change of heart was because 'the promoters have removed the whole of the homosexual theme', with the boy now being 'merely portrayed as a "cissy"' and 'no question of any accusation of homosexuality either with masters or with the other boys'. Additionally, 'The broad hint, so obvious in the play, that the headmaster himself is a homosexual, has been completely eliminated'.[13] Beaumont and Albery came to St James's to exert further pressure, threatening to open a second major theatre as a private club so that Anderson's play could run concurrently with *A View from the Bridge.*

> Having heard that a film of this play is to be produced they naturally want to get the play in first. They understand that the film is substantially the same as the Play. I understood that all objections which we had to the Play were removed in the film. They felt, not unreasonably, that if the film was the same as the play we might reconsider passing the play—or perhaps not demanding such rigorous cuts. I said I had not seen the film but that if they got hold of it and ran it though someone from here would, without prejudice, come and see it.[14]

The two impresarios also floated the idea of the Lord Chamberlain issuing a restricted licence, which, rather than making the play available to all, would be specific to 'a trustworthy producer' in a particular theatre and 'for a definite time'. Gwatkin agreed to look into this, but, since there was no provision in the Theatres Act for such limitations, he was not optimistic. Meanwhile, Beaumont and Albery raised again 'the general principle of Homosexual plays', offering 'the usual arguments' to suggest that the policy should be reconsidered. 'It was,' they insisted, 'no longer a hidden subject but mentioned in practically every paper, frequently by the BBC, in literature, quite a number of drawing rooms, and quite unconcernedly by the young.' Moreover, the plays under discussion 'could be seen in every capital in the world but in London'. Gwatkin dutifully countered that 'the Lord Chamberlain took a great deal of trouble to gauge the general feeling', and that his position was based on advice from a number of people whose views he had sought; but Beaumont and Albery had heard that argument before, and had their riposte prepared: 'They suggested, nicely, that the sort of people who the Lord Chamberlain asked were as likely to agree to licensing such plays as the House of Lords were to agree to the nationalisation of land.' Such people, they pointed out, had probably neither seen nor read the kinds of play they were being asked to judge. Furthermore, 'was it not more in the public interest to show good deterrent plays on a subject of great national and moral importance than to let them read juicy details on Sunday in the *News of the World*?'

The following week, Nugent, Gwatkin and Scarbrough attended a special showing of the film version of *Tea and Sympathy*, arranged for them by Beaumont and Albery. 'It was a very tedious two hours,' yawned Gwatkin—but Nugent disagreed: 'Not for me,' he wrote; 'I am simple.' But the licensing of the film could not help the play much, since all the homosexual references had indeed been excised. Gwatkin telephoned Albery and told him the Lord Chamberlain had no power allowing him to issue restricted or limited licences, and that 'If he (Albery) proceeds with the proposal of a second theatre under the Watergate umbrella the Lord Chamberlain would feel obliged to reconsider the position of such theatres'. The only concession he offered was an assurance that 'The Lord Chamberlain would consider the granting of a Licence to the play *Tea and Sympathy* if a script on similar lines to that used for the film, avoiding the matter of homosexuality, was submitted'. According to Gwatkin, 'Albery had little to say after this broadside', other than thanking him 'not ... for the substance of what I had said but for giving me answers definitely and quickly'.[15]

If there really had been plans to open a second club theatre along similar lines to the Watergate/Comedy venture, these were quickly shelved. But on 27 September, the General Manager of the Comedy officially informed the Lord Chamberlain's Office that the theatre would close to the public as from the 29th. The 'Rules and Regulations' of the New Watergate Theatre Club now gave the Comedy Theatre in Panton Street as its registered address, and it identified a single objective: 'to provide Members and their guests at the Comedy Theatre in London with stage productions of cultural value and of a character not likely to be seen at public performances.'[16]

On 11 October, the 'private' production of *A View from the Bridge* opened, directed by Peter Brook and with a cast including Richard Harris and Anthony Quayle. Miller's play would run for six months and 219 performances, and would help to inflict some lasting and mortal damage on the Lord Chamberlain. If 'private' implies any sense of secrecy or being out of the public eye, then such an epithet was never going to be appropriate to this production, which attracted all the newspaper publicity of a big film premiere. This status was guaranteed by the fact that the opening night was attended not only by Miller, but by his wife, Marilyn Monroe. That made it big news: 'FIRST-NIGHT CROWDS PULL AT MARILYN'S MINK' reported the *Evening Standard*:—one of many newspapers to focus primarily on Monroe and the audience's reaction to her:

> Crowds shouting 'Marilyn!' surged around Marilyn Monroe's car as she arrived at the Comedy Theatre last night with her husband, Arthur Miller, for the first performance of his new play, *A View from the Bridge*.
>
> The crowd pushed through a police cordon as Miss Monroe got out of the car—walking with difficulty in a narrow hobble skirt.
>
> Mr Miller, one arm round his wife, tried to force a way through. But he was unable to prevent crowds pulling at Miss Monroe's hair, dress and the mink tails fringing her stole.
>
> Miss Monroe was in tight red velvet, only a foot wide at the knees. Her matching stole was lined with mink.
>
> Inside the foyer half a dozen commissionaires struggled to control the crowds who closed in on Miss Monroe and Mr Miller ...

Said Miss Monroe, hair dishevelled but smiling: 'It seems like an enthusiastic crowd. I like it when crowds get enthusiastic about me.[17]

The *Daily Express* had a front page headline 'Marilyn arrives early' above a photograph of the moment, and a full page spread inside, with photographs of Monroe, Miller and other celebrities entering the auditorium. Even John Barber's review of the production began not on-stage but in the audience.

> They mobbed her, shrieking, as Marilyn Monroe fought her way into the lobby last night beside Laurence Olivier, Vivien Leigh, and the author of the play—her husband, Arthur Miller.
>
> Some of them burst down into the stalls to see her—dazzling in garnet satin and a cape lined with mink, with little mink tails dancing at her ankles.[18]

The images and publicity alone would have been enough to cause embarrassment at St James's Palace, but the fact that the play itself was also well-received—and that most reviews dwelt on the circumstances of its presentation—left the Lord Chamberlain looking even sillier. Cecil Wilson's review in the *Daily Mail* appeared under the headline 'ELECTRIC FIRST NIGHT':

> London's first season of banned American plays blazed into action last night with a savage, searing, and spellbinding drama that earned one of the greatest receptions I can remember.
>
> That one sickening moment has no doubt spread the impression that the play is all about homosexuality, which is much the same as saying that 'Macbeth' is all about banquets ...[19]

The *Daily Telegraph* was equally complimentary towards the play and implicitly critical of the Censorship:

> The New Watergate Theatre Club made a triumphant entry on the scene in its new form at the Comedy Theatre last night. And its purpose, of presenting controversial plays of merit, which have fallen under the censor's ban, was thoroughly vindicated by the choice of Arthur Miller's *A View from the Bridge* ...
>
> Like several other good (and completely decent) American plays, it was automatically banned because it admitted the existence of homosexuality, which we are officially forbidden to do.
>
> So, but for this new club, we should have missed the chance to see a strong and enthralling play by a major dramatist, vividly directed by Peter Brook and played by a distinguished cast of English players.[20]

The Illustrated London News weighed in even more directly, under the headline: HIGHBROW STUFF FROM MR MILLER.

> The pious attempts of the Lord Chancellor [sic] to spare London the shock of this play—a play New Yorkers withstood without pain for some months—has fortunately been foiled by a nice quirk of the law. What may go on behind closed doors is nobody's business, says the law, so a club may put on anything it likes. Accordingly, the New Watergate, installed in the recently renovated Comedy Theatre, have taken it over. True, anyone can join—for five bob—and over thirty thousand have done so. But the principle of Decency First has been preserved.
>
> The next two plays at the Watergate will be *A Cat on a Hot Tin Roof* by Tennessee Williams, and *Tea and Sympathy* by Robert Anderson. Both American masterpieces. Both about homosexuality. Both good box office. 'The ban seems silly, at this time in the world', says Miller. It certainly does.[21]

The Lord Chamberlain was exposed, and the Home Office contacted the Comptroller to advise him that the issue was to be raised in Parliament. The Home Secretary was to be asked 'whether in view of the recent performances of unlicensed plays in certain theatres, he will now abolish or modify the present system of censorship of plays'. How, they asked Nugent, should they reply? The Comptroller passed the query on to Scarbrough: 'Sorry to be a bore but a question is being asked in the House ... and I do feel that it must be you, and no one else, who acts in this matter.' The Home Office wanted to know whether a straightforward negative answer to the question was sufficient, and the non-committal reply from St James's was hardly helpful: 'the Lord Chamberlain has no comments or any alternative reply to offer.' Though Gwatkin did offer one further comment, not intended to be relayed to the House:

> As I told you on the telephone, the Lord Chamberlain has asked me to add for the information of the Home Secretary that recent developments of theatre clubs are being watched. It is too early to give any view as to whether some action may eventually be required.

The parliamentary answer did not satisfy the MP who had raised the issue. 'Surely it is time censorship was abolished and the performance of plays be permitted, subject only to the laws of the land,' he told the press.[22]

Meanwhile, despite its declared aversion to a 'pin-pricking prosecution', the Lord Chamberlain's Office asked police to carry out undercover checks to see if the Club rules at the Comedy were being fully observed.

On 31 October, Gwatkin wrote to the Commissioner of Police at New Scotland Yard:

> The creation of this Theatre Club raises a considerable issue which is being reviewed, and it may be decided by the Lord Chamberlain to bring a test case to establish what is in fact the law.
>
> A necessary precedent to any case being brought will be the provision of evidence that the premises are open. The Lord Chamberlain wonders therefore, whether it would be possible to arrange, for the next few weeks, that he should receive routine reports from the Officers patrolling Panton Street, perhaps three or four times a week, certifying that the premises are open, and that persons are entering to see the performance.

The police obliged with regular reports:

> On Thursday, 8th November, 1956, I kept casual observation on the New Watergate Theatre, Panton Street ... from 8 p.m. to 8.20 p.m.
>
> During this time I saw members of the public entering and purchasing tickets for the play then being shown, 'A view from the bridge' ...
>
> I entered the foyer of the theatre and a commissionaire approached me. I asked if I could book tickets for the show and he replied, 'Not unless you are a member ...' I took a membership form and left the theatre.

At the end of the month the Lord Chamberlain informed them it was no longer necessary to continue.[23]

In its annual report at the end of 1956, the Public Morality Council expressed 'no little anxiety' at recent developments:

> As the law now stands it is possible, by the payment of a nominal sum, for members of the public to become members of a theatre club which is not subject to the rulings of the Lord Chamberlain, nor the regulations of the London County Council. Such a club enjoys the privileges of privacy accorded to every ordinary dwelling house, and it will be appreciated that there is considerable peril in that situation.[24]

Most people had other things on their mind. In January 1957, the Suez debacle brought the resignation of Anthony Eden, and his replacement as Prime Minister by Harold Macmillan. Rab Butler became the new Home Secretary, and Scarbrough, whose attitude to the Watergate project was described by his Comptroller as 'aloof but friendly', had hopes that the new administration might back his wish for a change in the law.[25]

The 219th and final performance of *A View from the Bridge* at the Comedy took place on 20 April, but its closure afforded no relief to the

Lord Chamberlain. Five days later, *Tea and Sympathy* replaced it, and although reviews for this were much more mixed, Anderson's play would still run for 173 performances and five months. Its opening immediately generated new attacks on the ineffectiveness of the Lord Chamberlain, as press reports claimed that the New Watergate had already acquired some 43,000 members, and was increasing by 1,200 a week.[26] W.A. Darlington, theatre reviewer of the *Daily Telegraph*, and neither a theatrical radical or a spokesperson for homosexuals, stuck his knife in under the headline, 'Censorship Reduced to Absurdity':

> In the first place, the theme of the play is not homosexuality ... but charity ... In the second, if the play had been a serious and decent play about homosexuality, I should have been for it.
>
> And in the third, I believe that the Censor, from his own point of view (the protection of the public morals) has made a serious error in banning the three plays.

In Darlington's view, Scarbrough's strategy was misguided and now in tatters. In trying (and failing) to silence a subject, he had scored a spectacular own goal:

> These three plays are banned, not because they discuss homosexuality, but because they mention it. This, surely, is absurd. People are free to mention this subject anywhere but in the theatre, and they freely do. And because there are people about like the Censor ... young people discuss it more than they otherwise might, and condone it more easily than they would if they knew anything about it.

Since none of the plays championed the cause, what, asked Darlington, was the point of trying to repress them: 'homosexuality in these plays is definitely A Bad Thing, and I cannot see why the Censor should want to prevent them from making that point.' He also accused Scarbrough of inconsistency:

> why has he allowed the music-hall comic so remarkably impersonated by Laurence Olivier in John Osborne's *The Entertainer* to make all those blue little jokes on the forbidden subject? Does this mean that in view of the violent public reaction against his former decision the Censor has given ground? I hope so; but if not, then I repeat the question. In the name of all consistency, why, why, why?[27]

'Et tu, Brute?' as Scarbrough might have muttered.

Once again, attention in the press was not limited to the theatre pages. The *Telegraph*, for example, also published an editorial under the headline

Sense and Censorship, bemoaning the fact that theatre was still governed by an act passed over a hundred years earlier.

> The law of 1843 is thus not only out of tune with the times: it is also ineffective. Can anything be said in its defence? The only effective argument is put forward by some theatre managers themselves; that they would rather be at the mercy of one Lord Chamberlain than at that of any number of local licensing authorities. But to make a convenience of the censorship is not to justify the law as a whole. Nor do we hear publishers of books, who are free from licensing, crying for the benefit of similar protection from the public conscience. Moreover, the fact that his authority can so easily be flouted by the 'theatre club' device should make the Lord Chamberlain's department as ready as other interests to see the law revised or done away with. Does it wish to fall, with the theatre, into comic disrepute? [28]

The newspaper's letters' column developed the debate over the next few days, with one manager defending the use of theatre clubs and praising the Lord Chamberlain for 'protecting the author from self-inflicted wounds'.[29] But this was a minority view, and Richard Findlater's was one of a number of responses published under the headline 'Stage in Fetters':

> 'The censor knows best' has always been the motto of the managers. Without their devotion, the Lord Chamberlain would long ago have been freed from his obligation to umpire over the drama. No other section of the theatrical profession shows this rapt, fantastic faith in the Lord Chamberlain's indispensability ...
>
> I do not recall reading any pleas from publishers for a censor to teach authors how to behave, or to relieve them of moral responsibility for what they print.[30]

The Lord Chamberlain was on the ropes and struggling to survive. As Troubridge wrote to Gwatkin: 'It seems to me that our venerable institution of the Revels is under stronger attack at the moment than at any time since Percy Smith's Bill ten or twelve years ago.' He blamed it all on 'the constantly recurring provocation of that damned Comedy', and thought the situation had been mis-handled:

> I should myself have been sorely tempted to whisper in the licensee's ear that the owner of a hundred and fifty thousand pounds worth of property needing an annually renewable licence, was in a less strong position to adopt a policy of spitting in the Lord Chamberlain's eye than say the Arts.

However, even Troubridge recognised that such unscrupulous tactics might have provoked an even worse press: 'I suppose that would be called official blackmail.'[31]

In the *Daily Mail*, the playwright Ronald Duncan focused on another anomaly which 'makes nonsense of a nonsensical law':

> It has always been possible to drive a coach and horses through the law; if you go to the Adelphi Theatre you will see that *The Country Wife* can scuttle past it too ...
>
> How is it that *The Country Wife* can be shown to the public when such plays as *A View from the Bridge* and *Cat on a Hot Tin Roof* can only be seen by members of a club theatre?

Of the contentious male kiss in Miller's play, Duncan reported that 'not a single person has complained that they found this scene offensive' during the play's six month run; there had been, he said, 'no public disturbances in the stalls, no outbreak of immorality in Panton Street'. Rather, the interest in the play demonstrated 'our appetite for mature plays on adult subjects'. The club theatre strategy was a charade since each member could take three guests, thus allowing the membership subscription to be split at 1s 6d each. Duncan was not against theatre censorship *per se*: 'Of course nobody wants to upset poor Aunt Agatha's treasured prejudices when she comes up from Cheltenham and drops into a theatre, especially if she's got her young niece with her.' But he was adamant that 'the Lord Chamberlain's present position is both incongruous and untenable', and he threw his weight behind Henry Sherek's 'excellent suggestion that plays should be licensed in the same way as films are and given X certificates if restricted to adult audiences'.[32]

A week later, the new Home Secretary was asked in parliament whether he would introduce legislation to amend the law. Rab Butler said he had no such intention, but something had to change, and St James's Palace stepped up its campaign to persuade the Home Office that amending the law so as to allow the Lord Chamberlain to issue conditional and limited licences would be the best way to break the pressure. On 23 May, Gwatkin nudged Scarbrough by writing what was almost an ultimatum for him to present to the government: 'Having not much else to do I put the enclosed thoughts on paper in the hopes that you were thinking somewhat on similar lines!' His proposal made a case for amending the law; more surprisingly, it also held out the possibility of complete abolition of the 1843 Act:

> Over a hundred years have passed since this Act was placed on the Statute Book during which period we have seen numerous changes in human relationships and manners. The impact of time, wars, the cinematograph,

wireless and television could naturally not have been foreseen when this Act was initiated, and it is clear to me that its provisions are out of date and do not allow me adequately, or indeed justly to implement the powers which this Act gives me.

This state of affairs apart from being wrong inevitably leads to efforts on the part of some producers to find ways in which to defeat the censorship: such as the 'private theatre'.

I have the power either to give or to withhold a licence but there are a number of plays to which [I] should undoubtedly grant a licence but for the fact that I am advised, and I agree with this advice, that the presentation would be harmful to juvenile audiences.

I have no power to lay down restrictions on the type of audience which may visit a play.

It may well be thought that in the second half of the twentieth century, the censorship of plays should pass from the Lord Chamberlain to a Government department, to some other body, or that it should be abolished altogether.

If, however, it is considered that the Censorship should remain vested in the Lord Chamberlain, I must ask that an amendment to the Theatre Act of 1843 should be made to enable me to designate plays 'for adults only' and so to bring the principles of the censorship of plays parallel with those of the British Board of Film Censors.[33]

Scarbrough replied to his Assistant Comptroller by return, with a lengthy and 'most secret' memorandum, which is worth quoting at some length. What clearly emerges from this is that the Lord Chamberlain was taking seriously the possibility of significant change, and that he was ready to consult at the highest possible level:

Since the censorship of plays forms part of the Lord Chamberlain's job I have asked the Queen if Her Majesty would have any strong objection to the whole subject being examined, with the object of reaching a decision as to whether any change should be attempted. The Queen said she would have no objection to such an examination and I therefore feel able to proceed with it.

However, he was certainly not ready to go public:

It is of much importance that no inkling that an examination is taking place should leak out. The whole thing must be treated as very secret and for the present no one except the Comptroller and Assistant Comptroller should know about it or see this memorandum. Knowledge of it should not be extended without my permission.

Scarbrough was well aware of the difficulties which would be involved in altering the current system:

> It has to be recognised from the start that any substantial change will almost certainly require legislation, which would mean the assent and backing of the Government to any proposed changes and the approval of Parliament. All of these will be major hurdles, whatever changes may be suggested.

Despite this, he appeared ready to consider the most radical step of all, and to weigh the arguments on both sides:

> The first question to consider is whether the censorship of stage plays should be abolished completely. The arguments in favour appear to be—
>
> a) That no other country has a system of censorship. I wonder if this is wholly true. Have we any reliable information about what is done in other countries?
>
> b) That any form of censorship is out of date, and out of tune with modern life. Those who hold this view are vocal and I would say quite numerous, and for them it is one of the fundamental requirements of a free society.
>
> c) That with complete freedom of expression in the Press, and, with few exceptions, in books, it is difficult to justify the continuance of a censorship for plays.
>
> d) That more plays about subjects at present forbidden will be written, some of them good plays, that more and more criticism will be heard if they are banned, and that this will eventually end in the abolition of the censorship.
>
> e) That theatre clubs, unless controlled, will make the censorship a farce.
>
> f) That a natural desire to avoid giving material to the critics will tend to make the censorship ineffective and its continuance therefore unjustified.
>
> The arguments against complete abolition seem to be—
>
> g) That to give complete freedom to those who want to exploit sex in its many forms will arouse a storm of protest and will be regarded as a surrender to unrestrained immorality.
>
> h) That managers and producers would oppose abolition if it left them at the mercy of every local authority in this country.
>
> j) That there are other subjects besides sex which need control, eg royalty, foreign heads of state, living persons, blasphemy.

k) That the tone of the British theatre which at present helps to place London in the first rank, as far as the stage is concerned, will be lowered.

Scarbrough concluded that 'There are strong arguments on both sides and anyone who has not got to take responsibility for a decision will find it easy to come down on one side or the other'. But he was experienced enough to know that the decision would actually be taken on the basis of pragmatism rather than principle, and he doubted the courage and commitment of the politicians. What, after all, was in it for them?

> Personally I doubt whether any Government will be prepared to risk the storm which might arise if by its own action unrestrained freedom were given to sex exploiters on the stage. The Government is not much bothered by criticisms of the Lord Chamberlain as things are at present: it will very likely think it would be asking for trouble to change that happy state of insulation for a first class clash with the forces of morality.

But even if the government was not yet ready to take the ultimate step of doing away with stage censorship altogether, perhaps it might be persuaded to take one which would be only slightly less radical:

> Assuming, for the sake of argument, that abolition of the Censorship is not practical politics, the next question to be considered is whether the Lord Chamberlain should take the initiative in requesting that the censorship should be taken out of his hands—placed elsewhere.

Again, Scarbrough was familiar with the rhetoric

> The arguments in favour of this course appear to be—
> a) Censorship by the Lord Chamberlain is an historical anachronism which provides fuel for the critics and cannot be defeated with logic.
> b) No censor can avoid public criticism from one quarter or another and this brings the head of the Sovereign's household under frequent criticism at the same time that he should be setting an example to the rest of the household of unobtrusive, uncontroversial conduct.
> c) The Lord Chamberlain of the day may not be especially interested in or knowledgeable about plays.
> d) He is lampooned by critics as a kind of aristocratic blimp of the 1890s, who is quite unaware of the facts of modern life.
>
> These arguments can be countered by the following—
> e) It works well and has done so for many years.
> f) Most responsible people connected with the theatre prefer the

approachability of the Lord Chamberlain's office to a government department obsessed with the fear of parliamentary questions and the need to follow bureaucratic procedure.

g) To be an expert on the theatre or closely connected with one or other of its branches is precisely what is not wanted in a censor. Experience of public reactions which comes from experience in public life may be of more value, and the impartiality of a non-specialist seems essential.

h) Probably no Ministry would want to be responsible for censorship.

i) The long connection between the theatre and the Palace is prized by the former.

Scarbrough suggested that 'some form of board, like the board responsible for censoring films, would carry more public confidence'. While he doubted whether it would prove in practice to be 'more impartial, more approachable, more flexible and quicker in despatch of business than the existing system', its judgements might, in the present day and age, be received and accepted more positively. In his view, this seemed, on balance, the best option to encourage:

> with all the difficulties which are found to face the censorship as time goes on would it not be best to propose to the Government that the time has come to find a more defensible, I will not say a better, form of censorship? I am inclined to think that that possibility should be considered unless a means can be found to strengthen the present system by giving it wider powers which could make it less of a target for criticism from either side.

The only viable alternative he saw was to allow him the same flexibility as the film censorship enjoyed in terms of restricting audiences:

> We could give A licences—not for obscene plays and those tending to corrupt greatly—but for the better type of plays dealing with the unnatural vices. This would take much of the sting out of the vocal critics—authors and dramatic critics for the most part—and might allay for quite a long time the kind of outcry to which we are periodically subjected.

This innovation would simultaneously 'remove the incentive' for theatres to set up private clubs, and 'preserve for the responsible elements in the theatre those advantages which they seem to prize in the present system'. By sidestepping the confrontations over sexuality and morality, the Lord Chamberlain would be able to retain what mattered most: 'control over subjects such as Royalty'.[34]

Scarbrough doubted whether the government would be willing to introduce legislation to empower him with the authority to issue licences with restrictions attached. Yet perhaps there was a solution. Perhaps legislation was not actually required: 'I would like to know who says I cannot do this under the existing Act (1843)?' he wondered; 'Who would take me to task if I did it?'[35] Hill dashed this hope, citing an occasion in 1913 when a conditional licence issued to Herbert Tree for his production of *Parsifal* had been quashed by the Home Office, leading to considerable embarrassment for the Lord Chamberlain of the day. On a more constructive note, the secretary sent Scarbrough a proposed amended version of the 1843 Theatres Act which he had drafted, and which he thought might prove workable:

> I have ... interfered with it as little as I possibly could ... I have not attempted to give the Lord Chamberlain any additional specific powers, what I have done is to give him, I hope, a general power to make his permission conditional, and to establish a penalty for breach of such conditions as he makes.

It was a straightforward but precise revision. In section 12—which prohibited performances without express approval from the Lord Chamberlain of 'any play, or any act, scene or part thereof, or any prologue or epilogue, or any part thereof'—Hill proposed an extension, conferring on him the right to 'make his allowance thereof conditional upon the observance of requirements which he shall specify'. To the clause stating that 'it shall not be lawful for any person to act or present the same, or cause the same to be acted or presented contrary to such disallowance', he suggested adding 'without observance of such stipulated requirements'. In section 15, which stipulated that anyone guilty of the offence of presenting unlicensed material should be liable to conviction and to 'forfeit such sum as shall be awarded by the court', Hill proposed an additional offence of presenting material 'contrary to any of the requirements conditional upon the observance of which the same shall have been allowed by the Lord Chamberlain'. Finally—and thoughtfully—he took a long awaited opportunity and proposed increasing the readers' fees from 2 to 4 guineas per play.

Further to the changes in the Act, Hill identified four kinds of play which might be placed in 'restricted categories'. Namely:

i Those dealing with Perversion.
ii Those introducing the deity.
iii Those of a disproportionately sexual character.
iv Patently pornographic or sadistic.

But he was clear that 'The main object' was 'to exclude from plays on Perversion the impressionable sections of the community, and to prevent

Perverts from securing justification for their actions from them'. Not for the first time, he hinted at his doubts over Scarbrough's policies, observing that there was 'no way of excluding perverts' altogether, and that 'presumably there are still grave doubts whether plays on perversion will do harm'. Even though he had dutifully drafted a proposal for a new Act, he was not necessarily convinced it would prove workable on the ground:

> A category excluding children under sixteen is perfectly practicable but hardly of much use, since children rarely go to the theatre. To raise the age limit to a useful level say twenty one is impossible of application, that age not being determinable on site.

Moreover, he worried that an 'adults only' licence would translate in practice into a good selling point for less scrupulous managements, leading to an increase rather than a reduction in precisely the sort of material they were supposedly trying to outlaw. To discourage this, Hill suggested an additional clause which would give the Lord Chamberlain the option of restricting licences to specific and trusted theatres and managements. But although Hill recognised that 'the Lord Chamberlain's hand is being forced' by the Comedy/Watergate venture, he questioned whether this tinkering with legislation would remedy the situation or head off his pursuers:

> There is little praise or condemnation of the Lord Chamberlain by the general public. But an artificial situation is being created by a small group of vociferous and interested journalists and critics. They have really misrepresented the Lord Chamberlain, and they will both misrepresent his motives now and amplify the shortcomings of any category scheme. They will give the Lord Chamberlain no credit.

In his view, the problem of private theatres would still remain, and unscrupulous managements would still take financial advantage of the situation by 'Treating a play given a restricted licence as "Banned by the Lord Chamberlain" and putting it on, the Lord Chamberlain's ban now being highly profitable and making a closed performance pay better than an open one'. The restricted licence, argued Hill, would do nothing to halt the growing problem 'because if the Comedy is legal so is any other private theatre of similar proportions, and the market seems so great that a competitor must appear sooner or later'.[36]

At the start of June, Scarbrough attempted to initiate a process of change, as he reported in another memorandum marked 'MOST SECRET':

> I went to see the Home Secretary, at my request, this morning. I told him I had been reviewing the position with regard to the censorship, and had

come to the conclusion that it was desirable, if it were possible, that my
hand should be strengthened by an amendment of the law on one point.

This was: 'To give the Lord Chamberlain power to attach conditions to
licenses for plays, which would enable him to direct that certain plays
should be for adults only.' At the same time, Scarbrough also signalled
quite explicitly that he was now ready to shift his position on 'perversion':

> Up to now I had maintained a rigid attitude, as had my predecessors, on
> this subject, and allowed no mention of it on the stage. I maintained that
> attitude for one reason only; that to permit references or plays dealing with
> that subject would inevitably introduce some young people to a subject that
> otherwise they might never come into contact with. I doubted whether it
> would be possible for this attitude to be maintained much longer.

He did not, of course, concede that his previous policy had been mistaken,
claiming, rather, that the situation had changed. The subject 'had now
become one which was much talked about, and it was bound to appear as
rather ostrich like that it should never be mentioned on the stage'. Faced
with 'an increasing number of plays, some of them good' and 'dealing seriously with this subject', he conceded that 'it was bound to appear absurd
to quite sensible people to disallow any attempt to deal seriously with a
subject which had now become, unfortunately, one of the problems of life'.
Scarbrough also informed the Home Secretary that the private theatre clubs
were, in his view, 'experimental laboratories' and 'very useful adjuncts to
the British Theatre', and that 'I would be very sorry to see them interfered with'. It was a matter for regret that the recent actions of the New
Watergate 'had created a position in which the law and the censorship was
becoming rather farcical'.

Interestingly, Scarbrough's request seems not to have been quite on the
lines Butler had been anticipating:

> The Home Secretary said that his department had been much afraid that
> I was going to ask for a prosecution of the New Watergate Club and had
> given him a brief on that subject. He ... was glad to hear from me that
> this was not the object of my visit.

Butler told Scarbrough that the Home Office considered the definitions
and meanings of the 1843 Theatres Act to be 'obscure', and that a
ruling by Law Officers in 1903 that plays in theatre clubs also required
licensing was 'still more obscure'. He said he understood Scarbrough's
wish 'to move a little forward' in relation to plays dealing with the
'social question' of homosexuality, and suggested that the forthcoming

report from the Wolfenden enquiry might contain recommendations 'on which my proposal might easily follow'. Meanwhile, Butler recommended that a representative from the Home Office—'a new man called Gwynn'—should liaise with Scarbrough's department to discuss the Lord Chamberlain's proposal in more detail: 'he thought that we should find him very good indeed.' Overall, Scarbrough reported that the meeting had been a positive one:

> He stressed the difficulty of any legislation, which I told him I fully realised, but he was certainly willing to consider the proposal carefully. It seemed to him a sensible one and one which could be defended, and one which might possibly fall in conveniently with the Wolfenden report ... It was quite clear that he had got the whole idea in correct prospective [sic].[37]

With hindsight, it appears more likely that he was being fobbed off and that Butler had little intention of introducing legislation.

A week later, on 12 June 1957, Gwatkin wrote to Gwynne:

> You probably know that my master, Lord Scarbrough, had a talk with your master before Whitsun regarding the question of censorship of plays. This is really to tell you that I am at your disposal at any time if you wish to talk about the matter.

Apparently having heard nothing in response, he wrote again on 17 July:

> before very long the good old English habit of 'taking a holiday' will assert itself, and both your office and the Lord Chamberlain's will be on a second XI basis. It would seem to be a very good thing if we could have a talk about the matter before this happens.

They eventually met at the Home Office on 31 July. But although Gwynne began by suggesting that the Home Secretary broadly supported the idea of bringing licensing policies for theatre and cinema more in line, he went on to suggest—perhaps slightly patronisingly—that he 'held out very little hope' and was 'very pessimistic' about the prospect of anything happening in the near future:

> He then explained to me the difficulties attendant at getting a Bill through the House, and the very terrifying time lag that exists ... quoting the fact that he had known Bills to wait for ten years, and as this could hardly be called a very urgent one, it might be literally some years before it came forward. He did also mention that it would seem to be rather a difficult Bill to draft ...

Gwatkin urged Gwynne that 'it might not be a bad thing to get on drafting the Bill now, as at least that would be a step forward'.

In September, Gwynne did send the Assistant Comptroller a memorandum to look at, which he proposed circulating to the Home Secretary (and perhaps the Cabinet), and which proposed a possible amendment of the 1843 Theatres Act to enable the Lord Chamberlain to issue licences which restricted entry to persons over the age of eighteen. However, Gwynne's memorandum included a warning that although 'in themselves the amendments seem likely to be widely welcomed as a sensible reform', it was likely that 'A Bill making these amendments might stir up controversy in as much as it would bring the whole question of censorship under discussion'. In fact, despite its superficial advocacy for Scarbrough's plan, the tone of Gwynne's memorandum to the Home Secretary was, at best, ambivalent. Moreover, the most optimistic option he held out was the possibility of introducing a private member's bill on the subject—which would not itself be possible unless the relevant member happened to come top in a ballot:

> This draft was prepared on the basis that the Home Secretary might wish to support the Lord Chamberlain's suggestion. There are, however, [arguments] of some weight against it. First, although vocal opposition to the censorship usually comes from those who think it is too strict there is probably an at least equal body of opinion that would be ready to raise its voice against a too lax censorship; and a Bill incorporating the Lord Chamberlain's suggestion might disturb this body of opinion.
>
> Secondly, it is open to doubt whether the suggested amendment of the law would have the effect that the Lord Chamberlain expects. It is already said that one or two of the theatre clubs do not merely exist to get round the censorship but are deliberately designed to exploit it, even to the extent of arranging for an objectionable play to be submitted to the Lord Chamberlain in order that it can subsequently be advertised as 'banned'. It might well be that if the Lord Chamberlain had the authority to pass a play for adult audiences only, this would be exploited in the same way—just as some cinemas exploit 'X' Certificates for films as a special attraction.

Gwynne pointed out that while such exploitation in cinemas was merely 'an incidental and minor disadvantage of censorship' within a system that was essentially working well, 'it does not necessarily follow that the same would apply to a classified censorship of plays, having regard to the very different place of the theatre in the world of popular entertainment'. There was, he said, no easy solution:

> Clearly the Lord Chamberlain is in real difficulty, and it is not easy to suggest any satisfactory way out. Apart from the theatre clubs the

censorship of plays seems to work pretty well on the whole, and is accepted by theatre managements; and any proposal to abolish it would be highly controversial. But so would any proposal to extend the censorship to plays put on by theatre clubs.

It was at just this point that the Wolfenden Committee published its controversial report, and as debate about its recommendations raged, it gradually became clear that the government was not going to take the plunge and accept the Committee's recommendation to decriminalise private and consensual acts of homosexuality. That being so, it would have been unthinkable for the same government to support an amendment to the Theatres Act which, however it might have been presented, was essentially an attempt to save the Lord Chamberlain's bacon by giving him a way to license public performances for adults of plays dealing with that very subject. On 19 November, Gwynne told Gwatkin that the Home Office had 'encountered greater technical difficulties than we had expected' in drafting a possible bill, 'particularly in relation to Scotland, where legislation about theatres seems to be in an even worse state of confusion than in England'. Gwynne reassured him that they were still 'pursuing the matter so as to be ready for the next session', but this, as both sides knew, was diplomatic speak for kicking it into the long grass. Scarbrough waited a couple of months and then, having heard nothing, wrote two letters to Butler on 26 and 27 February 1958. In the first, he rather provocatively suggested that he, as Lord Chamberlain, should himself put down a motion in the House of Lords proposing that the 1843 Act be amended. In the second letter, having noticed that a question about theatre censorship was due to be asked in the House of Lords, he requested that the ministerial reply should state that 'the Home Secretary received a request some time ago from the Lord Chamberlain' to address the issue, and that an amendment to the Act was under 'active consideration'. Probably both letters were written in the hope of getting things moving again rather than as serious suggestions. Certainly, Butler was keen to prevent them:

> I think it would be a mistake for you, in view of your constitutional position, to take any public initiative in this matter or even to allow it to be known that you have put forward any suggestion for amending the law. I should much prefer, therefore, that you should not yourself put down a Motion, nor would I propose that any reference should be made to you in the answer to Lord Massereene and Ferrard's question. The answer to the question will be that the matter is now receiving consideration but presents difficult problems, and the Government do not propose to introduce legislation at present.

Butler assured him that things were progressing and that 'a scheme has now been worked out that could probably be put into a fairly simple Private Member's Bill if it were decided to proceed'. But it was becoming evident that the Government was less than enthusiastic: 'I am bound to say,' warned the Home Secretary, 'that in considering the matter I have been impressed by some of the objections that might be raised to your suggestion.' In the light of this, Butler suggested that 'a further discussion between us would be valuable'.

A couple of weeks later, on 17 March, Gwatkin sent a desperate and despairing memorandum to the Lord Chamberlain: 'Not in 22 years have I seen so many and so "wounding" references to the Censorship as have appeared recently in the Press.' The 1843 Act, he declared, was 'out of date', and one which 'forces the Lord Chamberlain into an impossible posi-tion'. Being 'a bad law' it also gave 'encouragement to circumvent it', and, said the Assistant Comptroller, the determination of some people to get round it 'has now reached such a proportion as to make a monkey of the Censorship and those who have to administer it'. Worse still, 'The Lord Chamberlain being the head of the Queen's household even brings The Queen into it'. Urgent action was required:

There is a very strong feeling against Censorship in certain quarters—there always has been but it has greatly increased ... Those against the Censorship are trying to kill it by ridicule and they are not doing badly ...

We are charged with being inconsistent and that is unavoidable if we judge each play on its merits—which we must do.

We are charged with having political bias—this is not true but we have no 'public relations' officer' to refute this.

Finally the main trouble—this flush of homosexuality.

It was this flush on which Gwatkin agonised the most:

It is, on the face of it, odd to disallow this on the stage when it is a subject for very widely read reports; discussions in Parliament (and jokes—the homosexual club tie), letters from prelates, doctors and what-have-you in the Press; discussions on the wireless ('Any Questions'—'Any Answers), and practically every other modern novel.

With the government clearly not willing to help, there was really only one possible recommendation to make—and Gwatkin made it: 'In view of this immense publicity I feel the time has come when serious plays on this subject must be allowed.' His only caveat was that they should carry a health warning:

I still maintain that it is an embarrassing and dangerous subject in a live theatre and that people are entitled to a warning that the play they consider visiting is out of the ordinary. If they go in spite of that warning they have little cause for complaint.

Nine days later, on 26 March, Butler invited the Lord Chamberlain to go and see him. As Scarborough doubtless anticipated, it was bad news:

The Home Secretary told me that his closest advisers had advised against him making any amendment of the Theatres' Act ... It would appear that his advisers thought that the Lord Chamberlain would be incurring greater criticisms if he were given the power to choose between what should be played before adults only and what should be passed for universal presentation; and that their anxiety was that in these days the Lord Chamberlain should not be exposed to increased criticism of that kind.

Scarbrough was stung:

I replied that in my opinion that situation had already arisen, and that it was a fact that the Lord Chamberlain, as Head of the Queen's Household, was already involved in undesirable criticism which had some reflection upon the Throne; and that it was on that account that I had put forward my proposal.

Butler asked whether he thought that responsibility for theatre censorship should be shifted elsewhere. 'I replied that I thought it would probably be a good thing,' reported Scarbrough, 'but that I would not welcome any move towards that end unless it were done decently and did not appear to have come about through any failure of the present system.' In other words, don't blame it on me—or on the Queen. Not that Butler had any practical alternative in mind:

It was clear that the Home Secretary had no intention of allowing his own office to be saddled with it, and he thought that if any change were made it would have to be in the direction of some kind of board under, perhaps, a distinguished retired Civil Servant. This, he recognised, would be more expensive than the present form of Censorship, and I added that it might be less expeditious; and that in any case, as he freely recognised, the problems before the censor would in no way be changed by changing the censor.

Scarbrough put forward the radical alternative, instructing Butler that

'A case could certainly be made out for abolition provided something effective was done to allay the anxiety of theatrical managers'.

The meeting ended with no firm conclusion. Butler actually agreed to take Scarbrough's request for an amendment to the Theatres Act to the Cabinet's Home Affairs' Committee, and promised to be in touch. 'He made it clear that this should be regarded as very confidential, and it was desirable that I should not let my own views leak out.'[38] It was another five months before Scarbrough heard anything official. But he knew what was coming—and what his own next step would be. In July, he met with the West End Theatrical Managers' Association and gave them a broad hint of what was—and was not—coming. He informed them

> that it was unlikely that any Government would willingly make any alteration in the existing Theatres' Act, which might involve it in considerable domestic trouble. That being so the Lord Chamberlain had already considered whether he should make any alteration in his present outlook on homosexual plays. The time might come, and not before long, when he might begin to pass really good plays on these subjects, but of course he would still keep a tight hold on any plays that treated such a matter with levity or condolence.

For their part, the Managers immediately made it clear they were opposed to any change in the law:

> Mr Carter then raised the matter of plays for adults only and the question of marking them as such. He said that, generally, the West End Managers were very much against any labelling. He put forward the argument that it would only encourage people to go rather than to discourage them; but really I think at the back of his mind was the fact that the difficulties of administrating this rule might fall on the theatres and might give extra anxiety.[39]

But the Lord Chamberlain's mind was made up. On 11 August, he received a letter from Butler:

> Dear Roger,
> Following our discussion about the censorship of plays, I have now discussed with my colleagues your suggestion that legislation should be introduced to give you power to make it a condition of your allowance of a play that it should not be shown to children.
>   Our feeling is that it would be unwise to subject the censorship of plays to Parliamentary discussion. Modest though your proposal is, Parliamentary discussion of it ... would inevitably lead to a debate on

censorship generally and might result in a demand for the substitution of some method of control less acceptable than the present arrangement. I am sorry to have to tell you, therefore, that the Government can not support your proposal for a Private Member's Bill.

He acknowledged that Scarbrough faced 'a real problem', and vaguely suggested that he would 'be glad to hear from you from time to time how the problem develops'. But even this offer reads as a subtle way of letting him know that he did not want to hear any more about it for the moment, and the matter was closed. By hand, the Home Secretary added a gracious sop of a postscript: 'This letter would be incomplete if I did not say that my colleagues marvel at your success and say in fact "leave it to the Lord Chamberlain and he will tighten up where he thinks fit".' It was a polite way of saying, 'you're on your own, mate.'

Scarbrough thanked Butler for his letter, and advised him that 'I will now consider whether I should slightly alter my policy and allow plays which deal seriously with homosexuality'. This would not solve everything: 'To do so will bring it's [sic] own crop of difficulties but I am inclined to think it may now be necessary.' And showing that he, too, spoke the language of diplomacy, he subtly warned Butler that 'I will, as you suggest, keep you in touch with any developments of interest'.

Scarbrough having finally accepted that his policy on homosexuality in plays must change, discussions at Stable Yard turned to how best to enact that change. 'I think there is really nothing for us to do, but to wait until we get a suitable play in and then pass it,' wrote the Assistant Comptroller; 'It will soon get around that we are changing our policy.' He recommended there should be no formal announcement, and no direct contact with playwrights or managers whom they had previously turned down.

> It is, of course, bad luck on the writers of good plays, which we would pass if submitted now, such as 'South', 'Children's Hour' and others, but I don't think it would be possible to make our ruling known to the writers of these plays, and say that we are now prepared to alter our rules. I think this would lead to too much complication, and it is quite possible that we might miss a suitable play and not tell the author, who would then have a considerable grievance that he was not told and other authors were.

A couple of months later, the Lord Chamberlain issued his famous minute, instituting and detailing the change. He knew as well as anyone that the new policy would not be straightforward to operate and would create its own problems. 'I think we must go on judging each play on its merits,' he confirmed, 'and this, I fear, will be forging another scourge for our backs, because playwrights will naturally resent any picking and choosing on our part.' But as he added: 'It is true to say they always have done—this is only an additional whipping.'[40]

For the time being, then, both the Theatres Act and the Lord Chamberlain staggered on, apparently intact. But their days were surely numbered. Both by government and by the Lord Chamberlain himself, a world without them had been imagined.

CHAPTER FOUR

Speaking the Unspoken:

Homosexuality and the Stage (II)

How can we differentiate between the aesthetic character and the active
pansy?[1]

On 31 October 1958, the Lord Chamberlain issued a memorandum to
his staff, stating that plays about homosexuality or including homosexual
characters would no longer be subject to an automatic ban. Henceforth,
licensing would depend on a series of provisos:

(a) Every play will continue to be judged on its merits. The difference
will be that plays will be passed which deal seriously with the subject.

(b) We would not pass a play that was violently pro-homosexuality.

(c) We would not allow a homosexual character to be included if there
was no need for such inclusion.

(d) We would not allow any 'funny' innuendos or jokes on the subject.

(e) We will allow the word 'pansy', but not the word 'bugger'.

(f) We will not allow embraces between males or practical demonstrations
of love.

(g) We will allow criticisms of the present Homosexual Laws, though
plays obviously written for propaganda purposes will fall to be judged on
their merits.

(h) We will not allow embarrassing display by male prostitutes.[2]

Following the damage inflicted on the Office by the Watergate/Comedy
experiment and the failure of the Home Secretary to support his request
for changes in the law, this was effectively the only step open to him.
Scarbrough did have some justification for asserting that his capitulation
was not an admission that his previous position had been wrong: 'I do not
regret the policy of strict exclusion which has been continued up to now,
and I think it has been to the public good,' he insisted.[3] He could, after

all, reasonably maintain that the context in which he was making decisions had significantly altered—not least as a result of the Wolfenden report—and that the Office was simply moving with the times. Nevertheless, there had for some time been suggestions within his own Office that his rigid and uncompromising adherence to a principle had been the root cause of a confrontation which had caused great embarrassment and threatened his continued existence as Censor of Plays.

It seems at first slightly bizarre that the play which brought the battle into the open—the first to be staged by the New Watergate Club in a West End theatre—should have been Arthur Miller's text, *A View from the Bridge*. Only a handful of relatively minor amendments had been asked for, and even these could probably have been negotiated. Plenty of other plays with more extensive references to homosexuality had been rewarded with licences once they had made the alterations required of them. Yet it was precisely the comparative innocuousness of Miller's play (along, to be sure, with its quality and bankability) which ensured that Beaumont would be widely cheered as he drove his coach and horses through Stable Yard. If even a play by a serious and reputable author like Arthur Miller, which was already running on Broadway, could be silenced in Britain, then it showed there really was something rotten in the state and in need of change.

The switch in policy announced in the autumn of 1958 rather conveniently assumed that homosexuality had been successfully and entirely excluded prior to that date. We have already seen that it was not quite as straightforward as that. For those with eyes to see and ears to hear, there were always coded ways of evading absolute boundaries, and censorship is always happier dealing with the literal than with the metaphorical. It is not only recent scholars who have pointed this out. Writing just after the policy change, Angus Wilson doubted that the stage was likely to see a sudden deluge of plays addressing the subject: 'the incentive for any writer to get his work presented, to communicate, is so strong that it is likely that a number of plays on this theme have already been modified or disguised to circumvent the Lord Chamberlain's ukase,' he suggested; 'Most playgoers can remember excellent plays in these last years that were clearly conceived in homosexual terms and presented in heterosexual ones.'[4]

Although codes may indeed have allowed playwrights to incorporate limited representations of homosexuality in their work, this does not necessarily mean that the Lord Chamberlain's ban (or the lifting of it) were irrelevant or unimportant. This chapter will concentrate on some of the practical effects of his policy during the period immediately before he formally jettisoned it. While the New Watergate was staging unlicensed plays 'privately' in the West End, and Scarbrough himself was trying to persuade the Home Office to make it possible for him to license plays about 'perversion' for adults only, what was his attitude to other new scripts that came in? Did he try to maintain his stringent policy until the last possible moment, or—away from the public eye focused on the Miller, Williams and Anderson plays—did he begin to shift his ground in order to pave the way for change?

Max Reitemann's *Hot and Cold in All Rooms* was submitted for licence just a couple of weeks before *A View from the Bridge*. A comedy set in 'a good class Kensington apartment house', it contained a problematic element right at its core: 'The point at issue,' reported Troubridge, 'is whether or not the character "an effeminate dress-maker" is permissible on the stage.' Given the current policy, he felt there was no argument: 'Cecil is a roaring Pansy who does not pretend to be anything else,' wrote Troubridge; 'and as he is a very central figure, under the present censorship policy as I understand it, the play is not eligible for a licence.' However, he also expressed some regret at not being able to recommend it:

> In a way I cannot help feeling sorry, for if it were conceded that audiences may be aware that some men are more effeminate than others, a fact quite often to be confirmed by a glance at the occupant of the next stall, then 90% of Cecil is quite funny and not really offensive adult comedy.[5]

This, after all, was not a serious play but a harmless comedy, and comedies depended on stereotypes like Cecil, whose first appearance is scripted as follows:

> *[Cecil] is elegantly and superbly dressed. His linen and other appointments are in exquisite taste, if a little exotic. His hair is beautifully waved, and he is aware of the impression he is creating, and loving every minute. He exudes charm, and has a flashing smile ...*
> CECIL: Oh, you're the American boy Mrs Danvers has been telling me about. How nice to meet you. You must tell me all about yourself. I just <u>adore</u> Americans. (*He takes out a slim gold case and flicks it open*) Cigarette?[6]

Troubridge tried to establish a distinction which he believed might provide a conceptual basis for easing the current policy—coining a new verb in the process: 'Only one scene, readily excisable, concerns not effeminacy but homosexuality (in the sense of the urge to intercourse with males).' The scene which worried Troubridge the most was one in which 'Cecil makes a sort of defence of his unhappy state'.

Gwatkin picked up the question of definitions:

> It is, of course, simple to ban a homosexual play or to insist upon the

deletion of homosexual passages. Both these courses lay the censorship open to criticism on one side and to credit on the other ...

However in recent years anything that is not blatantly male is immediately dubbed as 'queer'—there is no half measure such as there used to be thirty years ago when intolerance of the true homosexual was far greater than it is to-day: for although in those days the aesthetes and their like were, certainly, ridiculed, they were not automatically labelled homosexuals as they would be now.

Thus it is impossible for a playwright to include any character which is not 100% male without running very serious risks of being subjected to censorship for characterising a homosexual.

He endorsed the Reader's view that Reitemann's script could be easily amended so as to render it safe for easy consumption. However, he recognised that much depended on the acting and the production, and whether audiences might 'read in' something that would no longer 'really' be there:

it is quite unnecessary for the character Cecil to be a homosexual, he could perfectly well be a 'maiden aunt' type of man to whom homosexuality would be just as abhorrent as would be normal sex. He hasn't got to be a sodomite. If the passages on pages 55 to 59 were removed and the characters properly cast and produced, on paper there should be no reason to suppose a homosexual kink—on paper: but the fact remains that in the minds of the majority of the audience, because Cecil is not essentially male, he must inevitably be the other thing ...

It seems that both the Reader and the Assistant Comptroller were beginning to seek ways to gently nudge the policy on homosexuality away from the blanket ban imposed by Scarbrough, and towards something more flexible. In this instance, the order was given that 'Cecil should be changed from being admitted homosexual to being a "maiden aunt" type', and a revised script was submitted within a month. Troubridge thoroughly approved of it: 'The author has deftly performed the required trick of turning a roaring pansy into a maiden aunt,' he reported; 'the play is a pleasant and natural one, and with the new Cecil in the centre of it, I prophesy it will be most successful in Repertory.' To satisfy the Censorship, new notes had been inserted in the script for the actor playing Cecil, explicitly adopting their requirements and terms: these stipulated that 'At no time must his effeminate nature be allowed to become offensive', and that he must be played as a 'maiden aunt'.[7] Whatever might happen on stage within different productions and performances, the Lord Chamberlain's back was covered. More specific changes had also been demanded, crucially including the deletion of Cecil's 'defence' of homosexuality, and these were also met.[8] Unfortunately, we don't have the original script for a point of comparison, but in the revised and acceptable version, Cecil appears to be beyond and detached from any suggestion of personal relationships; he is the confidant of others, who devotes his time to sorting out their problems. Nevertheless, there is still a strong emphasis on his complete lack of sexual interest in women, and the freedom this gives him to help them dress up for other men. On one occasion he 'thrusts a very professional hand deep up inside the offending underskirt' of a young woman, with the line, 'Oh, don't be silly, girl! It's only me!' When another young woman is shocked at his suggestion that she should undress in front of him, he tells her, 'Oh, you've no need to worry about me, dear', and 'giggles hilariously'. Cecil describes himself as 'neutral'—but 'camp' might be the word we should use to describe him now. He personally demonstrates how a woman should 'flaunt [her] bottom' by letting it 'swing from the hips'. In one scene, a group of his young male friends return drunk from the pub and try to remove his dressing gown and pyjama trousers before carrying him to his bed: 'Cecil giggles and protests,' says the stage direction, 'but he's enjoying every minute of it.' And as he heads off to attend a wedding at the end of the play he tells us: 'the trouble with me is, I don't know whether I'm the best man or a bridesmaid.' Without even thinking of how the live performance might have accentuated it, the script alone would surely have left audiences with no doubt at all that they were watching someone of homosexual inclinations. Interestingly, although audiences were certainly expected to laugh at him, he was also an entirely benevolent and sympathetic character. On the other hand, the closest the revised script allows itself to come to any 'defence' of homosexuality is the following exchange between Cecil and a man in his fifties:

> POP: (*He finds this very difficult*) Er—I've always been a bit 'anti' to your sort. Probably because I've never been able to understand them.
> CECIL: That's the tragedy of it. Very few people do.
> POP: You know, you're the first person of that—er—type—I've ever come into close contact with, and I must say it's been a very interesting experience.
> CECIL: Well! That's the first time I've ever been called an experience![9]

While the 'small action where Eddie kisses the boy' was 'too forceful a homosexual implication' to be permitted in *A View from the Bridge*, the licence for the revised version of *Hot and Cold in All Rooms* was signed by the Lord Chamberlain without objection.[10] No doubt this was in part because the play was a light comedy in which audiences could laugh with affection at someone who might be 'perverse' but who was non-threatening, non-complaining, possibly non-active, and always cheerful. It was therefore a 'safe' play—and it might even be argued that a child or someone who had not previously come across the existence of homosexuality might have been none the wiser at the end. But it was probably equally significant to the securing of a licence that Scarbrough seems never to have had his attention drawn to it or alerted to the possibility of there being a problem. Certainly, there is no evidence that he was either asked to read the play or told anything about it. Effectively, then, it seems that the decision was taken by his staff not to involve him.

By contrast, in the early summer of 1956 the Office turned down *The Lonesome Road*, Philip King's follow-up to *Serious Charge*. The new play centred on a writer who is attempting to rebuild his life and career, living in a small Sussex village to which he has retreated after serving a short prison sentence for a mistake he made during 'one drunken afternoon'.[11] Unfortunately for him, Martin then finds himself idolised by a seventeen-year-old boy in the village, Jimmie, who has himself been thrown out of school for what we realise must have been homosexual activity. Falsely accused by Jimmie's father of having 'interfered' with his son, Martin is then prevented by his own agent—desperately trying to save his protégé from more damaging publicity—from opening his door to Jimmie, who is in despair at his father's plan to move him to the other end of the country. Martin knows he is the only person who could help Jimmie, and he makes an impassioned and powerful speech to his agent, which is very striking for the period in which it was written:

MARTIN: We're both on the same side of the fence ... Alex, can't you see it's my story all over again. When I was that boy's age I was living in a vicarage and my mother was dead ... I was afraid of my father, and I didn't seem able to do anything right for him. And he didn't trouble to disguise his disappointment with his one and only son. But it wasn't my failures that tormented my days and nights. I wasn't tortured by his displeasure. My agony came from knowing what the Prayer-book called 'the inclination of my heart'. When I heard beautiful music and my heart filled with a great yearning to love, I thought that the dazzling unattainable image that swung unbidden into my mind was a thing tainted and accursed. I thought that I was guilty of vileness even in my dreams. For my sin, a whole city had been destroyed. And while I struggled hopelessly to obliterate the image of my love, I thought God looked down and condemned my iniquity ... Didn't I go through hell on earth believing that apart from a few wretches expelled or imprisoned I was the only one in my village, in my class, in my school, in all my little world, I was the only one with this guilty longing? And when years later I discovered that it just wasn't true—I wasn't the only one on the wrong side of the fence, there were hundreds and thousands

like me who lived in fear and loneliness and there always had been—didn't
I react over-violently, stupidly, recklessly? ... if only I'd had someone I
could talk with about it, if only there'd been someone to help me along
that lonesome road I wouldn't have suffered one half as much ... I'm the
only person who can help him. And he's still young. If he's helped now,
he may reach the safe land on the right side of the fence and live without
fear of the sudden knock at the door, the intercepted letter and tapped
phone line, the blackmailer's threat, the sneers and contempt—the whole
trappings of life on the wrong side of it.[12]

But the opportunity to help has gone, and, believing himself rejected by
Martin, Jimmie commits suicide.

Even though Martin is shown desperately struggling to overcome his
own homosexuality and passionately wishing he could help Jimmie move to
'the right side of the fence', the script was not licensable. 'Homosexuality
is, at the moment, a forbidden topic for stage representation,' wrote Heriot,
'and this play is not a very powerful advocate in its favour.' In most
respects the script was far from radical, accepting many of the clichés,
assumptions, and easy psychology of its period. Nevertheless, the audience
is encouraged not only to feel sympathy for Jimmie and Martin and their
plight, but also to criticise the actions of several other characters which
contribute to the tragic denouement. This is made explicit when Alex, the
agent, acknowledges that he has become in effect a murderer, driven by
his determination to protect his financial investment. Jimmie's sister also
realises how her brother has been destroyed by the prejudices of their
family: 'I thought what Jimmie had done was ... I thought people like that
... I'd listened to every word Daddy said about them. And I believed him.
And now I've found out it just isn't true, and it's too late.'[13] Scarbrough
had few doubts:

> If plays dealing with the problems of homosexuality were allowed, this
> one could have no other objection ... But I remain—and definitely—of the
> opinion that the balance of advantage lies in continuing to refuse licences
> for plays which, naively and unmistakably as this one does—concern
> themselves with the subject.[14]

In early 1957, licences were refused for both R.D. Wood's *Foolish
Attachment*—'a stupid, badly written, banal play'—and Reginald Beckwith's
No Retreat. The problem with the former was that 'one of its main story
threads is a Lesbian relationship, the nature of which is made quite clear'.
Troubridge claimed: 'I often have some sympathy with plays that are
sincere and distressed studies of some aspect of sexual perversion'; but
in his view, this one was seeking to exploit the subject for gain: 'I must

resent the catch penny merchants.'[15] While there is nothing profound about *Foolish Attachment*, it now reads as an honest—if fairly simplistic—attempt to engage directly with the issue. Exploitation, surely, was in the eye of the Reader, who evidently found the notion of a lesbian police sergeant impossible to imagine, calling her 'a figure it would be hard to beat for absurdity.' Again, the play's psychology tends to the facile, with the strong suggestion that Vera has retreated into a lesbian relationship—her 'foolish attachment'—as a direct result of being jilted by a young man. She apparently comes to her senses, sees the error of her ways, falls in love with Michael, and rejects her long-time partner, Sandra, in a disturbing confrontation in which she cruelly denies and denounces their past relationship.

> SANDRA: What has changed you? I thought our love was forever.
> VERA: Don't talk such utter rubbish! There has never been any true love between us.
> SANDRA: How can you say that?
> VERA: How can I? For the simple reason you know as well as I do—it's not true. How can there be? ... We have degraded the word, love, using it the way we have ...
> SANDRA: ... You don't seem to have thought that in the past.
> VERA: No, because I accepted a cheap view of love.
> SANDRA: Cheap? That we have shared together! I think you have gone out of your mind.
> VERA: I said cheap, and I meant it.
> SANDRA: But how could it have been so—so—cheap?
> VERA: Because I accepted something which at the very best was only second rate.

However, the playwright leaves us space to question whether Vera's voice has quite the absolute legitimacy and morality it claims. Sandra, cruelly abandoned and unrepentant to the end, is never unequivocally condemned by the play, and we are given no absolute explanation of her supposedly abnormal feelings—though there are suggestions that they may have arisen as a result of her inability to bear children and thus achieve fulfilment. But Vera herself is divided, and, as Sandra realises, is fighting to overcome her own instincts and expressing views which have been imposed upon her.

> VERA: I shall love as it is only proper to love, with a man. This will cost me an awful lot. But because I intend to give far more than I can possibly hope to receive—I know I shall succeed. For love requires that of you.
> SANDRA: You—love a man?
> VERA: It may sound foolish to you, but my salvation can only be found there.

SANDRA: A man!

VERA: Because the end of woman's love must be in children.

SANDRA: Children! Can I believe that this is you speaking, Vera? ... Ours was a different experience.

VERA: That's what made it wrong—false—improper ...

SANDRA: Think of our love and our happiness.

VERA: So selfish though—to exclude that great fundamental purpose in our lives—procreation ... This love of ours which once meant so much to me—was only a sublimation of my desire for marriage and children. I was substituting my true and useful function in life for a misguided belief in self-satisfaction, choosing things for my own personal gratification. Can self ever be right? Can personal lust ever really give real happiness? You know it cannot. It corrupts one's self. It jaundices the proper view of life—until at last only the husk is left—a husk which is empty, useless and fit for nothing.

SANDRA: Michael told you all this? [16]

Moreover, Vera's certainty that future happiness lies with Michael is rendered completely ironic by the fact that we know him to be a serial liar, currently going through divorce proceedings and already in a relationship with Vera's sister, Anne! Even Troubridge was not convinced by the 'extraordinary final solution' which the play seemed to propose:

> This is that Michael shall go off with Vera, spend the six weeks before his divorce is through in convincing her in a horizontal position of the advantages of straight sex over Lesbianism, and then return to marry Anne, who, it is assumed, will by then be glad to have him back. [17]

Either way, the simplest thing was to ban it. The Reader recommended that was no need for anyone else in the Office to 'plough through all this nonsense', and Gwatkin agreed that *Foolish Attachment* was beyond amendment.

Also rejected in May was Reginald Beckwith's *No Retreat*, 'a thin, poor play'. Heriot found it 'entirely inoffensive in its treatment of the forbidden subject' since 'perversion is always "wrapped up" and oblique'. But he still felt obliged to recommend turning it down, 'since the subject is taboo'. *No Retreat* was partly a crime thriller, with a contrived and somewhat implausible narrative. Jack and Kay are married to each other, but are both having secret affairs with Jimmy, 'a borderline delinquent' whom they employ. [18] Jimmy is mysteriously murdered, and we eventually discover that Jack has killed him out of jealousy at having to share him. Jack has an alibi, but this has been provided by a senior judge with whom Jack had lived prior to his marriage, and proves to be false. Meanwhile, the detective investigating the case turns out to have been the boy with whom this same judge was in love at school! The references to homosexuality hardly seem 'oblique' now, and within the rather absurd narrative, there is some articulate—didactic, even—advocacy for the legitimacy of homosexuality. We are reminded of its history: 'We all know that this is an instinct, an emotion, which has been with us since the world began'; of its acceptability within the classical world—'I'm thinking of Socrates, and ... of Michelangelo, those sonnets to the young man.... a nephew re-edited them and turned all the "hes" to "shes"'; of its relationship to artistic genius—'you couldn't publish the Oxford Book of Verse without it ... there'd be no Greek Anthology and no sonnets of ... Shakespeare'; and of the hypocrisy which allows people to accept in art what they reject in real life: 'it's only the literary expression of that emotion which the world finds acceptable ... translate the words into actions and all the old professors who've spent their lives translating Catullus and Sapho will throw up their hands in horror.' In one scene, the Judge, Mackintosh, confesses to Haynes, the detective, the sacrifice and the lie on which his outwardly successful career and life have been based. What makes it particularly provocative is that the author has placed such transgressive material in the mouths of two of society's most respectable and secure guardians:.

MACINTOSH: I loved Jack. I have always loved Jack. ... I know of no moment, since first I loved, that my emotions lead me otherwise. It was congenital, fundamental; what are you to do with a man, when every particle of his marrow, bone and sinew, convinces him that this instinct is true for him ... I suppose I can say I conquered it—at a very great price ... I silenced that part of my life ... I became a barrister at an early age. ... I suppose it could be called a brilliant success. ... But it was empty and almost meaningless to me because I had no one to share it with me.
HAYNES: Not even ... discreetly?
MACINTOSH: No, not even discreetly... I've never been promiscuous, although, I know, that it's popularly supposed to be the besetting sin of my kind ... For years my life was entirely negative and then, I met Jack. The first comfort of my life, the first real companion. I was happy for the first time ... and so we made the fatal mistake.
HAYNES: What was that?
MACINTOSH: We decided not to be furtive about it, by that, I don't mean we advertised our relationship. That wouldn't have appealed to either of us—but we did decide to live together, to set up house ... It seemed madness not to try to snatch some little happiness out of life. ... We broke no laws and yet we lived a crime every day, every minute we breathed. We were two men together and people began to talk and went on talking.

Nor did the play shy away from making direct—if heavy-handed—propaganda:

> HAYNES: I must say it's difficult to see what harm you were doing to the social fabric, both useful members of society ... We've felt, a lot of us, and for a long time, that the law should be altered in the case of consenting adults—that the life they lead in the privacy of their own homes, should remain private. Why, a Government Commission has just advised a change of law.
>
> MACINTOSH: Yes, but the trouble is that no Government will be courageous enough to accept that advice and, can you blame them? ... No, easier to alter the law on Capital punishment than that.
>
> HAYNES: And yet we know, and the world knows the law is broken by millions every day, and to complete the hypocrisy we all could name a score of the famous among our friends, who should be in jail, if justice is justice and the law means anything.
>
> MACINTOSH: But the world averts its eyes, just so long as certain conventions are observed. In fact, the world is unjust to those who take life seriously, and kind, only to those who make a mockery of human relationships and buy their satisfaction in the streets and bars, the back alleys of life, sordid, but away from the respectable noses of the normal.[19]

It is not hard to understand Scarbrough's anxiety or his refusal to considering licensing *No Retreat*:

> This play seems to attempt a justification for homosexual tendencies, and although the treatment is inoffensive I think the arguments are likely to encourage or excuse rather than deter young persons who may have such tendencies.[20]

It was also Scarbrough's decision to reject *The Catalyst*, Ronald Duncan's poetic exploration of triangular love relationships involving husband, wife, and mistress. Troubridge's report had been ambivalent:

> This play fills me with the utmost perturbation. It has three characters, and in the somewhat unexpected ending the two women discover that they have lesbian tendencies, and the man realises that he more than possibly has homosexual tendencies. So, upon the application of the principles at present established, it would not receive a licence.

Yet with the Office seemingly digging itself into a deeper and deeper hole, perhaps it was time to stop digging. Duncan's play, said Troubridge, was based on 'a superb probing of human hearts', and he recognised an artistic integrity and quality in the writing: 'I do not think it would impair "the preservation of good manners, decorum, or of the public peace" anywhere with adults,' advised the Reader, 'and least of all with the Royal Court Theatre audiences.' Indeed, he proposed that Duncan's text might be the one which could allow the Censorship to draw a line and move decisively on to a fresh chapter: 'I advise that this is the exceptional play for which to loosen up,' he recommended.[21]

But although the poetic style seems to distance the text from the physicality of even Sartre's *Huis Clos*, Therese's revelation to her husband was too specific:

THERESE: Charles, it was I who made her cry.
CHARLES: What do you mean?
THERESE: It is I who Leone ...
CHARLES: What? You mean?
THERESE: Yes. And neither of us knew ...
    Because she was frightened of her feelings for me
    As I have been frightened of my feelings for her—
    So frightened that neither of us recognised what those feelings
     were ...
    I've got to learn to live with the person I now find I am ...
    All I know is that I do not want to live without her.[22]

It is not clear why Scarbrough felt obliged to turn the play down outright, rather than to seek specific amendments. Evidently, he was not yet willing to take the plunge:

I have read this play with great interest and I should think it could be a real success, but I am not prepared at present to pick and choose between the good and the bad plays which deal with the subject of homosexuality and lesbianism and so long as that policy prevails I regret I cannot license this play.[23]

Once again, *The Catalyst* would receive its first performances in a private production at the Arts Theatre.[24]

In the autumn of 1957, after nearly three years of taking evidence and opinions from a wide number of individuals and organisations, the Wolfenden Committee on Homosexual Offences and Prostitution finally published its report. The first of its recommendations proposed 'That homosexual behaviour between consenting adults in private be no longer a criminal offence'. All hell broke loose in the Press. 'It's the Truth It's the Answer IT'S LIFE' shouted the front page of the *Daily Mirror*, which urged readers,

'Don't be shocked by this Report', and demanded that the government should 'DECIDE ON ACTION NOW'.[25] The following day, its front page announced that the newspaper was to carry out a nationwide poll for readers to sign their agreement or disagreement with the proposals. Three of the four issues highlighted related to female prostitution, but the paper also did its best to nudge readers towards supporting the decriminalisation of homosexual acts committed in private between consenting adults, pointing out that this was 'generally speaking, the law in several European countries'.[26]

Even as disarmament talks with the Soviet Union broke down, and a 'COLD WAR CRISIS' was proclaimed when the US sent arms to Jordan,[27] debate raged around the Wolfenden recommendations, and dominated the press. As the *Daily Telegraph* reported in its leader of 9 September: 'Three days have sufficed to turn the Wolfenden Report into a battlefield so thickly shrouded in dust that the combatants can hardly see one another.'[28] However, the *Daily Mail* was soon announcing with satisfaction that 'Law for Men Unlikely to Change', and telling its readers that for the government to propose legislation on the legalising of homosexuality 'would strain party loyalty for many M.P.s beyond endurance'. The newspaper's own editorial columns also fulminated against allowing 'legalised degradation in our midst', insisting that the proposals were 'full of danger' and would, if enacted, 'certainly encourage an increase in perversion'.[29] On the other side, *The Times*—which had referred in an editorial six months earlier to 'the legal anomaly penalizing private sexual behaviour between men'[30]— now published a leader proclaiming that 'Nearly all civilized countries recognize the futility of making into crimes what are regarded as sins against morality', and that 'Adult sexual behaviour not involving minors, force, fraud, or public indecency belongs to the realm of private conduct, not of criminal law'.[31]

The separation of moral disapproval from legal restraint was strongly insisted upon by many supporters of the recommendation. To decriminalise homosexuality was not to condone it. Lord Denning told the Law Society conference that 'morals are not the law's business',[32] and as Wolfenden himself put it when interviewed on 'Woman's Hour': 'I want to make it absolutely plain that we do not think that men who behave like this are doing something that is right.' The crucial point was that while they might be doing something which society generally condemned, 'it does not follow that they should be sent to prison'.[33] The Archbishop of Canterbury, too, agreed that while 'homosexual offences are sins', and would remain so irrespective of legal changes, 'most sins are not and ought not to be treated as crimes'.[34] The act of adultery was sometimes referred to as an obvious equivalent or point of comparison. Although other Church leaders expressed fears that 'private homosexual indulgence' might come to be regarded 'with the same tolerance with which it now regards sexual aberrations which were not so long ago shunned as being shameful', a Church Assembly voted by 155 votes to 138 to give general approval to the report's recommendations on homosexuality.[35] Despite all this, when the government published its legislative programme for the autumn session, no mention was made of the committee's recommendations. *The Times*, probably acting as an unofficial voice for ministerial thinking, informed its readers that

> The Government feels that although the committee's recommendations on the law relating to homosexuality are logical enough they are very much ahead of public opinion. They therefore consider it best to wait for the controversial issues to be well aired in Parliament, probably in a discussion on a private member's Bill. But legislation on this part of the report in the present session may be ruled out.[36]

From the point of view of theatre censorship, Scarbrough's primary justification for suppressing references to homosexuality from plays had always been that they risked introducing the subject to people who had not previously encountered it. The furore which followed the publication of the Wolfenden Report quickly rendered the idea absurd. Yet there was no visible or immediate change in the Lord Chamberlain's policy. In December 1957, the Office received a script for a psychological crime thriller called *Compulsion*. Already running in New York, the play was based on a novel, itself derived from real-life events which had supposedly occurred in Chicago in the 1920s. 'As this is the story of a murder committed by two paranoiacally insane adolescent youths who have a homosexual relationship, I MUST DECLARE AGAINST IT', pronounced Troubridge. 'The homosexual relationship is not in itself greatly insisted upon,' he added, 'but it runs like a pervasive smell of drains throughout the play.'[37] The narrative and the structure of *Compulsion* contain echoes of a host of 1950s Hollywood movies. The play begins when a criminal is released from prison after a lengthy sentence, and the story is told mostly through flashbacks as he recounts the details and background of the crime to a journalist. It is an unsettling and uncomfortable piece, focused on two highly intelligent but sadistic young men, Judd and Artie, who lure a child away from his friends, brutally murder him, and bury him in a sewer pipe. The youths themselves come from rich families, and are articulate and sophisticated; their primary motivation seems to be a determination to transcend and subvert conventional morality, and they invoke Dostoyevsky as their guide and guru: 'Philosophy is meaningless unless you live by it,' declares Judd, insisting that 'Great men make their own laws'. To kill a human being without reason and for no material gain is a demonstration of the fact that you are free. In court, Judd vehemently denies any suggestion that there was a sexual relationship or attraction between himself and the victim: 'The choice of subject was left to accident so as to be purely impersonal. An experiment of this kind is no different than impaling an insect or mounting a bird.' His aim, he tells the court, was 'to seek the furthest limits of human experience. Not to be bound by mundane rules and conventions. To taste everything, to know everything in its pure form.' However, the suggestion is voiced that in exchange for assisting him in committing violent crimes, Artie agreed to take part in sexual acts with Judd.

Reading it now, *Compulsion* still comes across as a disturbing play, which perhaps sought to exploit fears and prejudices by linking the tendency in young males to homosexuality with an enjoyment of viciously cold-blooded criminal acts. Potentially a powerful and effective piece of theatre, the message is a disturbing and reactionary one—even if, by the end, there are voices in the courtroom pleading for medical help rather than just for punishment:

> WILK: Whatever happens in this case, and horrible as the clamor has been, I still hope the one purpose has been served. The world has heard, millions have read, of the dark forces within us. Perhaps other children, troubled as these, may recognize what is happening in themselves, may pause long enough to cry out, 'Help me! Take me to a doctor before I kill someone!'
> Your honor, if we could only help, instead of kill.[38]

Troubridge proposed a list of specific cuts to remove explicit homosexual references, and Gwatkin—doubtless wary of the publicity which would be generated by turning down yet another American commercial success—was keen to find a way to pass it: 'This isn't a very nice play,' he wrote, 'but I don't think we could ban it.' Scarbrough queried if the proposed cuts went far enough, and 'whether all the homosexual taint will have been removed' by them. Further amendments were proposed, but even so, no guarantee could be offered that this would do the trick: 'it has proved a difficult task, as there are a number of passages which would be hints of perversion once the main fact of the homosexual relationship is established and known.' Troubridge, however, was probably correct in his assumption that they might have done enough to achieve the goal of silencing the production without formally banning it:

> Personally, I would venture the opinion that the submitting management will not proceed with the production of the play thus eviscerated, as without the psychologically linking perversion thread, the action of the two boys will become merely lunatic, and therefore uninteresting. If my conjecture is correct, this would have in practice the effect of the ban I recommended.[39]

There is no evidence that the management responded to the request for amendments, or sought to proceed with their plans.

In early 1958, the Lord Chamberlain's Office and London County Council received protests about an all-male revue starring the popular dame comedians, Phil Starr and Terry Dennis. The saucily named *We're No Ladies* had been licensed by Scarbrough for the 20th Century Theatre, in London's Westbourne Grove, but several letters attacked the show's 'blatant and undisguised perversion', and demanded that steps be taken to 'clean up this nest of homosexuality in our midst'. Others condemned it as a 'disgraceful exhibition', 'A travesty of entertainment', 'a vehicle for the basest perversion', and 'a smutty badly performed homosexual orgy, in which the "converted" audience joins'. As this last reference suggests, the objections were not levelled exclusively at those appearing on stage, but also at the audiences: 'I believe that many of its members were homosexuals,' declared one complaint. One thing which clearly provoked outrage was that rather than constructing homosexuals as helpless inadequates in need of our sympathies, many of those on stage and in the auditorium of the 20th Century Theatre were neither hiding nor apologising for their apparent homosexuality—they were, if the letters are to be trusted, celebrating and flaunting it:

These 'men' with wigs, make-up, stockings and female dress, often transparent cloth that shows the most intimate female garments, are an insult to a great profession and the decent people who live in West London … Deplorable homosexual filth, in which the most sacred and lovely affections of men and women are mocked and debased as they all laugh at their private jokes. The effect on young people will be deeply disturbing and long lasting. I appeal to you, with all the power of your office to stop this lewd, nasty parody. It is offensive to me and, I am sure, to all other normal human beings. That these men exist and that they work their evil on each other we all know. But to stand and sing the 'National Anthem' in both 'soprano' and normal male voices, grimacing all the time at friends in the audience, is an insult to a gracious lady and great position, and an affront to English people.[40]

The Lord Chamberlain's secretary dutifully took himself down to Westbourne Grove to check out what was going on. He remained unconvinced that the show was breaking the law:

Some of the actors approximated to the dame type, others were pathologically effeminate, one if not two sang in soprano voices, and so on. In these times that could have a very obvious implication. Nevertheless, apart from one or two questionable gestures, the actors' conduct on the stage was simply that of women. There were no 'sissy' gestures or attempts to impose a male personality on that of the womanly one. There is no law which prevents female impersonation on the stage; it is in fact as old as the stage. Some of these actors were so good they might have been thought to be women.

Hill felt bound to pay attention not just to the performance, but also to the spectators. Goodness knows what they made of him:

Next the audience—I naturally looked at those present with some care. There was one almost certain homosexual but apart from him the company present all looked most respectable and there were many accompanied by wives or girl-friends who obviously had no perverted interest in the proceedings. I listened, and certainly in my vicinity there was no questionable conversation. I saw no undesirables making themselves conspicuous during the interval.

  As against this I have to record that:-

    1. The introductory remark 'This is Camp all right' which is specialised actors' slang for a homosexual gathering was greeted with a roar of laughter from the whole audience, who must thus be more familiar with the phraseology of the perverted than appeared.

The evident rapport between stage and auditorium was a cause for concern—though one wonders whether this may also have reflected Hill's limited exposure to theatrical forms which favoured direct address over the fourth wall convention:

One could sense that there was a rapport between audience and stage—in some cases Christian names were known e.g. shouts of 'bravo Wally' at some pieces of acting. Either those present had been to many shows of this sort or they met the actors socially or anti-socially elsewhere.

While Hill did not find evidence to support all the accusations, there was enough to make him suspicious—and anxious:

It is possible to speculate a good deal upon the implications of this but on my one visit I can offer no concrete evidence of the Twentieth Century Theatre becoming a focal point for pederasts. At the same time my impression as to the habits of some of the actors, whilst not given here, is pretty firmly formed in my own mind.[41]

A warning shot was promptly fired across the bows of the 20th Century Theatre, in the form of an official letter to Miss Compton-Burnett—the licensee—and Philip Starr—who had submitted the script. Rather than confront them directly with the real issue, the letter warned that a secret inspection had discovered that additional and unlicensed lines had been included, and threatened prosecution if the offence was repeated. In response, Starr claimed that the worst offence (probably the burlesque version of the National Anthem) had only occurred once, and was entirely the fault of a single performer. The Lord Chamberlain's Office was not completely convinced: 'Me thinks he doth protest too much and hides a guilty heart.' But the last thing they wanted to do was allow themselves to become embroiled in another conflict which could be manipulated by the press to turn not only Scarbrough but even the Queen into figures of mockery. Much better to shift responsibility for policing both venue and the performance on to the London County Council by sending them a copy of Hill's report, and a letter in which they would 'point out tactfully that we can't refuse to license a piece on the grounds that it may be performed by pansies'. It was the LCC's rather than the Lord Chamberlain's responsibility to deal with what happened next: 'It is up to them to watch the Theatre and if improper characters assemble there, to take appropriate action.' Gwatkin duly wrote to advise the Council that following observation of 'the large and enthusiastic audience' during the performance, 'his Lordship is not altogether satisfied that the piece was being received purely on its dramatic merits'. Happily, dealing with this was beyond the remit of St James's Palace:

> The Lord Chamberlain finds himself in some difficulty over pieces of this kind. He has no apparent grounds for refusing to license a play merely because it is to be performed by female impersonators, female impersonation being in this country as old as the stage. Nevertheless the increase in homo-sexuality could give such performances a new implication.

In the event of receiving a 'similar play from this Management' in the future, Gwatkin promised he would inform the Council at once, so that 'preliminary official or police enquiries could be made to see if there was any danger of the theatre becoming a meeting place for undesirable characters'.[42]

January 1958 also saw the opening of the third Watergate/Comedy production of an unlicensed play, Tennessee Williams's *Cat on a Hot Tin Roof*. In fact, homosexual references were only one of the reasons this play had been turned down by the Lord Chamberlain, and it would continue to be rejected long after the Lord Chamberlain's shift in policy, but inevitably, much of the discussion centred on this particular aspect. The script had first been submitted by the Arts Theatre in the autumn of 1955, but there was already a history between the Office and Williams. Some forty cuts were demanded, including references to 'boobs' and 'ass-aching', 'menstrual period', 'pair of homos', 'sodomy', 'fairies', 'homosexual hints', 'homosexual discussion', and 'the extended anecdote about elephants'. Scarbrough also stipulated that the playwright must 'eliminate the suggestion that there may have been a homosexual relationship' in the past.[43] Williams was unwilling to comply, so the play remained unseen in Britain until the Watergate production.

Yet the ground was beginning to shift. In May 1958, two new plays by Williams were licensed, with Scarbrough actually over-ruling the recommendation of his Reader. Though it has not generally been identified as such, it can be argued that it was actually Scarbrough's unexpected decision to license *Suddenly Last Summer*—the plot of which centres on a middle-aged artist who is torn to pieces and eaten by a group of poor boys in a Spanish holiday resort in revenge for his sexually predatory behaviour towards them—which marked his policy change. Alan Sinfield describes this as 'Williams' most homophobic play', and maintains that its critical success was based primarily on 'misogyny and homophobia'.[44] Was it this, too, that made it more acceptable to the Lord Chamberlain than some he had recently turned down? Troubridge originally advised rejection, but admitted that he was 'not altogether happy about such a recommendation'. Rather, he felt obliged to make it 'In accordance with what I conceive would be the Lord Chamberlain's wishes and current practice'. The moral lesson he drew from the narrative probably caught Scarbrough's eye: 'Though I should always view with horror any approval of or incitement to sexual perversity ... what could be more cautionary than the story of a homosexual who is not only killed by his victims but literally devoured by them?' Scarbrough confounded his expectations: 'Strange as the theme is, I do not think it calls for banning,' he wrote; 'I think it is a question of banning the whole play or allowing it all. I will allow it all and a licence can be issued.'[45]

Suddenly Last Summer was to be performed on a double bill with the same author's *Something Unspoken*, which was also licensed without difficulty, even though the entire play skirts around the subject of lesbianism. As the title indicates, the play is built on the fact that while Cornelia and Grace have lived together as employer and secretary and as companions for fifteen years, they have never talked about the nature of their relationship or named what it might become; a stage direction tells us that 'There is between the two women a mysterious tension, an atmosphere of something unspoken'.[46] In fact, Cornelia longs to bring out what is hidden, but knows this will be resisted:

CORNELIA: I've felt for a long time something unspoken between us.
GRACE:—Don't you think there is always something unspoken between two people?

CORNELIA: I see no reason for it. ... there's something unspoken between us that ought to be spoken.—Why are you looking at me like that?
GRACE: How am I looking at you?
CORNELIA: With positive terror.[47]

For Grace, 'some things are better left unspoken'—an opinion which happily coincided with the views of the Lord Chamberlain: providing its subject was never named, the Office was prepared to read the text's subtlety as vagueness, and license it to be performed:

What is unspoken between the two women is what is now termed ambivalence, a love-hate relationship. There is a tiny little undertone that they might have become lovers if things had gone differently many years ago, but there is no dubious line or sufficient nuance-suggestion in the play that would justify the refusal of a licence.[48]

In the same month came the possibly surprising decision to license Shelagh Delaney's *A Taste of Honey*. Shellard tells us that Delaney had written the play specifically 'as a response to the attitude to homosexuality evident in Rattigan's insipid *Variations on a Theme*',[49] but Heriot found it 'a surprisingly good play—though God knows it is not to my personal taste'. In his view, 'the problem of Geoff' had been 'delicately conveyed', and he was more inclined to sympathise than to condemn him:

Geoff has the reputation of being a pervert—and he confesses that there is a little flame to the immense amount of smoke; but he explains that he is really quite a normal young man, only not very strongly sexed, and with a very real desire to marry and settle down and have a family ... The curtain falls and we are left with the slightest hint that this is the end for him and that he will never get another chance to prove himself normal.

Heriot identified specific lines which would require cutting, including 'where Helen calls him a pervert and a castrated little clown', but advised that these could 'easily come out'. And his conclusion again indicated that some in the Office were now actively seeking a text which they could identify to mark a revolution in policy:

The point I wish to make is that this play is balanced on a knife-edge: it is the perfect border-line case, since it is concerned with the forbidden subject in a way that no-one, I believe, could take exception to ... But I think that the Comptroller and the Lord Chamberlain should both read the play carefully themselves.[50]

Not everyone at St James's agreed with his judgement on Delaney's play: 'I think it's revolting, quite apart from the homosexual bits,' wrote someone else; 'To me it has no saving grace whatsoever. If we pass muck like this it <u>does</u> give our critics something to go on.'[51] But Scarbrough made the decision to license it with minor amendments. Of course, *A View from the Bridge* could have been licensed if the author had accepted the minor amendments demanded.

The press announcement in August 1958 that the Watergate private theatre experiment was coming to an end was met with grim satisfaction in the Lord Chamberlain's Office, and spun by the Comptroller as a vindication of their policy. He wrote to Scarbrough to inform him of the Comedy's plan to revert to its public status:

> I do not know whether you take the *Daily Telegraph*, but in case you do not, I am sending you this article which will interest and amuse you. I had no idea that the Watergate Theatre Club had been a failure, and it is rather satisfactory from our point of view that it should be so.

Under the headline 'WEST END THEATRE CLUB TO CLOSE', the *Telegraph* had published a copy of a letter sent out by the Watergate to its 68,000 members:

> We have tried to provide you with productions of the highest quality and to live up to our stated intention of presenting 'controversial plays of unusual interest.' ... however, it has been found that to present new plays in a full size theatre in a manner which can compare with other West End productions is not an economic proposition if we are to rely exclusively on a club membership, however large.
>
> Rather than compromise our standards of production therefore it has been decided to suspend the activities of the club and to close membership.[52]

However, there was really no case for breaking open the champagne at St James's. Even if a private club operating on this model could not survive in the long term, the damage had been done, and the Lord Chamberlain's enemies would have noticed the potency of the weapon used. Moreover, on the specific issue of homosexuality on the stage, they had surely been defeated. Having begun to pave the way, the Office was now in search of a play which they could use to mark the change more explicitly. The honour fell to a somewhat old-fashioned and in many ways unremarkable text called *Look on Tempests*.

Joan Henry's script fitted the bill perfectly. The entire plot centres on the trial of a man for illegal homosexual activities, but, most conveniently from the Lord Chamberlain's perspective, none of the activities, the man, or even the trial are ever seen on-stage. The focus falls rather on his family, their anxieties and the damage done to them by his actions. The setting, the structure and the language all made this a relatively safe and comfortable play; yet it named homosexuality, and addressed the 'issue' of the married and closet homosexual directly and with serious intent. Homosexuality is not seen as necessarily a fixed identity, or endemic to British society; rather, Philip has succumbed to the wiles and temptations of a young Italian man (homosexuality, by implication, becomes an essentially foreign and Latinate disease) and his tragic fall threatens his 'normal' married life. The 'sin' has been committed before the play starts, so what we witness is not the provocative excitement of a temptation, but the sad aftermath, and the anti-hero's determination to overcome and start again.

Henry's play is set in a wealthy flat in Knightsbridge, where the wife (Rose) and the mother of Philip Sinclair wait for news of the court's decision. We learn that Sinclair 'has been charged (a) with writing letters to a young Italian boy and (b) indulging in "physical intimacy" with him'.[53] But as the title tells its audience (assuming they are familiar with Shakespeare's sonnets) at the centre of the play is the testing of the wife's feelings for a husband who has fallen; can her love survive 'when it alteration finds', and remain 'an ever-fixed mark,/That looks on tempests and is never shaken'?[54] Place your bets, please. The play also asks who is to blame for the husband's fall; is it, as his mother initially insists, down to his wife for failing to satisfy his needs? Or is she a blameless victim? Yet while the text cannot for a moment let itself condone or defend homosexuality, the emphasis is on understanding rather than condemning the 'weakness', and it insists that an older generation must rethink its values and certainties:

MRS VINCENT: You're determined to make me believe that my son is homosexual.
ROSE: (slowly) I've become used to horrible phrases. My life is full of filthy words. But nobody has made one word sound dirtier than you have now.
MRS VINCENT: It is dirty.
ROSE: There are degrees in everything—there are degrees.
MRS VINCENT: I don't understand you. You talk in riddles.
ROSE: You don't want to understand. You only want to hear pleasant things in your black and white meaningless existence.
MRS VINCENT: Be quiet! Be quiet at once. I've been brought up to believe in certain things. You're not going to twist them for me. That's the trouble with your generation. You've no standards—no religion—nothing.
ROSE: You're saying that you've been brought up to condemn? Surely that's a terrible thing to say.

Or as Philip's defence counsel expresses it: 'it's time the public learnt that labels are for luggage—not human beings.'

On the tactical advice of his defence counsel, Philip is eventually persuaded to plead guilty, and is sent to prison for two years—though his stepfather (whose existence is probably intended to hint at one of the origins of Philip's 'problem') questions the wisdom of society's response: 'in many other countries what Philip has been found guilty of is not a criminal offence,' he points out; 'Even here, everybody knows that it can't help anyone with these—these tendencies to be sent to prison.' Meanwhile, Rose declares that she is prepared to wait for Philip, having no doubt of his love for her, and Philip's mother realises that her own prejudices and assumptions have been mis-placed. The play ends with an image of the two women clinging together in comfort. As Sinfield observes, the play is actually 'about the problem of everyone other than the unfortunate gay man'.[55]

Heriot reported on the script in early October 1958: 'This is what is known as a "sound" play on a forbidden subject,' he commented; 'It is serious and sincere.' Despite this, he did not think it could be allowed: 'It could never, I believe, be a suitable point d'appui for any change of policy. It is therefore Not Recommended for Licence.' Gwatkin saw it differently:

> You will see that Heriot does not consider this a worthwhile enough play with which to inaugurate a new policy. He is rather in favour of waiting for one by a better known author. I don't agree. I think it might well be a good thing to license a play by a little known author—we would not then lay ourselves open to charges of favour or snobbery!

The Comptroller sided with Heriot, and advocated waiting for a better play:

> I am afraid that I agree with Heriot that this play is not a worthy vehicle for so momentous a change of policy. It may be sincere and serious, but to my mind it is a very amateurish affair ... the dialogue is banal ... the Play is most unconvincing. The author generalises about the likely action of the Law without any regard for factual truth: for instance, there is not a shred of evidence put forward of any Homosexual Acts; nor is there any corroboration. The author's idea that any judge would give a lighter sentence because a man pleaded guilty to such a flimsy charge, is puerile and an insult to the judiciary. I am sorry to disagree because I think your point about licensing a play by a little known author, rather than by some 'swell', is a very good one; but I think that the change of policy, when it comes, should be heralded by a really worthwhile play, which I fear I do not think 'Look On Tempests' to be.

Indeed, Nugent worried that passing this play could rebound on them since 'the authors of such plays as *South*, *The Children's Hour*, *Tea and Sympathy*, etc., would have a justifiable grievance; and I think the critics would have a good deal to say'. But Gwatkin continued to argue his case with conviction:

> This is not, of course, a great play—we might have to wait years for one—but I still think it a good play for a starter.
>
> It is serious: it brings out the differences in the consideration of homosexuality by separate generations: it brings out the strength of deep love: it avoids the unpleasantness of seeing the principles as neither the boy nor the man appear on the stage: it draws attention to the two sides of homosexuality, mental and physical, and I don't think the play could cause anyone embarrassment.
>
> We cannot go back or we could license *South* which was in many ways a much better play, though *Look On Tempests* is a more human one. *The Catalyst* also.
>
> I do not see that the author of any previously turned-down play would have any cause to grumble because we were not passing homosexual plays when his was submitted.
>
> I don't know about the legal errors in the play but everyone who has dealt out justice prefers a plea of guilty and, subsequently, is apt to be kinder in his sentence!

Scarbrough gave his momentous ruling:

> After I have seen the West End Managers on Nov 4th and have informed them of this change in policy with regard to plays concerned with the theme of homosexuality, this play—being a serious and not offensive attempt to deal with the subject—will receive a licence.[56]

Probably the Lord Chamberlain's decision took everyone by surprise, including the management who had submitted it. Ironically, he then found that he was unable to sign a licence since no actual production of the play had been scheduled—a pre-requisite for issuing permission. It was almost another year, in the autumn of 1959, before *Look on Tempests* actually received its first performance, when Vanessa Redgrave portrayed the wife trying to come to terms with her husband's betrayal.

Having made the decision that from now on they would be prepared to 'pass plays which deal seriously with the subject of either sex homosexuality', the Lord Chamberlain and his senior staff needed to fix more precise details of what they would and would not allow:

Subsequent on the passing of the first homosexual play will come enquiries as to our change of policy. It would help if we could have certain points clear in our minds. ...

Would we pass a play that was violently pro or con?

Would we allow a homosexual character to be included if there was no need for such inclusion?

Would we allow any "funny" innuendos or jokes on the subject?

How can we differentiate between the aesthetic character and the active pansy?

Will we allow the word pansy?[57]

On 31 October, Scarbrough wrote an official minute outlining the new policy, and explaining the thinking behind it:

I have decided to make a change in the policy of the censorship, and I think it desirable to place on record as clearly as possible the nature of the change so that all concerned may be fully aware of it.

First, the reason behind this change. For some time the subject of Homosexuality has been so widely debated, written about and talked about, that it is no longer justifiable to continue the strict exclusion of the subject from the Stage. I do not regret the policy of strict exclusion which has been continued up to now, and I think it has been to the public good. Nevertheless, now that it has become a topic of almost everyday conversation, its exclusion from the Stage can no longer be defended as a reasonable course, even when account is taken of the more effective persuasion which the living Stage can exercise as compared with the written word. I therefore propose to allow plays which make a serious and sincere attempt to deal with the subject. It will follow also that references in other plays will be allowed to the subject which appear necessary to the dialogue or the plot, and which are not salacious or offensive. Licences will continue to be refused for plays which are exploitations of the subject rather than contributions to the problem; and similarly references to the subject which are unnecessary or have merely an exploitation value will be disallowed.

The instructions and guidelines issued to Readers (included near the start of this chapter) inevitably left considerable space for interpretation and argument. Scarbrough was not so naïve as to suppose that arguments over homosexuality on stage could be consigned to the past: 'I do not imagine that this change of policy will eliminate all difficulties with regard to this question. I have, in fact, little doubt that we shall continue to be faced with problems which it will be difficult to resolve.' Yet it was an important step, and one which immediately gave the Office more room for manoeuvre.

Scarbrough sent letters explaining his decision to the Archbishop of Canterbury, the Home Secretary, the Press Secretary at Buckingham Palace, and the British Board of Film Censors, as well as to his Readers. The Archbishop expressed some regret: 'It is to my mind not at all a good thing that dramatists seem so ready to bend their energies to dramatising the least pleasant things in life, to wit adultery and homosexuality.' He reluctantly accepted that Scarbrough had had little choice, but he forecast challenging times ahead for the Lord Chamberlain:

> Homosexual vice is still a criminal offence, and I understand that the Government are not likely to adopt the Wolfenden Report recommendations about it. That does put a different slant upon the introduction of references to homosexuality in the theatre: it might be said that they would be incitements to breaking the law ... Would you be in danger of finding yourself taken to the Courts for allowing incitements to homosexuality ...?

On 4 November, Scarbrough called a meeting of leading West End Theatre Managers to inform them of the change, explaining that homosexuality was now so widely discussed that 'the subject must be common knowledge to most people, and the possible corruption of innocent persons was negligible'. Sycophants to a man, they applauded his decision as a master stroke:

> The meeting expressed their great approval ... and thought that it might well have the effect of cleaning up the theatre by running out of business those theatre clubs which traded in the production of erotic plays.
> They also considered that a spate of homosexual plays would be unlikely as it would be bad business, theatrically, to have too many plays on this, generally repugnant, subject.

Scarbrough originally intended to make no formal press announcement about the change, in order to avoid drawing publicity to it. He hoped to rely on the select handful of managers invited to attend the meeting 'to pass the word around'. But they persuaded him that this would upset other managers, and that he should write officially to Charles Killick, the Chair of the Theatres' National Committee. By 7 November, the story had been broken in the national press. Scarbrough received some telegrams and letters of support—'Your decision announced today represents important step forward for the theatre many many congratulations—Sam Wanamaker'—and others of denunciation—'God will hold you, my Lord, and Mr. Killick's association responsible at the day of Judgement, a day which ... may not be far off.'

On 12 November, the Assistant Comptroller told Scarbrough that managers were beginning to seek licences for various plays which had previously been refused. This raised an unfortunate financial problem which no-one had thought to allow for:

> I think that such plays, which were submitted before you came into office and which have been read by an Examiner no longer here, should be read again. But if they are exactly the same as the originals we cannot, legally, ask for another Reading Fee. This is bad luck on the Examiner, but there it is.

In some instances, the Readers stood to get a particularly raw deal:

> Plays which were obvious 100% homosexual, and therefore automatically banned, might not, possibly, have been read with such attention to details as we should require if the play was to be considered for licensing.
>
> It seems, therefore, that all banned plays will have to be re-examined in some degree and that no fee can be charged.

There is no record of how Heriot and Troubridge responded to the news that they were expected to undertake additional work without additional remuneration.

Less than three weeks after the Lord Chamberlain had announced his change in policy, the House of Commons finally debated the Wolfenden report. The Home Secretary let it be known in advance that while the government was ready to follow many of the recommendations in relation to prostitution, there was 'no hope of bringing in a measure to change the law referring to homosexuality in the present state of Parliamentary feeling and public opinion'.[58] One MP attacked the media for granting Wolfenden so much publicity, and spoke of an 'evil thread' he had detected which 'runs through the theatre, through the music hall, through the Press, and through the B.B.C.'[59] Another speaker also made direct and disapproving reference to the stage, and to what could now be seen and heard on it:

> I am of opinion that there are too many presentations on the stage, either in private or in public, portraying homosexuality as their central theme. I notice that the Lord Chamberlain has recently permitted the public performances of certain plays. I regret that. After all, those who use the Lord's Payer and who pray 'Lead us not into temptation' are entitled to ask what are we doing when we throw open to the public gaze both of the mature and immature, on the stage and on television … performances centring round a subject which can do as much damage as subliminal advertising?

The message can be presented in most attractive and dramatic terms. Anybody who knows of the actions, and the personalities ... of some homosexuals knows that some of them are very ingratiating. They have powers, and sometimes occupy places of influence, whereby they can exercise an effect on the minds of those who would not otherwise be interested in this subject ... I am not talking only of adolescents, but of adults too, and we should hesitate before doing anything which might permit this business to expand and extend. That is why I feel so strongly on this matter and particularly about the public presentation of plays dealing with homosexuality.[60]

As for the Lord Chamberlain, he had been desperate to draw a line in the sand which would allow his Office some respite from the ridicule and criticisms to which it had been subjected by the Press. But as so often happens when concessions are made, it seemed too little too late, and it bought him very little credit. Overall, the retreat showed him as weak rather than strong—on the one hand trying to catch up with a world that was passing him by, and on the other giving in to the forces of decadence and evil. At best, the press were grudging. Under the headline 'Lord Blue Pencil lifts stage ban', the ever with it *Daily Mail* told readers that his 'sudden change of heart after a long and stubborn opposition against plays with even the vaguest reference to homosexuality' meant that Scarbrough had finally fallen 'into step with the enlightened new times'; his change in policy was thus seen as a somewhat belated attempt to catch up: 'managers will welcome this new broadminded step by a Court official whose views on what playgoers should and should not see have hitherto seemed to belong to some remote Puritan age.' Yet the paper suggested that the decision had been made too late, and 'ironically at a time when the supply of plays with homosexual themes or references has run so low that the new Watergate Theatre Club formed expressly to present them to privileged members has had to disband'.[61] Angus Wilson's assessment for the *International Theatre Annual* was no more inclined to offer congratulations:

The recent decision of the Lord Chamberlain to allow the serious representation of homosexual themes upon the English stage has hardly been greeted with any marked feeling, either gratified or hostile ... the decision, like so many official decisions in England, has come as an anti-climax.

Public interest in the issue of male homosexuality was past its peak and on the way down, insisted Wilson:

it may well seem an irony that the Lord Chamberlain should give his licence just at the moment when the subject is becoming a trifle 'old hat'. One might even suppose that the authorities had waited for such a moment in the hope that censorship would no longer be needed when the topic had lost its news value. One might suppose, that is if one was not sure that governmental bodies seldom act from such subtle motives and nearly always arrive on the scene late in the day from sheer ignorance and sloth … The Lord Chamberlain's office may suppose that they have bravely and democratically permitted the stage representation of a 'controversial theme' because the 'controversial theme' has by now largely been relegated to a small column on the back page.

Still, Wilson did not underestimate the importance of the change, or the damaging effect of the policy which Scarbrough had previously applied. Although some playwrights had managed to sneak homosexuals onto the stage in disguise, 'There is little doubt, I think, that they were the poorer for the transformation'. Even more interesting is Wilson's assessment of how the ban had not silenced but shaped and distorted the subject:

how weary we all are of plays in which adult people have homosexual emotions, or wake to the discovery in adult years with shattering results. Why is all this tedious? Surely because it is so false. There are adolescents and even adult people in naïve milieux who suffer such pangs and their predicament is a tragic one. But the greater part of men over eighteen in England today are a good deal more informed than play censorship has allowed them to appear. They may be deeply concerned at the discovery of homosexual tendencies in themselves or in those around them, but not with the kind of half innocent, tongue-tied horror that they show in most stage representations.

Then again we are so often given plays in which after all the labour of conscience we learn that homosexual tendencies have been little more than some schoolgirl crush. This again was a ridiculous circumvention imposed by censorship. There are many homosexuals in this country whose consciences have denied them physical expression of their feelings. A very interesting play might be written about whether such abstinence strengthened or dessicated a man's life. But simply to present the phenomenon as interesting, surprising or horrifying in itself is to lag absurdly behind public sophistication.

Wilson cited *Cat on a Hot Tin Roof* and Peter Shaffer's *Five Finger Exercise* as recent examples of plays suffering 'from an improbable naivete' and an 'inability to speak upon the central theme of the play'. And he celebrated the fact that 'the new licence to the stage will rid us of this gentility, this once necessary fiction'.[62]

But if Scarbrough imagined the policy change would provide his Office with significant relief from attacks, and a quieter life, he was going to be disappointed. An important decision had been made in relation to an issue which had become extremely contentious, and he must have hoped to gain some respite. But throwing a pack of hounds off a scent they have in their nostrils is a tricky business. A wounded Lord Chamberlain could run, but he couldn't hide.

CHAPTER FIVE

Not Always on Top

The Lord Chamberlain's Office
and the New Wave

The English Stage Company is a fine affair, and I used to be a highbrow once myself, but it is quite an affliction to an examiner with its predilection for blasphemy (in all languages) and sexual perversity.[1]

The Theatre Workshop people from my experience in Court where they all lied openly and unashamedly, have no compunction in taking the Censor for a ride and I think they are doing it here.[2]

It is a pleasure to read a play these days in which all the characters are attractive.[3]

While critical debates may continue about the extent of the British theatre revolution in 1956, and the relative impacts of the English Stage Company, Theatre Workshop and the Berliner Ensemble, it is beyond dispute that the second half of the decade brought a new energy and a new generation of theatre-makers, determined to challenge and uproot much of what they found. It was therefore inevitable that the Censorship would find itself under heavy and sustained attack. The attack did not need to be co-ordinated; it came from different sides and took the form of a series of skirmishes rather than a decisive battle. But while it was not always obvious at the time who was winning, it is clearer in retrospect that the Lord Chamberlain was on the retreat and in effect looking for a way to escape gracefully and with some dignity intact. One long battle was fought on the site of the Comedy theatre as part of his determined but doomed campaign to keep homosexuality off the stage. But there were some other heavyweight contests, and this chapter will concentrate on some of the most bruising encounters which took place between 1957 and 1958.

Theatre Workshop on Trial

In 1958, the Lord Chamberlain's Office took Joan Littlewood and Theatre Workshop to court, following an undercover inspection by members of his staff which revealed that the Company's production of the aptly named *You Won't Always Be on Top* included new material which had not been submitted for licence. Superficially, St James's Palace won the case, with a court of law ruling in their favour and against members of the company. But, as we shall see, it was the hollowest of victories, which undoubtedly hurt St James's Palace much more than it did Theatre Workshop.

You Won't Always Be on Top was submitted for licence in October 1957.

> Setting: A building site in the south of England.
> Time: Not very long ago.
> Story: A day out of many.[4]

Heriot was impressed neither by the real-world ordinariness, or the structure:

> It is difficult to see the point of this play. It is about a gang of workmen on a building site who grumble and squabble and complain and loaf through three acts. There is no plot and no development and has about as much entertainment value as a tape-recording of real workmen on a real job.[5]

Both dialogue and dialect were certainly different from what you might hear in Loamshire. This was hardly surprising since the playwright, Henry Chapman, was a former builder, and the actors had spent time observing at building sites and talking with builders before embarking on a rehearsal process which involved improvising and devising in order to create a performance text. 'There are more "buggers" to the page than in any other play I have read,' noted Heriot; 'They must all come out.' Other distasteful phrases included 'sodding', 'on the piss', and ''ad your nose stuffed up 'is arse'. But the Company accepted the cuts, the play opened without delay, and that might have been the end of the story, had not an enthusiastic newspaper reviewer reported the following:

> This play—by a building-trade worker, about a day's work on a building site—isn't really a play at all, in shape or construction: it is a raw, realistic 'slice of life'.
>
> What makes it more so, but has so far escaped the notice of the press and the Lord Chamberlain (I hope he won't mind), is that the play varies every night. The actors, really living their parts, genuinely improvise, introducing their own new gags and fragments of dialogue.[6]

Scarbrough did mind. Or, to put it more precisely he *had* to mind, now it had been brought to his attention. One can only imagine what Joan Littlewood may have said of (and probably to) the reviewer who gave the game away. It is possible that St James's Palace already had an inkling of Littlewood's approach to performance, and that blind eyes had been judiciously turned. But once an infringement of the law had been placed in the public eye, they could hardly ignore it.

Two members of the Lord Chamberlain's staff were promptly sent to watch a performance incognito, licensed scripts in hand (or possibly up their sleeves), to check the truth of the reviewer's claim. As a result of what they found, the Assistant Comptroller wrote officially to the company's general manager, Gerald Raffles:

> I am desired by the Lord Chamberlain to inform you that it is reported to him that the Stage Play '*You Won't Always Be On Top*' as acted at the Theatre Royal, Stratford on Thursday, October 31st and Friday, November 1st, 1957, differed very materially from the version allowed by him. His Lordship is also of the opinion that some of the unauthorised dialogue allegedly spoken on these occasions was grossly offensive. In consequence I am, at his direction, now enquiring into the practicability of taking legal proceedings against those concerned.

Raffles insisted that the script as performed did not 'differ materially from the version allowed by you', and protested moral (if not actual) innocence:

> It is inevitable with a play of this type that actors should vary the words slightly each night, but I am fully convinced that on no occasion were any substantial alterations made, nor any words spoken that could be construed by an ordinary person, as in any way offensive.

The sting, doubtless deliberate, was in his reference to 'an ordinary person'.

As Raffles well knew, the Theatres Act did not allow additions of any kind to a licensed script—whether offensive or not. Anyway, his claim did not quite match the evidence of the Lord Chamberlain's staff, who had reported 'two grossly offensive interpolations'. One of these was a reference to a baby sitting on a pot, but the more serious one was 'an impersonation of Sir Winston Churchill opening a public urinal'. The company would deny in court that any specific impersonation had been intended, claiming that they could not control how an audience read a character. But Hill's account of the scene was probably fairly accurate:

> The actor ... continues his speech in imitation of Churchill, saying in Churchillian tones, 'It is my pleasure and honour to declare this building

open. May God bless all those who function in them'. Then, as a finale, he lifts a watering can between his legs and sprays the ground in front of him as though urinating. All the time he has a small black bowler hat on his head and is pretending to smoke a cigar.

In private, the Censorship had little option other than to accept the fact that since they had no system of policing performances on anything like a regular basis, it was effectively impossible for them to ensure that actors kept faithfully to the text they licensed. 'The public can no more be protected from sudden interpolations in the written script, than they can be from occasional murder,' Gwatkin had admitted to someone complaining about a production of Robert Bolt's *Flowering Cherry*.[7] But this present case was much worse than a couple of interpolated gags, pre-meditated or otherwise. In fact, it seemed that almost an entire new act had been added and played, without even bothering to submit it for licence.

Gwatkin sent the licensed script to the Director of Public Prosecutions, along with the performance reports of Ronald Hill and David Buchanan, and a covering letter in which he explained that although Act One had been played more or less as scripted, Act Two had contained 30 per cent of unallowed dialogue, and Act Three approximately 90 per cent. He requested that legal proceedings should be taken against the licensee of the theatre (Mr John Bury), the General Manager of the company (Gerald Raffles), the producer of the play (Joan Littlewood) and the actors, Henry Chapman and Richard Harris, who were 'responsible for the most offensive and obviously rehearsed pieces of unauthorised dialogue'. Gwatkin explained why prosecution was vital:

> It is true that the majority of this unallowed dialogue and the new theme of action are innocuous and would have been passed had they been submitted. Despite this the changes are of such magnitude as to constitute what is tantamount to a new play, and represent a flagrant disregard of his authority ... The offence is aggravated by the fact that some of the unallowed additions and action are of a grossly offensive kind which would not have been licensed had they been submitted to him ... they are not the result of some lapse of memory and 'gagging', but are rehearsed incidents which were repeated at two performances.

And all this in front of the children: 'It may also be remarked in this connection that at the performance on 31st October some thirty to forty schoolgirls of approximate age fifteen were present.'

In March 1958, detectives from Scotland Yard walked into rehearsals of another show at Stratford East to serve summonses on those involved. Potentially, the resulting court case could have destroyed Theatre Workshop completely. The company's strategy was therefore to go on the offensive—admitting their guilt, casting themselves as martyrs and marshalling support for a campaign on the basis of principle and the future of theatre. On 27 March, Joan Littlewood wrote a public letter:

> Dear Friends
>
> As you may know four members of our company have to appear in court on April 16th for breaking the 1843 censorship law. We are guilty and can only ameliorate our case by attempting to prove that this law is obsolete and by having a show of public opinion on our side ... We are asking for your active support, not only for our sakes (although we may be fined five hundred pounds and have our theatre closed), but because it is more than ever necessary to free our English theatre from obsolete practices ...
>
> If any among you feel that you would like to make an individual statement or protest on our behalf, our solicitor ... will be pleased to hear from you.

There were plenty of voices in the Arts ready to speak up for Theatre Workshop and against the Lord Chamberlain. One powerful piece of advocacy was a letter sent to the press, with signatories including Frith Banbury, George Devine, Richard Findlater, Peter Hall and Kenneth Tynan:

> Theatre Workshop, the company concerned, is famous in this country and abroad for fertile and original work in both contemporary and classical drama. It is out of the West End and lives, as such experimental companies have always lived, on a shoestring. It is completely without reserves to meet the cost of its defence in court and would almost certainly have to close, whatever the verdict, unless it receives financial help.

The letter linked this specific case to a much broader context:

> The Home Secretary recently announced that he was going to study the law of theatre censorship ... it seems likely that the law is about to undergo one of those concentrated inspections by public opinion to which we in this country periodically subject our more controversial institutions. For this reasons, as well as for the great intrinsic merit of Theatre Workshop itself, we should like to see the defence conducted in the best possible way, and appeal to your readers to contribute to a defence fund.

In the event, the appeal raised considerably more money than the defendants would need. The accused, represented in court by a QC taking no fee, pleaded guilty and were duly convicted and fined. But they were not the real losers. Several speeches were made in court which exposed the anachronism of the law, and the fines imposed were relatively minor and easily covered by the defence fund. It seemed that the magistrates, while obliged to convict in law, sided at least partially with the defendants. Raffles, as general manager of Theatre Workshop, was fined £8, John Bury £5, Littlewood £2 and the two actors each £2 1s 6d. Hill thought St James's Palace had been stitched up:

> The defence lawyer Mr Gerald Gardiner then addressed the Court. He said that the English Stage was the only form of entertainment subjected to Censorship (which is of course untrue and he knew it), that his clients must admit they had broken the law but they denied doing anything obscene. That the two fingered gesture complained of was used by Sir Laurence Olivier in '*The Entertainer*'. He read a letter from Michael Redgrave saying that they had put many lines into '*A Touch of the Sun*' without the consent of the Lord Chamberlain.
>
> He then went on to say that the Company was more or less bankrupt … the actors got no more than £2 to £8 per week … he added that he was appearing without a fee (which statement I should have thought a professional impropriety) … I got the impression that, but for the statement that the Theatre and Actors were bankrupt the fines would have been heavier.[8]

Hill later claimed that 'The Theatre Workshop people' had 'all lied openly and unashamedly' in court.[9] He also blamed the referee, describing the magistrates as 'a very parochial looking pair' and 'not very articulate'. About the most positive light he could put on the experience was to tell Scarbrough that 'So far as I am aware we succeeded in escaping without being photographed'. Gwatkin suggested that the outcome of the case had probably been 'about as much as we could expect'. In reference to the rather embarrassing revelation that adding lines in performance was almost standard practice, he noted dryly: 'We must watch for M. Redgrave's next appearance.' To which Nugent added, even more dryly: '*Hamlet* at Stratford! He can't put anything new into that!'[10]

Ostensibly, then, the judge had endorsed the Lord Chamberlain's case against Theatre Workshop. But St James's Palace must have winced at the press coverage they received. Several newspapers printed photographs of Theatre Workshop staff celebrating on the set at Stratford, while the *Daily Mail*, under a banner headline 'Workshop Drinks Toast To "Victory Over The Censor"', reported as follows:

> At Theatre Workshop, the East End home of serious drama, they drank last night to 'victory over the Lord Chamberlain'. Earlier, three members

of the company were fined for presenting parts of a play which had not been passed by the censor.

'But we have really won a tremendous victory,' said general manager Gerry Raffles, glass in hand.

'I don't think the Lord Chamberlain will dare bring another case.'

He was not far wrong. The paper also reported that because the fines had been less than the money donated by supporters, Theatre Workshop had been left with a surplus:

> 'Now we are wondering what to do with the money left over' said Mr Raffles. 'The fines were nominal and counsel appeared for us free.
>
> 'We are thinking of using the money to form a League Against Theatre Censorship to bring pressure to bear against the present system'.[11]

There was more bad publicity for the Earl and his colleagues at St James's when several newspapers also reported the speech of the defence counsel, Gerald Gardiner, which had painted the Lord Chamberlain as a figure of privilege, out of touch with ordinary people.

> After referring to the language used by building workers in the play, Mr Gardiner said: 'It may be that the Lord Chamberlain, Lord Scarbrough, is less familiar with the real-life men of that kind than with the speech he heard in the apartments of St James's Palace which he is privileged to occupy.'

Gardiner had also informed the court that Britain was 'the only civilised country in the world' to impose restrictions of this kind on the stage, and observed that those who enjoyed the 'means to pay an annual subscription in a West End theatre like the Arts or Comedy' could effectively buy themselves free of the Lord Chamberlain's control.[12]

Other newspapers, equally ready to play up the sense of class conflict, quoted from Joan Littlewood's evidence that Chapman's play appealed to audiences because 'for the first time they heard the speech of the English people put down in beauty and simplicity as they had never heard it before'.[13] Several quoted the letters of support from Michael Redgrave and Alec Guinness which had been read out in court, while the *Daily Herald* pointedly took the play's title as its headline, following it with a rallying declaration: 'Now the actors who use the language of the building site know it's true.'[14] The *Glasgow Herald* suggested that the case would prove a significant marker:

> The outcome of the Theatre Workshop case ... is not regarded at all

gloomily by the critics of the present system of theatrical censorship. It seems to be hoped that it will help to focus the interest which has been expressed recently among the theatrical avant garde in the prospects of a change in the Lord Chamberlain's powers.[15]

Of all the reports, possibly the most wounding for Stable Yard was that in the *Daily Mirror*, which described the court case as 'one of the most ludicrous prosecutions we had seen for months'. Their account appeared under the headline THE ST JAMES'S EAVESDROPPERS:

> the actors did a certain amount of ad-libbing, in a rather earthy sort of way, which included some fairly obvious and cumbrous remarks about public lavatories. It was the old ribald tradition breaking out on the theme that has the blessing of such amateur writers as Chaucer and William Shakespeare.
>
> The Lord Chamberlain's office then sent down a couple of Professional Earholes who listened to a performance ... and decided that the Lord Chamberlain's office and his miserable department of Examiners of Plays would be on Top.
>
> The Eavesdroppers reported back to the Lord Chamberlain who authorised that the whole miserable legal action should be put in motion.

It was also the *Mirror* which drew the most forceful conclusion:

> The Lord Chamberlain, in his capacity of 'Examiner of Plays' should be scrubbed out completely, and his little eavesdroppers should be sent packing to do a more useful day's work than extracting miserable penalties for non-existent offences.[16]

To be fair to the Lord Chamberlain's Office, it would have been very difficult for them not to take action once the original report of the ad libbing had been published in the press. After all, this was not an argument over a few words or an impersonation, but a challenge to the basic principle of a script requiring a licence. But Lords Chamberlain had generally—and increasingly—found that avoiding confrontations and public exposure was the best approach to most situations. It is not surprising, then, that after this discomforting affair, Scarbrough issued a pointed instruction to his staff: 'In the present state of affairs I wish to be consulted before any steps which might lead to any prosecution are taken.'[17] He was clearly furious that crucial decisions about *You Won't Always Be on Top* had been taken at a lower level and without reference to him.

The Entertainer

Open warfare between the Lord Chamberlain's Office and the Royal
Court was still a few years away, but the arrival of John Osborne, and
his vituperative attacks against a complacent establishment, were bound
to lead to collisions. In 1956, *Look Back in Anger* required only some
more or less minor alterations of language. Heriot acknowledged it as an
'impressive and depressing play' which 'breaks new psychological ground'.
More surprisingly, the Reader went on to link it with Sartre's *Huis Clos*,
suggesting that the play's main interest lay 'in its careful observation of
the anteroom of hell'.[18] *The Entertainer* caused more acrimony the following
year. Troubridge's report was dismissive: 'In the modern fashion it has
scarcely any story at all,' he wrote, though he also detected that 'the author
has come under the influence of Brecht's epic technique.' Troubridge
identified 'traces of blasphemy and disloyalty' in the text, and described
Osborne as 'the acknowledged head of the Angry Young Man school (or
racket) of dramatists'. Indeed, it was really the arrogance they perceived
in him which the Office most resented. 'Who does this Osborne think he
is?' they demanded, when he asked for 'balls' to be reinstated as a direct
equivalent of the 'not bloody likely' famously used by Bernard Shaw. 'No.
A thousand times no!' Other examples of Osborne's 'verbal dirt' in *The
Entertainer* which they considered 'too raw' to be permitted included 'arse
upwards', 'vicar's got the clappers', 'poof', 'shagged', 'right up', 'rodgered',
'poke the fire', 'always needed a jump at the end of the day', 'screwing
himself silly', 'wet your pants', 'have you ever had it on the kitchen table',
'turds', 'camp', 'bloomers', 'fried eggs' (according to the Examiner, 'the
lowest word for breasts') and 'the lines referring to Archie being a "seven
days a week man"'. On the grounds that 'guying religious programmes will
give offence to a number of people' they also objected to the juxtaposition
of 'Lift up Your Hearts' with the prominent display of a brassiere. 'It is
to be understood,' wrote Troubridge, 'that the whole play is impregnated
with sex, sexy references and half references and general lavatory dirt.'
There was also concern about a nude Britannia, which knowingly evoked
the living statuaries of the Windmill and revue tradition. 'She must sit
more sideways—no sexuality,' they inscribed on the body of the photograph
submitted by the Royal Court.[19] As they later explained when justifying the
decision: 'In the case of *The Entertainer* the nudes were expressly approved
in side views concealing the pudenda.'[20]

While it was the language and sexuality on which the Censorship
primarily focused, they knew that there was something more threatening
in Osborne's writing which was aimed at the world they were part of.
Troubridge recommended that *The Entertainer* should be licensed, but
he did so 'with aversion and disgust, as an angry middle-aged man'.

Though, he evidently enjoyed a bit of rough, telling the Assistant Comptroller: 'I prefer to examine such plays rather than this morning's arrival, "Lord Byron's Heritage" for amateurs.'

Given that *The Entertainer* was built around extracts from a music-hall performance, there was clearly a risk of ad-libbing and interaction between stage and audience. Certainly it occurred to the Lord Chamberlain's Office to question whether the ESC was following their rulings as conscientiously and meekly as appeared to be the case. The Assistant Comptroller went to see the show, and in fact enjoyed it enough to recommend it to Troubridge: 'It is a very good caste [sic],' he noted; 'you ought to see it if you can.' Gwatkin also took the opportunity to speak with the star of the show: 'Larry Olivier hates "The Examiner" for cutting out his best line "The Vickers' got the Clappers",' he reported, 'but is very grateful for being allowed his ballet dancer and Men's Tights story.' Gwatkin added, thoughtfully: 'I can't say that I recall a story about ballet dancers and their tights,' and wondered, 'Could it even have been an interpolation by the Angry Young Man? I wouldn't put it past them.' Judiciously, the Office chose not to enquire too closely, and when a member of the public wrote to complain about the 'torrent of obscenity and bad manners', Gwatkin issued a robust defence of the Lord Chamberlain's decision:

> This play, which is by no means a comedy, is written by a very modern playwright in the genre of the times. It is not attractive but it is, at least, honest in its choice of word and phrase …
>
> There are however limits beyond which the Lord Chamberlain cannot allow honesty of speech or action to go and it may interest you to know that over a score of alterations were required in places where the Lord Chamberlain considered that a less violent word or passage would be adequate.

Such answers did not satisfy everyone, and one woman wrote to Scarbrough in sarcastic and contemptuous disgust:

> This young man is to be congratulated on bringing off the two biggest money making hoaxes in the history of the theatre. In 'The Entertainer', mixing up 'Rock of Ages', 'The Cross of Jesus', 'Christ the Royal Saviour' with bloodys, bastards, bleders [sic], having a blow through, having a bit on the table, etc. [sic]
>
> How he must have enjoyed getting all this past the dear simple old Censor! Perhaps he thought 'having a blow through' was a children's bubble game! … Then the well-timed publicity of the man in the audience calling out something about Communistic rubbish, and leaving the theatre. Just enough to register without disturbing the play.

This is a magnificent piece of rubbish which enables the author to sit back and drink quarts of Bass and know that he has taken his place amongst the greatest theatre audience hoaxes of all time, as well as provide the newspapers with a large piece of cake.

For this sort of thing, the real stuff has to take a back seat and it is not fair—not fair at all.[21]

Endgame

Troubridge told Gwatkin that the gag they had denied Olivier in *The Entertainer*—'The Old Church Bell won't ring tonight as the vicar's got the clappers'—was 'about the hottest single line' he could remember being submitted, 'Samuel Beckett's <u>conneries</u> always excepted'. These 'conneries' had featured in the original French text of Samuel Beckett's *Endgame*, submitted by the Royal Court as *Fin de Partie* in February 1957. Troubridge was generally contemptuous: 'This is the new play by the author of *Waiting for Godot*, which controversial work appears a masterpiece of clarity compared with this one,' he warned; to stage it in 'the original French will provide one extra layer of fog to the general mystification of the audience'. The Reader struggled to produce a synopsis and summary from 'the nightmare of meaningless, inconsequent talk', the 'lunatic scraps of action', and 'the intense pessimism of such philosophy as is comprehensible'. However, he eventually recommended a licence, subject to a handful of amendments:

1. 'Con' (p. 102) This is simply 'cunt'.

2. 'Conneries' (p. 110) This is a made up nonce word, as it might be 'cunteries'.

3. Various tenses and parts of the verb 'foutre' (pp. 37, 62, 65, 76, 91, 98, 103). Though 'foutre' means 'to fuck', in my by no means expert view, it has in French no more than half the obscenity value of the English.

4. 'Faire pipi' (pp. 40, 51). Here again, I believe this is much less strong than 'to do a pee', as it is the accepted French nursery expression, which softens it.

5. 'emmerdé (p. 107) is roughly 'shitty'.[22]

Troubridge suggested asking 'a friendly native of the Foreign Office' for advice, but only 'conneries' seemed to concern Scarbrough. The Royal Court offered 'betises' but Beckett said he would prefer 'aneries', and St James's Palace, not without reluctance, agreed ('This, I suppose, is the equivalent of "assing about". O.K.')[23] Unfortunately, Troubridge had failed to spot the line that would provoke the real trouble.

In December 1957, the Royal Court submitted the English version of

Beckett's play, and this time Troubridge queried the passage in which a collective silent prayer to God ends with Nagg's line: 'the bastard; he doesn't exist.' The theatre was asked to alter this, but the playwright himself refused to withdraw or amend the line: 'I have suggested the amendments for the passage on p. 28 we discussed together to Mr Samuel Beckett,' wrote the Court's director, George Devine, to the Assistant Comptroller, 'and he replies that he cannot agree to what he considers, rightly or wrongly, as grave injury to his work. He therefore states he is obliged to maintain the passage as he wrote it.' A couple of weeks later, Devine, accompanied by Lord Harewood, the Chair of the English Stage Company, called on the Assistant Comptroller:

> They came, as far as I can see, to try and blackmail us into passing the passage on page 28, because the Press would make an uproar if this Play could not be given in public for that reason. It has been done in French and was likely to go on the Third programme in English. I said that none of these points would influence the Lord Chamberlain to change his mind, and as for the Press, the Lord Chamberlain was used to their mostly inaccurate fulminations.

It was *A View from the Bridge* all over again: 'I stressed that the Lord Chamberlain had not banned the play, but only required a small alteration which could be made with no detriment to the play if its author was not a conceited ass.'[24]

However, once the press got hold of the story, it was not likely to be Samuel Beckett to whom such epithets were applied. Harold Hobson wrote a stinging denunciation of the Censorship, describing it as 'This quaint and dangerous institution', and referring to 'Thirteen months' work without parallel even in its own long and ridiculous history'. Matters had reached such a pass, he suggested, that 'We are now rapidly approaching a situation in which a dramatist will hear that his play has been licensed with disgust and despondency. It will practically be a guarantee that his work is feeble minded.' Turning to the latest episode, Hobson pointed out that

> Mr. Beckett has been recognised all over Europe and America as one of the greatest, the most serious and the noblest playwrights of our time. *End-Game* ranks among his best and profoundest work. It has already been seen in French, and at the Royal Court, without, so far as I know, provoking any outburst of crime or increase in public or private indecency, though French is a notoriously inflammatory language. Even so, the censorship now demands that the dialogue in its central scene should be emasculated before it can be produced in English.
>
> Here is one of the chief works of one of the chief writers of our age,

a man regarded in honour throughout the Western world. How long shall we endure not being allowed to see it?[25]

Gwatkin wrote to Troubridge, rather ruefully: 'We are being stoned a little over the play *Endgame* or *Fin de Partie*.' Though he was ready to argue in public that there might be legitimate reasons for applying different standards in different languages, the Assistant Comptroller knew full well that intervening over a passage in English which they had just allowed in French had made the Censorship look extremely foolish:

> I feel that people erudite enough to go, understanding, to a French play can take a great deal more dirt (I use the term broadly) than an average English audience seeing a direct translation in English. Quite apart from the fact that the French words sound more delicate than the English equivalent.
>
> But when it comes to blasphemy then I think it is different: and whether you refer to God as a dirty person or as a bastard it is blasphemy. I agree that the English word is more deplorable than the French, quite apart from its theological inexactitude.

What Gwatkin really wanted to know was why on earth Troubridge had not picked up the line in the original text:

> I think that matters that are basic in French and English should receive the same treatment and I know the Lord Chamberlain would have insisted on the French passage being cut had it been brought to his notice, as he did when you noted it in the English translation. We should then have been a little more consistent.

Troubridge held up his hands:

> Dear Brigadier,
> I fear there is no doubt that I owe the Lord Chamberlain an apology over the blasphemous passage in *Endgame* and *Fin de Partie*.
>
> While it is true, as you agree, that 'ce salaud' rings less harshly than 'the bastard' it is certainly blasphemous to revile God with rude words in any language, and I should have drawn attention to this in French as I did in English. I am less in agreement with the point raised by George Devine in one paper about 'il n'existe pas' and 'he doesn't exist' if the latter was in fact cut. This is atheism, not blasphemy, and disbelief in the Deity has never been censurable—or not for centuries.

He asked Gwatkin to 'convey my deep apology to Lord Scarbrough for having unwittingly but negligently placed him in a position of apparent inconsistency'. The Lord Chamberlain graciously accepted his Reader's contrition: 'What a nice letter. Thank you for letting me see it.' Troubridge was (more or less) forgiven, and Gwatkin wrote to tell him:

> Thank you for your letter about *Fin De Partie*. I've shown this to the Lord Chamberlain who wishes me to tell you that he quite understands how very easy it is to miss a line now and again—indeed the only wonder is that amongst such a forest of words so few queer trees escape the axe.

As always when it found itself going head to head with someone refusing to do what was expected of them, the Office was unwilling to back down—and especially to be seen to back down—on a decision they had made. In June 1958, Devine invited the Assistant Comptroller to attend a private reading of the English version of *Endgame*. Gwatkin advised Scarbrough that while it was 'always well to "show willing"', he doubted if would serve any useful purpose to attend since it was hard to see where any possible compromise might lie: 'The definition of blasphemy is "indignity offered to God", and if calling him a bastard is not an indignity what is?' The difficulty, as Gwatkin conceded was that, 'Unhappily, of course, we did let him blaspheme in French!' He wrote to Devine:

> I have talked to the Lord Chamberlain who, whilst perfectly agreeable to my attending a private reading of the Play, wishes me to point out the extreme unlikelihood that he would allow the passage about which we are thinking.
>
> So much so that he feels you should not be put to the trouble of arranging a reading.

As a sort of halfway house, or concession, Troubridge—who, as mere Reader, had no official status or authority—was sent to attend a reading in early July. Devine, meanwhile, continued to press his case with sometimes dubious interpretations:

> In my opinion, and that I think of others, this is a profoundly moral play, and in view of the fact that Clov's answer to Hamm's comment 'He doesn't exist' are the word's *[sic]* 'Not yet', the dramatist is implying that man is not yet worthy of God, but that he should become worthy, and that part of the message of the play is that if man made an effort to earn God, he would then be worthy of Him.

Devine also played the sincerity card:

I am sure that the Lord Chamberlain will appreciate that I am not making these efforts to obtain a public licence of this play for commercial or scandalous reasons. It is far from likely to attract much public, and ... we all feel it is a profoundly important work, which should be done.

Gwatkin briefed Troubridge: 'We should not worry about "He doesn't exist". But we do draw the line at calling the Almighty a bastard,' he insisted. From the Lord Chamberlain's perspective, the solution to the impasse was straightforward: all Devine and Beckett were being asked to do in order to secure a licence for the whole play was to make this one change; and, in Gwatkin's view, 'its [sic] such a simple alteration to make'.

Troubridge duly sat in on the reading on 5 July, and subsequently reported what had transpired:

I attended yesterday afternoon as the Lord Chamberlain's representative a reading at the Royal Court theatre of the English version of Samuel Beckett's play *Endgame*. There was an audience of some 12–15, whom I understood to be Court Theatre authors, and who were urged by Mr Devine to avoid any communication to the Press.

Though I still contend that the play is great nonsense and largely incomprehensible, I saw nothing truly objectionable except the specific line about God 'that *[sic]* bastard he doesn't exist'. This was spoken by George Devine as Hamm in a low, quick voice, not as avoiding it, but as desiring not to overemphasize it—'half thrown away' is the theatrical term.

Though we should probably take some of what Troubridge was told with a fairly hefty pinch of salt, the Court was now ready to back down:

Afterwards I had a brief and discreet talk with George Devine ... I gathered that as Mr Devine now feels that it is likely to be solely or mainly the word 'bastard' that stands between him and the licence he quite properly desires on grounds of theatre prestige, he intends to bring further pressure to bear upon his author Samuel Beckett to make the change of this word. ...

In bringing the pressure to bear, he will, I think, rely upon,

1) The argument that as the English text is at best a translation from the French, there must surely be other and less blasphemous or offensive variants of 'salaud'.

2) The fact (as he hinted to me) of Beckett's vanity, which will make him desire London production when his original pettish reaction to the banning of his play has subsided.

Troubridge foresaw 'a possible happy outcome', and Gwatkin thanked him for his efforts: 'Let us hope that Beckett will come to his senses—and alter one word—which he can so easily do.'

At the end of July, Devine conceded defeat. Beckett had agreed to substitute 'swine', and Gwatkin recommended approval. It was a significant concession by the playwright, and provided the Office with what was probably going to be the best opportunity to extricate itself from the situation, and to claim a victory on points: 'I think we had better let this go—it is an improvement, though it is still rude.' Scarbrough reluctantly agreed: 'It's still offensive but in this sort of play I suppose it will pass.' Other substitutions were quickly agreed—('botch' in place of 'balls'; 'I want to relieve myself' and 'What about that relieving yourself?' in place of 'I'd like a pee' and 'What about that pee?'; 'rump' instead of 'arses'). In early August, the Office formally confirmed that the licence could be issued, once they were advised of the venue and date of performance. Devine had the last word: 'I have no immediate plans for the presentation of the play, but now that I know that it is possible, I will begin to think about it, and let you know in due course.'[26]

A month or so later, he submitted *Krapp's Last Tape*. 'Mr Beckett's mind is like a mournful decayed public convenience in which elderly smelly men ... defecate the standing pool of thought,' wrote Heriot. In his view, there was 'neither art nor nature' in Beckett's text, but merely 'a crumpled ninth carbon of his master Joyce'. This time, the Office objected to just two phrases: 'the iron stool' and 'let me in'. Devine conceded the first but remonstrated about the latter: 'There will be nothing of an erotic nature in the phrase in question which is delivered quite cold over the tape-recorder.' Gwatkin finally conceded the point: 'As it is clear that the passage to which objection was taken referred to the eyes, no alteration will be required by this Office.'[27]

Ionesco and Genet

'I detest this pretentious rubbish worse than death or the taxes,' wrote Troubridge of *Endgame*, and the Office was generally disdainful and suspicious in roughly equal measure of the French 'nouvelle vague'.[28] 'I'd sooner die,' wrote Heriot in November 1956, when invited by the Cambridge Arts theatre to attend the private production of Ionesco's *The Bald Primadonna*, which the theatre hoped to transfer to a public venue. His report on the script was equally confident in its jingoistic bigotry.

When the French go crackers they do it, being a logical nation, in a logical way. If we are to laugh at madness we can only laugh at real madness. Synthetic madness, so to speak, is unfunny. Like this play ... The wonder is, not that any maniac should produce such a play but that anyone should bother to pay to see it.[29]

In this case, only minor cuts were required. However, in January 1957 the Office received 'Another crazy effusion from the pen of the Franco-Rumanian avant-garde writer Eugene Ionesco'. Though Heriot struggled to come to terms with the 'repetitive and meaningless' text of *The Lesson*, there was something about its violence that made him suspicious: 'If this means anything at all,' he mused, 'it is a clumsy allegory of the sexual act.' As such, it needed careful handling—especially in relation to the images and physical action which might accompany the spoken text:

> though it may kill the whole play I think the Lord Chamberlain will agree with me that the body of the girl must not fall into an immodest position, that the professor must not stand (as he cannot fail to do if the stage directions are followed) between her legs to deliver the second blow, and that the second blow must not in any circumstances resemble the male sexual act.

The endorsement on the licence duly specified that

> 1. p. 50, the Stage Direction 'then falls, crumpling into an immodest position', to be altered, so that there is nothing immodest in the position of the girl.
> 2. p. 51. The girl must not have her legs apart as described in the stage direction, and the thrust of the knife must not be in any way suggestive.[30]

There were fewer problems in April over *The Chairs*—a play bizarrely identified by Heriot as 'Simple symbolism for thoughtful corporals'. He was worried by 'A reference to the old woman baring her breasts', noting, 'I hope [it] is symbolical'. Hoping was not enough. 'LET US SEE THAT IT IS SO,' declared Gwatkin.[31] The following month, commenting on his latest play, *Amédée*, the Lord Chamberlain's Reader described Ionesco as 'a leading member of the Dustbin School of dramatists'. The playwright's outlook, he said, was 'negative, though less abysmally so than Beckett'. The Reader did at least acknowledge that the text was written with 'a certain zany gusto', but to provide a précis or analysis of such a text was too much for him: 'an Examiner can only recount the happenings, and add some tentative speculations as to what, if anything, it may all mean'.[32] In January 1958 came 'Another insane play by Ionesco'—*Victims of Duty*—from which the Censorship demanded the excision of 'All references to and business about the detective evacuating in his trousers'.[33]

However, plays by Beckett and Ionesco were hardly the most troublesome parts of the wave of French drama hitting the London stage at this time. For the most part, their plays needed what the Readers and Examiners considered only a handful of minor amendments. Genet was another matter. In the spring of 1957, the Arts Theatre staged a private production of *The Balcony*, and submitted the script for licensing for public performance. On a philosophical level, Heriot found this more accessible than absurdist drama: 'If this play has a thesis it is that reality is an illusion and that real symbols ... can be replaced by false symbols and no one will be any the wiser.' He felt he could get more of a handle on some of the ideas behind Genet's text:

> The author, self-confessed as having been in and out of gaol since the age of ten, is, I think, setting out to separate himself from vulgar humanity by a complete and inverted philosophy—rather like the Marquis de Sade whom Swinburne (and others before him) honoured with the adjective 'divine'.

But the expression of those ideas in practice was a different matter: 'pathological nastiness is larded throughout with words like "sod" and "shit" and "bugger",' reported the Reader; indeed, he added, it would be 'a waste of time to enumerate all the improprieties' to be found in the script.[34] Nevertheless, he urged Scarbrough and Gwatkin to accept the invitation to attend a private performance, and a licence was not immediately ruled out. The management was informed that 'words such as bugger would have to be altered and the constant references to brothels and whores reduced', but it was probably their more vague and general demand which ensured—as it was no doubt intended to—that the application would be dropped: 'The Lord Chamberlain would be prepared to consider giving a licence to this Play if the major themes of blasphemy and perversion were eradicated.' Unsurprisingly, the Arts Theatre baulked a bit at this. For once, St James's Palace had shrewdly placed itself in a situation where it could legitimately claim not to have refused a licence, and to have left plenty of room for negotiation.

In November 1958, the English Stage Company submitted a new translation of Genet's play. Heriot saw this as a positive sign reflecting a willingness to compromise.

> This is the controversial play which was performed at the Arts Theatre Club last May and which neither received nor was refused a licence. The printed edition differs in some considerable detail from the manuscript we originally read. There is, surprisingly, less indecency of language—with the inevitable result that the play gains tremendous force. The unspeakable M. Genet, apparently unlike Mr. T. Williams, does not think of his work as holy writ.

It now seemed possible to compile a list of specific improprieties which, if removed, might earn approval for *The Balcony*:

p. 7   The huge Spanish Crucifix must not be visible in the brothel room.
pp. 8–9 and 22   Cut all references to the flagellatory screams off-stage—and cut the screams as well, of course.
p. 31   Alter 'The Immaculate Conception of Lourdes'.
p. 33   Cut ... from 'The Immaculate Conception' to 'Saint-Theresa'.
p. 37   Alter 'a Madonna'.
p. 39   Cut 'Do you give him your breast' and 'showers of shit'.
p. 41   Cut 'Their seed never ripens in you and yet ... if you weren't there'.
p. 43   Substitute 'He' for 'Christ'.
p. 44   Cut 'or of the birth of Christ in the manger' and 'Put your hand there'.
p. 46   Cut '... and Christ in person'.
p. 59   Cut from 'One hand on the trigger' to 'Must you use such language?'
p. 87   Cut the entire business of the photographer using a monocle to impersonate the Host in a faked picture of the bogus prelate administering Holy Communion.
p. 110   Alter the entire business of the shadow Chief of Police castrating himself and all speeches referring to it and business concerning it.

However, Scarbrough and the Assistant Comptroller were less sanguine about Genet's play, and ruled that even the changes Heriot proposed would hardly touch their fundamental objections: 'Even if the more lurid bits are cut this play remains about nothing but the queer perversions of certain characters who frequent a brothel which specialises in that sort of thing.' By now, the policy of automatically refusing references to homosexuality on stage had been reversed; but there were still limits, as Scarbrough now pointed out:

I should have thought this play would embarrass a number of people and I don't think the censorship should give the impression of letting everything go by just because it now allows homo plays.

It would be the mid-sixties before Scarbrough's successor, Lord Cobbold, would agree that *The Balcony* could be publicly performed—and significant cuts would remain in place even then.[35]

The Hostage

The last major struggle for St James's Palace in 1958 was a return match with Theatre Workshop. It centred on Brendan Behan's *The Hostage*, and while much of the fight may have been conducted in masks of good humour, underneath it was as serious and bitter as ever. When the first version of the script was submitted at the end of September, an unsmiling Troubridge called it 'a filthy play with nothing to recommend it', and dismissed the plot as 'a mere excuse for anti-English, anti-Catholic propaganda and a series of stupidly indecent songs'. Most of the thirty or so cuts he proposed were on grounds of obscenity or blasphemy, but there were also political ballads which he deemed likely to cause a breach of the peace. He concluded:

> All this adds up in my opinion to a bare faced attempt to see just how far the Lord Chamberlain's nose may be twisted by a company who have voiced their contempt for him far too loudly and too often in the past. I think it is fair to take this into consideration. I am absolutely convinced that the play is worthless. I believe it to be likely to inflame political passions. It is therefore not recommended for licence.[36]

Though Heriot seconded this view, senior staff, wounded by the fiasco over *You'll Always Be on Top*, and wary of Theatre Workshop's ability to inspire support and cause trouble, reckoned it would be impolitic to refuse a licence. The Company, they said, would 'make too much of such an action'. But there were more ways to skin a cat than by banning it. Once again, the Office sent out a long list of the 'essential deletions', as marked by Troubridge. 'The large number of cuts will give them a headache,' noted Gwatkin, approvingly. These included individual words and phrases considered blasphemous or obscene, all references to a male prostitute, the ballad 'Who Dares to Speak of Easter Week' (described as 'anti-British propaganda' and 'likely to cause a breach of the peace with a Stratford E. audience'), 'references to Lord Scarbrough' and 'the last verse of "I Am A Happy English Lad"' for obvious reasons, bearing in mind where this is being performed'.[37]

Perhaps surprisingly, amendments were quickly substituted and agreed, and *The Hostage* opened in October. It received a number of particularly strong reviews, with some linking it to the work of Sean O'Casey, and the *Manchester Guardian* offering an intriguing image by suggesting it was like watching O'Casey and Brecht 'sharing a slum bed' together. The *Daily Telegraph* said Behan's script was 'the most pungent to be heard in any London theatre now', and Tynan described the event as 'a Commedia dell'Arte production'.[38] Perhaps most enthusiastic of all was Harold Hobson, writing in the *Sunday Times*: were Shakespeare to return to earth and 'demand to be shown the best that we are doing with the British theatre' said Hobson, this production should be high on the list of things to take him to:

> I would not, if I could help it, permit Shakespeare to return to wherever he came from without seeing also Brendan Behan's *The Hostage*, as given by the inspired chuckle-headed, aggravating, devoting and magnificently alive company of Theatre Workshop.

He considered the whole thing 'a masterpiece', and 'an honour to our theatre'.[39]

Raffles gently taunted the Office: 'I hope you will be able to spare the time to come down one night. It is a most remarkable show and I am sure you will find it interesting,' he wrote. 'No,' added someone in the margin, underlining the word four times. Since the licence had been issued, there should have been no reason for the play's success to embarrass the Lord Chamberlain's Office. But the game continued. One of the cuts the Office had insisted on was a verse of a song which ran:

> I met with a Gaelic pawnbroker,
> By Killarney's waterfalls,
> With sobs he cried, I wish I had died,
> The Saxons have stolen my only box of matches.

The Censorship had spotted that the use of a pause in the last line would allow an audience to make up its own mind about what had been stolen. More surprisingly, they had then agreed to the proposed alternative verse:

> I met with a Gaelic pawnbroker
> A pathetically sad little runt
> With sobs he sighed I wish I'd died
> The Saxons kicked in my shop front.

Most probably with the knowledge of Raffles, Behan and the Company, the actress who was to perform this song, Eileen Foster, now wrote directly to the Lord Chamberlain to complain about the lines he had passed: 'I find the insinuation in the rhymes of this version both unfunny and offensive,' she told him. She also requested that the original version should be permitted instead, promising that 'There is no pause between the words "my" and "only" nor is there any gesture or facial expression which could make the line offensive.' She concluded: 'I am quite sure that the way in which I might perform this version of the song would be in better taste, indeed less offensive than any in which I could perform the alternative version.'

Since the Office never liked to back down, it fell to Gwatkin to try and find a way of justifying the decision: 'I am answering your letter to the Lord Chamberlain I am afraid rather bluntly,' he wrote to the performer, 'but you must forgive me.' He then explained:

The original rhyme contains in the last line an aposiopesis, I think it is called, which makes it obvious, even if there is no pause, that the Saxons have stolen very vital parts from the Pawnbroker.

The second rhyme, is, at least, a rhyme, 'front' rhyming with 'runt'. Any such rhyme is potentially dangerous, but it was considered that as pawnbrokers are invariably male the obvious rhyming word would be so inapplicable as to be perfectly safe.

Gwatkin concluded: 'I know the wretched censor is supposed to find a third dirty meaning even if only two are intended, but in this case we thought we had played safe—apparently not.' He then informed Raffles that he had received a complaint about the licensed version, and that 'The Lord Chamberlain would be glad if you can think of some verse which will not be misconstrued as the obvious rhymes with "falls" and "runt". It took ten days—during which the play continued its nightly performances—for Raffles to respond:

Dear Sir Norman,
I hope you will not think me rude in not replying to you for so long but I have been trying to find a solution to the problem ... The actress who sings it refuses to sing the words that you are prepared to accept and I have been trying to get an alternative from the author but so far without success. I will however keep on trying.

He took the opportunity to have a further dig at the Lord Chamberlain, carefully disguising it as a casual compliment:

I do hope you will find time to come down to see this show one night. You will probably be amused to hear that many people are amazed that your office should have been sufficiently broadminded as to pass the script, but I have not had a single complaint ... We normally have a few complaints even when we present Shakespeare.

The Assistant Comptroller replied that he was 'quite delighted to hear that the actress refuses to sing the words which we passed, I think, in error—all power to her!' But the Office had no intention of being drawn into another public confrontation with Theatre Workshop, preferring to put the weight of trust and responsibility onto them: 'I don't know what lines you are using, if any, to complete the end of the song, but I am sure you will realise that if they have not been passed they should not be used.'

In December 1958, the Public Morality Council wrote to protest 'that a play containing such derisive and blasphemous, dialogue about God, the Bible, and Religion should have been licensed'. In particular, they objected to the fact that 'Prayer is ridiculed' and that 'the Moral Welfare worker is a caricature, immoral herself and held up to derision'. Gwatkin informed them that *The Hostage* had been licensed only 'after a very great number of excisions', and that checks would now be made as to whether any of these had 'crept back' since. 'The Lord Chamberlain has ordered that the play be kept under review and future productions will be checked by the police,' he claimed.[40] In the event, the production closed soon afterwards, as planned, after its eight-week run. But as we shall see in the final chapter, it would not be the last St James's Palace would hear of Behan's play—or his aposiopesis.

CHAPTER SIX

Dirty Business

Sex, Religion and International Politics

The censorship of plays is not without its difficulties
R.A. Butler, Home Secretary, 1958[1]

In November 1956, as British and French troops were landing in Port Said, Soviet troops were taking hold of Hungary and anti-war demonstrators were marching in London, the Arts Theatre Club held an open debate on the question 'Do We Need a Censor?' Leading the attack on censorship was the journalist Richard Findlater. A similar debate had already been broadcast on television, and Findlater had also published an article condemning the Censorship for its exaggerated protection of the House of Windsor, which, he said, ensured that any images of Royalty depicted on stage must 'never be less than perfect'. He observed with disapproval the fact that portraits of Queen Victoria and Prince Albert

> hang ominously in the Lord Chamberlain's waiting room, where angry playwrights—waiting to consult the umpire of their work—look at large gilt albums with photographs of 'the Chapel Royal as prepared for the wedding of the Duke and Duchess of York in 1893'.

Censorship, he said, had 'a long and odious tradition of pettifogging, paralysing interference', and was now 'halfway between a standing joke and a standing insult'. It was no longer even effective, and the Watergate venture had managed to 'make a monkey out of this absurd relic of a bygone age'. Rejoicing that censorship was 'once again ... under heavy fire', Findlater was confident that its days were numbered:

> Seven years ago the Lord Chamberlain had a narrow escape when his benevolent despotism was threatened by Parliamentary action ... But now a new resistance movement is growing against the direction of the English drama from St James's Palace.[2]

Scarbrough himself had turned down the offer to participate in the debate, and his champion at the Arts was the 'Leonine and smiling' West End impresario Henry Sherek.³ Sherek described the Lord Chamberlain as 'the best of all possible censors', the buffer who 'stood as the barrier between young playgoers and a flood of cheap plays and reviews [sic] exploiting homosexual subjects'. But the debate did not focus exclusively on homosexuality and the monarchy. And if, as Sherek stated, the Lord Chamberlain would probably refuse to license a play criticising South Africa's system of apartheid, what chance was there that he would allow one about Suez, or other contemporary political conflicts involving Britain?

The Empire and Beyond

Generally speaking, international politics surfaced comparatively rarely as a major issue for the Lord Chamberlain to deal with. Even if there were playwrights who might have wanted to write more directly about them, they knew it was likely to be a waste of time trying to get their work put on. In January 1956, Troubridge did recommend banning an obscure farce called *Rory Pavlova* from production in the Orkney Islands. The central conceit of the play is that a Jacobite party has won the British General Election and transferred the seat of government to the Hebrides. But it was the climax which made the Reader uneasy, for the final curtain falls as the President of the United States arrives on a visit, and turns out to be black:

> I know there is nothing in the U.S. constitution to prevent a Negro becoming President—indeed I believe Booker Washington was once nominated—but I regard this as in most abysmal taste. I know also that Dingwall is a long way away, but I know best of all that if there is a U.S. Air Base in that vicinity, there will be a very grave breach of the peace.

Scarbrough's solution was to change America 'into a mythical country not too easily identifiable with the USA', and, rather wonderfully, the licence was duly issued 'on the understanding that the "United States" is changed to Utopia'.⁴

In some cases, it was more judicious to avoid intervention. In May 1956, Heriot drew attention to the 'very doubtful taste' of *Iron Duchess*, a comedy by William Douglas Home: 'The Gimaltans, inhabitants of an island in the Commonwealth are agitating for freedom and self-government, but a reactionary Prime Minister refuses to allow them anything at all. There is a general strike, followed by riots and general disorder.' Heriot felt this was too near the nub for comfort: 'The name Gimalta (possibly from Gibraltar and Malta) is in itself unsuitable; but the parallel, on farcical lines, with

Cyprus about which feeling is so very high at the moment, seems not only distasteful but dangerous.' As it happened, the Comptroller also disliked both the play and the playwright: 'I have known William Douglas Home for a great many years. He is very conceited, very tiresome and has rather naïve left wing views,' wrote Nugent; 'I also think he is an extremely bad playwright.' But he was wary of exposing the Office to accusations of political bias, and unconvinced that there were adequate grounds for refusing a licence:

> I am certainly not prejudiced in William Home's favour, but at the same time I don't quite see on what grounds the Lord Chamberlain can ban this play.
>
> That it will inflame the feelings of people against our policy in Singapore or Cyprus? I hardly think this argument is tenable because he keeps entirely to a world of farce and his rather puerile views on freedom are uttered by a comic duchess.
>
> That it is improper to guy the politicians including the Prime Minister? But surely politicians including Prime Ministers are fair game for caricature on the stage in the same way as generals and admirals.

Nugent concluded that 'Much as I would like to, I cannot honestly recommend that it should be banned', and Scarbrough agreed: 'Although it is concerned in a general way with a kind of Colonial issue which is familiar today, it bears no identifiable resemblance to Cyprus or Ceylon or Singapore in particular.' And he pointed out that since 'neither Gibraltar nor Malta are trying to leave the Commonwealth', even the name Gimaltans was 'innocuous'.[5]

At the actual height of the Suez Crisis, Troubridge objected to 'a fanciful, semi-expressionist, bitter American pacifist play of World War One' written by Paul Green, which was submitted by the county of Essex's Education Committee. While lacking the form or power of Theatre Workshop's subsequent denunciation of first world war leaders in *Oh What a Lovely War*, *Johnny Johnson* may well have had the potential to provoke and upset. The script, said the Reader, was 'a pretty curious affair to bob up at this time of day, especially under the auspices of a County Education Committee'. He queried 'whether, when the State demands two years National Service of its sons, a County Education Committee should spend ratepayers' money on pacifist propaganda drama'. More specifically, Troubridge expressed concern about a scene which 'travesties a meeting of the allied high command', and which featured historical figures, including Foch, Pétain, Haig, King Albert, Lloyd George and Clemenceau. 'I think these distinguished persons should be allowed to rest in peace in their graves.' Again, Scarbrough was keen to avoid confrontations, and, in the circumstances, was prepared to be liberal. As for historical figures, it rather depended on what you were going to say about them: 'It should be explained to the applicant,' he wrote, 'that if it is the intention to lampoon the war leaders in scene five, their names must be changed to fictitious ones. Otherwise the names can stand.'[6]

One example of a play about recent political history which actually reached the West End was *The Shadow of Heroes*. This, however, did not feature Britain or British statesmen, being 'a long account in dramatic form of the history of the Communist movement and Government in Hungary between 1944 and the Hungarian revolution of October 1956'.[7] Written by the American playwright Robert Ardrey, it was eventually directed by Peter Hall at the Piccadilly Theatre in the autumn of 1958, with a cast which included Peggy Ashcroft as Julia Rajk, the widow of the Hungarian Communist leader executed in 1949. The script had been submitted some seven months earlier under the much more explicit title *The Murderers*, and Ardrey's text would be variously described by reviewers as 'documentary', 'semi-documentary', 'a living newspaper' and 'an illustrated lecture', and by the playwright as 'A contemporary historical drama in the Elizabethan manner'.[8] Again, it was the direct representation of actual people and events which alarmed Troubridge: 'The characters are the real Hungarian and Russian protagonists in these events (mostly now dead, though some live)'; since the focus was on recent and still contested history, there was a considerable risk that 'powers with whom this country is in friendly relations' would take offence:

> The murderers of the title are the present Hungarian government and three named members of the Soviet government. It must, therefore, be considered as a possibility, that there might be a diplomatic protest against the licensing of this play. It could, of course, be answered that the events concerned are now historical and that anyone desiring to put forward an opposite view in play form would be at liberty to do so. At the same time I should think it likely that this is a case in which the Lord Chamberlain would wish to have some prior consultation with the Foreign Office who would be the first recipients of any such protests.

Gwatkin commented: 'I should not have thought that these rascals need any personal protection in this country', but on this occasion Scarbrough was inclined to take the advice of his Reader:

> Since many efforts are being directed at the present time to a summit Conference with Russia, I think the Foreign Office should be asked whether they would wish me either to refuse a licence, or to postpone the matter for as long as possible.

The script was duly sent to the Foreign Office who confirmed that 'so far as the contents of the play are concerned, there is no reason to raise any objection to the issue of a Licence'. However, they did suggest that calling the play *The Murderers* might be injudicious and recommended that this should be altered: 'if a more specific title could be substituted (e.g. "Murder in Budapest") it might be easier to deal with any protest that might be made by the Hungarian Government.'[9]

Shadow of Heroes opened in the West End in October, and the advance press reports proclaimed its significance: 'the Lord Chamberlain does not commonly allow the representation of politicians living or recently dead,' noted the *Guardian*, voicing surprise that Scarbrough had approved it: 'The Iron Curtain, it seems, covers many things.'[10] Then, on the very day the production was due to open, the Hungarian Charge d'Affaires made vigorous protest to the Foreign Office. His objections were passed on to Scarbrough:

> Monsieur Nyerki said that according to the press the Lord Chamberlain, after consulting with the FO, had passed the play without cutting a single detail ... Monsieur Nyerki said that his Government took strong exception to the production of this play and that they resented the depiction in the play of Monsieur Kadar ... Monsieur Nyerki then said that according to some newspapers it was unusual for plays staged in this country to refer to living or recently dead foreign statesmen ... I declined to be drawn into a discussion of the history of political plays on the British stage. I agreed that the play was unusual. Monsieur Nyerki then said that in Hungary, plays of many kinds were staged; but plays about foreign statesmen were not ... Monsieur Nyerki then said that the émigré counter-revolutionaries were supporting and taking advantage of the play and that its production undoubtedly served certain interests. He also questioned its historical accuracy.

Gwatkin sarcastically observed that 'The Hungarian Charges d'Affaires is unlikely to appreciate the irresponsibilities of a free Press, whose inaccuracies he quotes on two occasions'. He pointed out that, contrary to these claims, changes had been made (if only to the title). Moreover,

> the rule about the portrayal of living or recently dead persons applies almost entirely to British personalities or to those foreigners with whom we have close ties. Our Statesmen qua Statesmen are by no means sacrosanct, indeed being political figures they are more liable to publicity than are normal people.

It seems clear that a decision was consciously taken in relation to *Shadow of Heroes* that the Hungarian/Soviet regime was not worthy of the protection normally accorded to countries officially designated as international allies: 'I remember before the war that we were at pains to tone down plays featuring Hitler and his "jackals" because it was the national policy to avoid upsetting those rascals,' wrote Gwatkin. He found this play 'a grim evening's entertainment and not one to sit through if one had a guilty conscience over what it portrayed', and recommended that the Foreign Office should meet the protest with a dead bat. In any case, further argument would only draw attention to a play which would otherwise be little noticed:

> The play is only on for three months at the Piccadilly and I should be surprised if it moved elsewhere. If blazing publicity is to be avoided I think the incident should end with the fact that you have implemented [the] promise to bring the Hungarian protest to the notice of the Lord Chamberlain.[11]

Shadow of Heroes did have some impact in influential circles—most especially because of the potential of its form: 'We are mesmerised by the potency of fact,' said Tynan in his review; 'All lovers of a truly contemporary drama will wish for more like it.' Pointedly, he added that he had 'left the theatre filled with a phantom hope that someone, some day, might give us a similar treatment of Suez'.[12] The *Guardian*, perhaps responding to this, questioned 'whether the censor would allow another about Suez'.[13] The answer to this question is almost certainly 'no'. In the early sixties, the Office would receive a request for information from Harry Street, a Professor of Law at Manchester University, who was working on a book about civil liberties; Street asked about the Censorship's attitude to the depiction of politicians on stage, and received the following response:

> The sort of thing that we might get might be something of the order of a play entitled 'Suez' with Anthony Eden and his colleagues impersonated, the whole written by one of the well-known Left Wing playwrights and staged at The Royal Court Theatre. Under the present regime a Play expounding all the political principles involved would probably be passed provided the setting was Saxonia and Pharoahstan and the Characters were general ones. But there is surely a case for avoiding the attribution of fictional words and actions to living individuals which must be the case in a play of political descriptions where Cabinet Meetings and Lobbyings and so on would have to be described.[14]

These words were written nearly six years after the Suez crisis had occurred. No such play ever appears to have been submitted.

Religious Orders

Dominic Shellard draws attention to the surprising fact that in the same month as *Look Back in Anger* was easily approved, *The Life of Christ*, 'a gentle Christian drama', was refused a licence for amateur performance.[15] The Reader called it 'a perfectly reverent, dignified and accurate life of Our Lord', in which 'Jesus says nothing that is not in the Gospels'.[16] But it could not be performed because the Censorship did not permit anyone to openly represent the figure of Christ on stage. In 1957, a licence was issued for *The Road To Emmaus* only after Christ had been deleted from the list of characters: '"The Stranger" who is Jesus does not now appear,' reported the Reader with approval; 'He is observed off approaching, and is referred to as the Holy Man.'[17] Even Scarbrough found such conventions incongruous, given that the York Mystery Cycle put Christ, God and Satan on stage for all to see and required no licence. Ironically, because a Welsh translation of the medieval *Everyman* was designated as a new text, God was required to speak his lines from the wings, even though in the original English he could have been centre stage.[18] As Troubridge noted on another occasion: 'The longer I hold my appointment, the more I come to think that questions affecting blasphemy are the most difficult aspect of the examiner's task.'[19]

Sometimes, the Lord Chamberlain cast aside his Readers' doubts. In 1956, Heriot objected to an adaptation of Old Testament stories written in 'contemporary, idiomatic, slangy English', though it was written by a churchman and obviously attempting to spread the word to new audiences:

> The author introduces a Messenger to announce the imminent destruction of Sodom and Gomorrah. He uses the first person singular and takes upon himself to bargain with Abraham ...: in fact he is God, and uses the words put into the Deity's mouth in the Old Testament ... I do not think that the Lord Chamberlain can permit this personification of Deity so thinly disguised.

Scarbrough over-ruled him: 'Leave,' he wrote. 'In this kind of religious play it does not seem objectionable.'[20] The following year, Troubridge disapproved of *The Leader*, which transferred the events of the Passion to 'the disagreeable and highly unsuitable guise of matters seen from a Committee Room in a contested election'. Again, Scarbrough was more broadminded: 'I do not find this irreverent or offensive and I do not think it can be regarded as blasphemous,' he ruled. And he set down a more general marker: 'I do not think it is the business of censorship to be strictly orthodox in religious matters.'[21]

While it is highly improbable that an overt attack on Christianity could ever have been passed, there were occasions when Scarbrough chose not to intervene over lines or images which many would have considered irreverent and insulting. In 1958, for example, Troubridge was worried about the blasphemous use of the Evensong/Magnificat in N.F. Simpson's absurdist comedy *A Resounding Tinkle*: 'It may be just possible to consider that the whole thing is so raving as to be beyond blasphemy,' he mused, 'but I doubt if the Lord Chamberlain will take that view.' But in fact he did: 'I expect some people will be offended by it,' wrote Scarbrough, 'But on the whole I am prepared to pass it—seeing that the whole play is so "zany" as the examiner says.'[22] More surprisingly, Nigel Dennis's *The Making of Moo* was licensed for the Royal Court, even though it constituted a full-length satire on religion. 'This is one of the most unusual plays I have read for a very long time indeed,' reported Troubridge; 'It is intelligent, adult, completely irreverent and anti-religious, without being in my view blasphemous.' He added that 'it is also funny, so it will please both middle-high and middle-lowbrows'. Actually, the basis on which the Office made its decision seems even more laudable from where we are now:

> Much of this play about what makes religions tick will offend deeply religious folk; the Catholics will not like the business of making a pope of the native butler, and putting a Cardinal's hat on him; the Protestants will not like the Old Testament texts twisted to the service of Moo. But I am taking the attitude in this matter that where there is specific mockery of or blasphemous references to the Church of England, but a more general questioning of the premises of all revealed religions, then, if the dogmas and faiths of such religions cannot stand up to this kind of hard-hitting, barbed banter, so much the worse for them.

To someone who complained, Gwatkin offered a diplomatic but unapologetic reply, in which he insisted that the decision had been a very considered one and entirely rational:

> When this play was passed it was realised that it would give some umbrage, although there is no specific mockery or blasphemous references to the Church of England.
>
> It is more of a general questioning of the premises of all revealed religions. It was felt that the dogmas and faiths of these religions should be proof against this form of hard-hitting, barbed banter. Indeed by the mere fact of making people think about, and possibly resent, this type of writing it might even be that 'we gather honey from the weed and make a moral of the Devil himself".[23]

Yet Scarbrough would not allow a guard to refer to Christ as a 'blighter' in *The Rock*, and for an adaptation of Graham Greene's *The Power and the Glory*, he insisted on checking with 'a high up Roman Catholic Ecclesiastic', to ensure 'that the Mass performed in Act One would be alright from a Roman Catholic Priesthood point of view'.[24] Another script which went just too far was *Valmouth*, and Sandy Wilson's musical was only approved for the English Stage Company after extensive cutting. Troubridge disliked it intensely:

> the play is fairly equally divided between the attempts of a lecherous old woman of nearly 60 to seduce a young farmer, which she achieves finally in a Catholic chapel, and a series of jeers and jives at the Catholic faith ... Personified by two old ladies of over 60 who still need to scourge themselves to mortify the lusts of their flesh, a Catholic priest with apparently a penchant for footmen, and a Cardinal who is ex-communicated towards the end of the play for having once baptized a dog.

He warned that 'Considerable offence will be given to Catholics', and thought it 'quite likely that the whole play will be booed on the first night'. But he had been over-ruled several times before on religion, and held back from recommending refusal:

> as nowadays the Lord Chamberlain's refusal of a licence almost always falls only on themes of perversion—here mentioned only in some occasional lines—, I opine that, after extensive revision and deodorization [sic], this play should probably be allowed to take its chance.

The Censors imposed more than twenty cuts, including 'the Catholic ceremonial from Sister Ecclesia down to "Mrs Hirstpierpoint is ecstatic"', and a general requirement was issued that 'There must be no ridicule of religious things'. However, the playwright persuaded them to revoke the ban on references to 'the sin of christening a dog', since this was apparently genuine and 'the most famous incident in Cardinal Pirelli's career'.[25]

In January 1959, *Follow Me*, Tyrone Guthrie's transposition of the New Testament story to contemporary Scotland, was submitted. 'This presents a perfectly straightforward decision of policy for the Lord Chamberlain,' suggested Troubridge; 'how far the central events of the Christian faith, the Passion of Christ, may be presented on the stage without blasphemy or gross offence in a fancy setting.' He himself was opposed to licensing:

> fancy settings of the basic dogmas of revealed Christian religion, seem to me to be most dangerous, not only because they will give deep offence to religious people in an audience ... but also because such things represent not only the thin end but a good deal of the thicker part of the wedge.

However, the Reader was still bristling over 'a not dissimilar case' when his recommendation to reject *The Leader* had been over-ruled: 'it is possible,' he now acknowledged, 'I am not seeing eye to eye with the Lord Chamberlain.' This time there was also a very specific racial agenda behind the Reader's wariness: 'If the Incarnation is to be postulated to have taken place in Scotland now, then why not in the Congo now,' he warned, 'in which case the questions of "decorum" and "breach of the peace", upon which the stage censorship truly rests, would most certainly be imperilled.' Gwatkin was inclined to back his view: 'I am not very religious,' he wrote, 'but I do resent tampering with or denigrating beliefs whose teachings offer us about the only chance of a decent future on earth.' However, before the decision could be passed to Scarbrough, it was discovered that Guthrie's script had been submitted in error, having already been licensed in 1932—on the specific advice of the Bishop of London and against the recommendation of the then Reader! Though Troubridge still maintained that 'the different immediacy of colour questions' changed the context, he conceded this was 'hypothetical, no such Congo Incarnation play having been submitted as yet'. Moreover, 'Personal opinion must always yield to informed authority, and it would be folly and impertinence for me to presume to set up my views on blasphemy against those of a former Bishop of London'.[26]

Though he didn't say so, Troubridge may well have had in his mind an American text written nearly thirty years earlier and not yet licensed, which imagined God as 'an idealized Negro preacher', smoking cigars. *Green Pastures* had first been turned down by the Lord Chamberlain in 1930, with the explicit support of the Archbishop of Canterbury and the King. However, a successful Warner Brothers film version had been released in 1936, and the playscript had been re-submitted to St James's Palace several times. In the early fifties, Lord Clarendon had accepted the view of the Archbishop of Canterbury, who, while confessing himself charmed by what he called the 'negro-child idea of God', recommended refusal on grounds of political sensitivity:

> I wonder what the negro world in general would think of this play being on the stage? One of the open sores of the world at present is the position of the negros in the United States. Will they appreciate it if while in the United States their treatment presents a grave moral problem they are being represented on the London stage as a primitive race somewhere between the pitiful and the ridiculous.

To license such a play might be to invite trouble at home:

> There are many Africans in London and presumably they or some of them would see the play. Knowing the temper of African nationalism at

the present time I wonder if this play would strike Africans as helpful or would not rather inflame their feelings. When all around negros and Africans are claiming the rights of mature people is not it rather a grave thing to have a play which represents them as a child race?

When Bernard Miles resubmitted *Green Pastures* in 1957, the Assistant Comptroller thought this was perhaps the moment to lift the ban—though his memorandum also reflects a shocking—if hardly unexpected—level of continuing racist assumptions:

> I never saw much objection to it. It is merely the black man's conception of God, and being a simple sort of chap he has to project his God into a body and clothes which he can understand. That really basically is the objection, because we would not allow our own God as we know Him, or think we know Him, to appear on the stage and, therefore, we can't allow a 'nigger' to let his God appear.

Echoing the Archbishop's point made six years earlier, Gwatkin added: 'there is also the question of the feelings of "Afrikaans". One doesn't want to give the impression that we think them elderly babies.' Scarbrough agreed that 'the licensing of this play now would bring down on our heads a double thunderbolt', and doubted the 'wisdom of portraying negros as sentimental and ignorant children'. As he pointed out:

> This has acquired much more point during the last few years on account of rising African nationalism and the efforts that are being made to impress on Africans that we regard them as equals. I would expect much criticism of this play over here and of the special step of allowing it to be played after it has been banned for so long, and that criticism would be supported by all the friends of African emancipation in this country.[27]

Issues of religion and international politics were not always unconnected.

Paul Raymond

In December 1956, a female revue artist sent the Lord Chamberlain a series of unsolicited pictures of herself in performance. 'Dear Sir,' Im [sic] writing to ask if you could please censor my photographs,' she wrote; 'Could you oblige by sending me them before the week is out.' What she was seeking was the security of knowing she could perform her poses in any town or city in the country with the immunity against prosecution that the Lord Chamberlain's licence was often thought to confer—in practice, if not in principle. Of course, the system did not work quite like that, as the title of the Lord Chamberlain's file indicates: 'MISS WALKER INFORMED HER ACT CAN ONLY BE CENSORED IF INCORPORATED IN A STAGE PLAY.'[28] But the producers of revues and touring road shows, increasingly competing for dwindling audiences by pushing back the boundaries of sexual display, had begun to play a more subtle version of the same game. The strategy was to include a verbal sketch in a show which would otherwise have fallen outside the Lord Chamberlain's jurisdiction, in order to oblige him to consider it for licence. Rather than trying to find a way out of censorship, such managers were seeking a way into it! Having done whatever it took to achieve that licence, and effectively guaranteed themselves against local prosecutions, the least scrupulous and more audacious managements—knowing how impracticable it was for the Lord Chamberlain to police performances effectively—were quite capable of adding material they had never shown him, and cutting the material which he had approved and which had brought their show under his control in the first place. The title of the show would remain as it appeared on the licence, and though almost everything else might have been changed, the management could claim to demonstrate that their show enjoyed the official approval of the Censorship. One leading exponent of this strategy was Paul Raymond, with whom, as we have seen, St James's Palace had already clashed on more than one occasion.

In February 1956, Raymond submitted a revue script under the title *Les Nues de Paris*, which he hoped to open in Hull. The Lord Chamberlain ruled that it fell outside his jurisdiction, and instructed the Hull police that since the performance was not a 'stage play', it did not require a licence from him. While in one sense this left Raymond free, it also opened him to much greater risk of prosecution. He therefore added a sketch which rendered the entire script liable to licensing, and resubmitted it. Scarbrough realised he and the system were being manipulated by a shrewd and cynical operator. 'I object to giving this a licence,' he wrote. 'It seems to me farce to pretend that this is a stage play.' He sought advice from his senior staff: 'What would the implication be of refusing a licence?' But as Gwatkin told him, Raymond knew the rules of the game.

> I am afraid it is a fact that anything that has a play in it and which has a script ... is considered a stage play and before it can be given in public it has to have a licence, and you are the only person who can license it. You can refuse, as you know, on various grounds, none of which I am afraid would cover the existing little play in this script.

Gwatkin also pointed out that Raymond was by no means the first person to have played it: 'For many years producers have put in a small stage play in order that they can get the Lord Chamberlain's licence for the whole production, which they regard as a form of insurance, and I don't think there is anything we can do about it.' As an example, he cited the comedians who worked as the Crazy Gang: 'They always include a stage play in their production although a great deal of it, as you know, has no pretentions [sic] of being a play within the meaning of the Act.' Scarbrough had no choice. All he could do was to flex his muscles over the title of the show ('the name must be changed to something less prurient'), to make a few specific cuts ('The girls may only enter the lion's cage if they are clothed') and to attach a general veto (on 'indecorous lack of clothing or offensive gesture in any of the Production Numbers').

Raymond seemed to have won the battle. But on this occasion, perhaps through arrogance, or simply lack of care, he then blundered. When, at Scarbrough's request, the Hull police inspected the performance to ensure that it matched the script he had so reluctantly licensed, they discovered not only that the show's comedian had included unlicensed verbal material, but that the sketch, which had been specifically added to oblige the Lord Chamberlain to accept authority, had been taken out again. Rather than threatening prosecution, the Lord Chamberlain simply withdrew his licence as being no longer relevant to the performance, leaving Raymond to face the consequences of not enjoying the crown's seal of approval:

> The omission of the sketch 'Las Vegas Hotel', the sole dramatic item, materially alters the nature of the piece. This quite definitely ceases to be an 'entertainment of the stage', is not subject to the control of the Lord Chamberlain, and is presented presumably under the authority of the Theatres, Music and Dancing licence.
>
> Mr Paul Raymond knows these facts. He was originally informed on the 19th July, 1956 that the entertainment as then conceived was not subject to the Lord Chamberlain. For the specific purpose of securing the Lord Chamberlain's licence for it, he then introduced the sketch 'Las Vegas Hotel'. The omission of this sketch for all performances in Hull was obviously intended to remove the piece from the Lord Chamberlain's control ...
>
> The Lord Chamberlain will take steps to inform Mr Paul Raymond of the danger of representing this entertainment in its current form to be 'an entertainment licensed by the Lord Chamberlain'.[29]

If it hadn't been before, Raymond's name was well and truly etched in the minds of officials at St James's Palace.

In January 1957, they clashed again when Raymond submitted a script for a play entitled *The Nude*. Heriot was immediately suspicious: 'I don't believe this play. I don't believe that it is a translation from the French.' While the title referred to 'a picture over the mantelpiece that has no other connection with the plot', Raymond had had the witty idea of replacing the painting with a live performer. The Censorship ruled against this:

> In the face of a great deal of criticism the Lord Chamberlain can only permit the employment of nudes on the stage to continue if certain principles are observed.
>
> Amongst these principles is one to the effect that the nude shall be part of an artistic setting.
>
> This cannot apply to the nude which you are considering whose inclusion is an unnatural addition to a straight play.

Not trusting Raymond to observe their ruling, they also asked police to check the performance: 'The producer in question makes it a practice to introduce naked or near naked women into his productions, and use unpleasant or indecent "business".'[30] This time, Raymond seems to have toed the line. Or perhaps he just knew which nights the police were coming.

But stage nudity was spreading. In 1957, a Town Clerk in Derby wrote to Scarbrough to express concern at the increasingly explicit nature of the touring Road Shows visiting the town. Most of them, he said, were produced by Paul Raymond. Gwatkin replied that Road Shows were not under the control or licence of the Lord Chamberlain, but that he was all for local authorities taking action themselves:

> It is of the greatest help to the Lord Chamberlain in maintaining his stand against undesirable performances to find that local licensing authorities are prepared to take action where entertainments not coming within his control are concerned, since if too great a disparity between the 'dramatic' and the 'variety' stage is allowed to become established, he will be unable to maintain his rule, which he strongly believes to be the only practicable one in this context.

He also offered the low-down on Raymond and his methods of work:

> Paul Raymond is well known to this Office, and has in fact been prosecuted at our instigation. He is an astute man, who, since his trouble with the Lord Chamberlain, has been careful to divide his productions into two categories.
>
> (a) Purely variety shows in which he is as extreme as he dares to be, knowing that he is immune from the Lord Chamberlain's control and relying on the fact that since he is only in any location for a week the reactions of local authorities are unlikely to be severe.
>
> (b) Dramatic entertainments which perforce have to be decent by

reason of the Lord Chamberlain's control, but which he endeavours to make enticing by means of the most lurid advertising.[31]

Sexual Stratagems

Of course, Raymond was by no means the only manager involved. In June 1957, the Chief Constable of Norwich wrote to the Office to complain about a touring performance—*Show Girls*—which had been licensed. 'You will observe,' wrote the Chief Constable, 'that my officer feels that the play itself was very crude and objectionable and no credit to the profession it represented,' and he pointedly voiced his surprise that an inspection of the script suggested that 'the presentation appeared to be in keeping with that approved by you'. Gwatkin agreed that the play contained 'a degree of coarseness, themes of sex of relative crudity, and equivocal remarks', but suggested that the Chief Constable was being unrealistic:

> That such plays are in bad taste and that they do not enhance the status of the acting profession is true. But nowadays considerations of good form, or propriety, induce little restraint in the use of language or the discussion of subjects once thought impossible. The Lord Chamberlain must exercise his powers of censorship judicially, and in this atmosphere he feels that this play and others like it have little effect and do not induce to crime or vice. He can and does ban those plays in which real viciousness or obscenity is present, incurring much public odium for doing so. When these elements are absent, however, his Lordship, although he may personally view a piece with extreme distaste, does not feel able to take the severe measure of destroying the author's property in his work by banning it.

However, the Association of Municipal Corporations took up the case:

> The committee found the report from Norwich very disturbing, and members from other parts of the country referred to incidents of a similar kind. The committee appreciated the explanation of your attitude ... but have expressed the hope that something could still be done to stop this type of performance.

Again, Gwatkin insisted that the Lord Chamberlain was 'continually taking action' against the worst examples, but that a stricter and more interventionist policy was simply not feasible in the current climate:

> Since they do not see those parts of Stage Plays which he forbids public performance, your Association will not know the true extent of the problem, and the Lord Chamberlain feels that it will help evaluate it if

he explains the situation. I am, accordingly, to tell you that nowadays
Theatre Managers and Authors assess the limits of public tolerance so
widely that in the last few years they have based the themes of plays on
what one would consider such unacceptable subjects as homo-sexuality
or heterosexual activities founded on the Kinsey report, such sadistic
occurrences as the Christie murders, or reduced to the level of animal
appetite. They nowadays do not hesitate to include in full in their works
the sort of obscene song which traditionally figured only at men's smoking-
concerts; and words I can only hint at as being the anglo-saxon for the
natural functions of the body are used with freedom. All this it becomes
the Lord Chamberlain's duty to excise, and your Association will, perhaps,
understand how it is that by comparison much of *Showgirls*, objectionable
though it may be, has passed.

Responsibility should be more broadly shared, said Gwatkin, and it was
unreasonable to lay the blame at the door of St James's Palace:

plays of this kind are received with approbation by audiences in the
so-called private theatre. Additionally, language and incidents of a similar
nature appear in some classes of contemporary literature without action
being taken either under the Common law or Statutes relating to indecency.
    The Lord Chamberlain must have regard to these facts, and to what
is apparently decent or obscene according to the law of the land. He has
obviously some freedom of decision, but even so he cannot govern the stage
in isolation from public opinion and entirely according to his personal
views. From what I have said, and your own observation, you may agree
that today public opinion seems to be liberal to the point of laxity.[32]

Meanwhile, in the hunt for cheap publicity, canny revue managements
knew the advantages of invoking the Lord Chamberlain. Camberwell
Palace made headlines when the press reported that a supposedly static
performer in *A Happy Nude Year*—'The delicious, singing nude'—had
involuntarily broken the regulations when a mouse ran across the stage.
'Blonde nineteen year old Peaches Page … stifled a scream, and dashed off
the stage.' According to the newspapers she was immediately sacked by the
manager for breaking her contract. 'Said eighteen pound a week Peaches
"I did what any girl would do".'[33] It seems quite probable that the entire
affair was a put up job to gain publicity.
    Other managements were increasingly prepared to take the risk of not
sticking to the licensed script, knowing that the chance of being found
out was relatively small, and that if they were they could probably escape
punishment by apologising for their 'mistake'. *A Girl Called Sadie*—a play
about 'a sensual slut, married to … a crooked little twerp'—ran into trouble

in Oldham, when a careful investigation by the police discovered that the line 'are you coming up later' was now being played as 'are you coming up for a bit later'. When challenged, the management claimed it was an accident, caused by the fact that the roles were being played by understudies. The Lord Chamberlain insisted on the removal of the 'offensive interpolation', and Hill was dispatched northwards to check that all the rulings were observed. Even he was surprised at some of what had been approved—'episodes such as a woman practically having a miscarriage on the stage which can only be characterised as disgusting', and especially 'the commencement of sexual intercourse between Albert and Sadie on a couch which we know ... to offer overwhelming temptation to certain types of actor before certain types of audience'. But at least on the night he was in, the performance 'observed meticulously all the conditions' the Office had imposed on it. In any case, according to Hill 'the acting was so inept that the erotic, pathological and tragic climaxes of the play became nothing but bathos leading to laughter all round'. Overall, he reported, it was 'A not unfunny evening', and no further action was required.[34] It is, of course, perfectly possible that the Company had been tipped off about Hill's presence and adapted their performance accordingly.

Another touring play which provoked interventions over the introduction of unlicensed business was *Free Love*. In August 1956 the Office wrote to the manager of the Company to advise them that the police in Newcastle had reported a discrepancy between the stage directions as licensed and some of the actions in performance:

> As played it closes with 'Mary lying back on the settee with Mario lying on top of her and the pair are squirming in a passionate embrace and kissing'.
>
> The Lord Chamberlain requires that Mary remains upright and that Mario does not lie on top of her ... After Mary says 'I tell you I'm packing up and leaving' Mario follows her into a bedroom after taking off his leather belt; screaming is heard and the sounds of a beating being administered. Mario enters replacing his belt'. All this unallowed action must cease at once.
>
> Finally on page 65 of the MS where Mario is assaulting Susan, he again adopts a most questionable position, forcing her to the ground and lying astride as he kisses her. The Lord Chamberlain requires the deletion of this business, and forbids Mario at any time to lie on top of either of these actresses.[35]

In May 1957, the censors were 'a bit worried about the lady's orgiastic cry', in *Odd Man In*, 'A nasty, leering, little three-handed comedy of Who-sleeps-with-Jane'. However, since 'to do anything about it would, virtually, reduce the play to nothing', and given that the producer was their old friend and supporter Henry Sherek, they entrusted him with the responsibility for ensuring it stayed within the bounds of the acceptable: 'I am sure that you will see that this item is played as decently as possible,' they told him; 'I hope we don't get bombarded with angry letters.'[36] *Vampires from Venus*—'A ridiculous and vulgar play about a threatened invasion of Earth by Amazonian troops from Venus'—also tested the Office's liberalism. 'Venus is a matriarchy and is short of men,' explained Heriot, but 'their technique is very different from ours since one of them, after only a few minutes, causes the death of the professor's son, an experienced debauchee, from sexual exhaustion.' A series of cuts was imposed, to the annoyance of the playwright who claimed he had written a serious and scientifically informed script: 'I was surprised at your cutting out the passages dealing with the activities of the praying mantis as <u>my sixteen-year old daughter has given me this information</u>. It is apparently included in one of her school books.' In a spirit of compromise, he agreed that rather than dying from sexual exhaustion, Julian could instead be shot by a ray-gun.[37]

'Of recent years the Lord Chamberlain's refusal to grant a licence has mostly fallen upon plays with themes of sexual perversity,' wrote Troubridge in November 1957; 'straight sex has been treated with tolerance.' But as he observed, 'there are limits'. The question was where those limits lay. The Lord Chamberlain's problems over sex were by no means confined to the popular or 'lowbrow' end of the market. Troubridge's observation came in his report on Ugo Betti's *Crime on Goat Island*, which, with its emphasis on the 'biological urge in women to have intercourse of some sort, whatever the deficiencies of the man', he considered 'too farmyard to be permissible'. The Reader listed 'minor objectionable lines' which he believed must be cut even if his general recommendation should be ignored, 'which I hope will not be the case'. He was particularly thrown by one moment 'which I might describe (with some surprise) as sodomy in reverse, about goats trying to make physical love to their goatherds'. The limits had indeed shifted. 'Personally I cannot see great reasons for banning it,' wrote Gwatkin; 'It is true that it is most sordid and a very revolting theme, but it does not break any of the Lord Chamberlain's rules and I think that to ban it would expose the Lord Chamberlain to the charge of being narrow-minded.' He also suspected that rejecting it might play into the hands of the management: 'I imagine that a play of this sort will have no commercial value and probably they are anxious that it should be banned so that they can put it on at the Comedy Theatre as a banned play.' Scarbrough agreed: 'I cannot see it injuring anyone's morals,' he wrote. But, just in case, he cut the line about the goat.[38]

The following year, they intervened over Giraudoux's *Judith*: 'I think the affair of the Queen of Aleppo with a donkey should be omitted,' wrote

Heriot, and Gwatkin agreed: 'We must draw a line at a donkey.'[39] And responding in December 1957 to a new translation for Theatre Workshop of *Man Beast and Virtue* ('a horrid early play of Pirandello'), it was felt that 'Mrs Perella's exhaustion after repeated intercourse seems to be more emphasized than in the other version'; the Office asked for this to be modified, and also deleted 'The business of the boy of eleven eating a part of the aphrodisiac'.[40] Troubridge was even more disparaging about Tennessee Williams's *Camino Real*: 'At a few moments it reminds one of Strindberg at his battiest,' he fumed; 'but even when Strindberg is climbing up the wall, there is a rustle of mighty wings in the background.' Actually, he seemed to find the text all but incomprehensible: 'I invite any reader of this report to read any two pages of the play at any point—and then he will know as much as I do.' Once again, Scarbrough licensed the play—though he did cut all references to menstruation and warn that, 'The rites of fertility must not be made suggestive'.[41] However, the decision to approve *Camino Real* for public performance provoked some forceful protests and accusations:

> Once again the Office of censorship of Plays has been exposed in all its foolishness and stupidity to an amused (and irritated) public! The above play has been licensed for public performance, though one of its cast impersonates the notorious Baron de Charlus! Can it really be that whoever read (and condescended to 'pass' this play) was so lacking in general information as to be unaware of this Proust character and his actions. It is evident that the Lord Chamberlain's staff have little time for the wide reading, still less for the acquiring of any general culture, which one would suppose to be a requisite for their unenviable task—scanning multitudes of manuscripts must befuddle their brain ...
>
> Surely the time has come to abolish entirely the unintelligently administered anomaly which is the 'censorship' (as in more civilised countries, e.g. Denmark). Staff made redundant could perhaps be found sinecures as Co-Wardens of the Badgeries or something.[42]

Lysistrata

The Greeks could still give the censors a good run for their money, too— especially when a new version of Aristophanes's best known comedy turned up, as it did in the summer of 1956 for a production at Oxford Playhouse. As Troubridge reported,

> it presents to the Lord Chamberlain (and to a lesser degree to the examiner) a problem of considerable difficulty. On the one hand, any censorship places itself in an invidious position open to ridicule in banning a work that has been an acknowledged comic masterpiece since the year

411B.C., and a version of which was given in London in 1910; on the other hand a censorship of the stage can hardly be justified in licensing for public performance a play in which ... all the male characters are suffering acute physical distress from the strain of prolonged continence, while commenting on this freely, and indicating it by the nature of their gait and even the disposition of their lower garments.

Troubridge came down against licensing, but listed about twenty specific cuts to be made if his general recommendation was ignored. He divided his proposed cuts under two headings—one consisting of lines spoken by the women as they planned their conspiracy—('I will not lift my slippers towards the ceiling'; 'A reference to "Widow's Delight"'; 'We'd have to fall back on ourselves')—and the other, lines referring to the men's physical state ('Up? I've been up for ages'; 'You don't walk naturally, with your tunic poked out'; 'Take them by the hand, women, or by anything else if they seem unwilling'). Once again, Scarbrough over-ruled his Reader's general recommendation: 'I cannot overlook the fact that seven versions have been passed since 1910,' he wrote, 'and that this translation appears to be a scholarly effort.' Given the play's history, he thought that any new version, 'would need to be particularly outrageous to deserve banning'. However, Scarbrough accepted most of Troubridge's individual objections, and added 'a severe warning about indecency' in general.[43]

The following year, the ESC staged the same text at the Royal Court (they originally hoped to include Marilyn Monroe in the cast), and then transferred it to the Duke of York's in the heart of the West End. The production was well received by the majority of critics, though a number of them expressed amazement that something so 'breathtakingly bawdy' should have been allowed on the commercial stage.[44] 'I think that if Aristophanes ... were alive today, we should see his work only if we belonged to a club theatre,' suggested one reviewer, while the *Sunday Times* found 'Joan Greenwood's rich, deep, river-of-butterscotch voice' to be 'so gloriously thick with sex that I should not be surprised to hear at any moment that the Lord Chamberlain has banned it'.[45] A moral campaign was launched against the production, and on 3 March 1958, the performance was interrupted by a demonstration in which three men, protesting against 'filth' on the London stage, dropped leaflets from the gallery onto the heads of the audience below. The leaflets carried 'AN APPEAL TO THE BRITISH PUBLIC', and urged them to 'WRITE TO YOUR MP AND DEMAND THAT THE LORD CHAMBERLAIN IN FUTURE REFUSE HIS LICENCE TO DISGUSTING PLAYS LIKE THIS'.[46] According to press reports, the intervention followed the discovery of 'a mysterious note', signed by 'The Blue Button Boys', which had been 'found pinned to the call board inside the stage door last Thursday'. The note apparently declared that although 'There will always be sufficient people in London to support sex shows', it was important to bear witness to the fact that 'a very great number of people in this country are utterly sick of the bawdy muck which is presented to the public as an "attraction"'.[47]

Of course, the attempt to stop 'the show the critics called "the hottest in town"' made the front pages of the national press, and Gwatkin immediately went to see the production on behalf of the Lord Chamberlain. He admitted to finding it 'very amusing in parts', but confessed he was 'astonished that we have had so few complaints'. Though it was too late to do much about it, he now had serious doubts as to whether the licence should ever have been issued, or whether it might have been better to accept the Reader's advice:

> I think it is an embarrassing play for a mixed audience, unless it is taken for granted that everyone there has suffered from the pangs of unrequited love and has passed the 'eleven plus' on the facts of life, with honours ... It was a mixed audience of both sexes, young and old, and it seemed to me that people were avoiding each other's eye, although there was plenty of applause and dirty laughs.

He added: 'Some bits were really very rough, and I should be most careful of who I took.'

For his part, Scarbrough—suffering under sustained attacks for his ban on the Miller and Williams plays—claimed to be delighted by the protest: 'This is just what was needed,' he wrote '—a blast from the other side.' Even though criticism was aimed at him for having approved the play, this still strengthened his position: 'Katherine [Scarbrough's wife] was at Lambeth Palace today and was asked, not by the Archbishop, but by an old friend what was I thinking of? Splendid!' Gwatkin felt empowered to send a severe warning to the ESC:

> Should it prove that this demonstration originated in revulsion from any indecency of gesture accompanying the language then I am to remind you that His Lordship's views on the subject are made plain to you on the Stage Plays Licence form. In this it is stipulated that no indecency of dress, dance or gesture, nor anything calculated to produce a breach of the peace is permissible.

He also asked Devine to 'review your presentation of the play to ensure that it is not offensive' and reminded him that a licence could always be withdrawn:

> Should investigation prove that the demonstration originated as surmised

you would, in view of the double warning of this letter and your licence, have no justifiable grievance were His Lordship to invoke the powers which he holds under Section 14 of the Theatres Act 1843 to forbid the acting or presenting of any part or the whole of any play, even though originally allowed.

Devine replied immediately to say that nothing had been added since the licence had been issued, and to assure him that the demonstration 'had no relationship to any particular piece of business which was taking place on the stage at the time'. However, he promised that, 'In view of the Lord Chamberlain's feelings in this matter ... we are conducting a review of all the business to make sure that it is not offensive'. But when he telephoned St James's to ask for more information about the particular actions to which the Office objected, he received a rather vague reply: 'I told him that as a general principle anything that raised a "dirty" laugh rather than a hearty one was to be avoided.' Slightly more concretely, he was advised that it was 'unnecessary for men to go about clutching themselves' or to 'look behind each other's shields and make faces'. In practice, it is unlikely that the Office would have seriously considered withdrawing the licence. To do so was almost unknown, and would have exposed them to another very public confrontation and considerable derision. When they received another letter protesting about the 'suburban and quite revolting distortion of Aristophanes' play', and asking to be 'informed why actors and producers are encouraged to such exhibitionism on the stage', Gwatkin's principled defence—presumably approved by Scarbrough—could hardly have been bettered by Devine himself:

> The theme of the play is not unnatural, and at the time at which it was written people were more outspoken on certain matters than is customary even in these days. Thus one is left a choice of either not producing the work of the greatest of Attic, if not of all comedians, or of so emaciating it as to make it entirely unrecognisable and false.
>
> The theatre is, amongst other things, supposed to be the mirror of the times, and it is of interest to learn that over two thousand years ago people were capable of robust outspokenness and a natural honesty which, in principle, might compare favourably with the present time.[48]

In April 1958, the English Stage Company staged another public debate on theatre censorship. Not for the first time, the Lord Chamberlain was invited to participate, and not for the first time he politely declined: 'He undertakes the Censorship by virtue of an Act of Parliament and it is not open to him, therefore, to enter into any discussion of the merits or demerits of the public duty thus laid upon him.'[49] Scarbrough would hardly have had a sympathetic hearing at the Royal Court. A few days later, Lord Harewood asked if he might visit St James's to discuss how 'the whole knotty problem of the Censorship' might best be solved. The reply to his offer, as originally drafted, would have revealed a lot about the current thinking at St James's Palace:

> The Lord Chamberlain has recognised for some considerable time that the provisions of the 1843 Theatres' Act do not allow him legal authority to make such alterations in the present system which he considers necessary to enable him to deal with certain contemporary aspects of Censorship.
>
> With this in view he has been in touch with the Home Secretary to discuss the implementation of the necessary legislation required to amend the Act. As the details of this matter are still sub judice it would clearly be a breach of confidence to discuss them at the moment; but if they come to fruition they will go a long way to remove the present anomalies and unsatisfactory state of affairs which the Lord Chamberlain is the first to recognise as existing.

Probably it was considered that this risked giving slightly too much information to the Chair of the English Stage Company, and the letter seems to have been replaced—or censored—and a slightly more cautious and judicious version substituted:

> I should certainly be glad to see you ... if for no other reason than to hear some home truths about the censorship—although I know most of them already! ...
>
> The Home Secretary has been aware, for some time, of the views of the Lord Chamberlain but it would, of course, be a breach of confidence for me to divulge them to you at the present time.
>
> As the Lord Chamberlain has to administer the law as it stands and has no authority to alter it or to go outside it, would it not be better for you to let the Home Secretary have any suggestions for altering the present arrangements which you have in mind? [50]

Even this offered a pretty broad hint that Scarbrough was hoping for government action to relieve the situation. However, he was well aware that it would take more than a change of policy over homosexuality to alleviate his difficulties.

Tasteful Vulgarities

Overall, Scarbrough was doing his best to pedal the Office quietly away from confrontations, but without abandoning the field entirely. This was also the case in respect of 'bad' language. Reporting on Brendan Behan's *The Quare Fellow* at Theatre Workshop in 1956, Troubridge wrote:

> I have allowed this play much latitude over a number of 'bloodies' and lesser oaths. To cut them out would make nonsense of the speech of a lot of low Irish in a play not basically censorable; The language will cause no offence whatever in Stratford E, and ... I draw my liberal line at only three points.[51]

These were 'chamber pot', 'sod you' and a song about the Governor. Like 'bloody', 'arse' was right on the edge—allowed in certain circumstances but not generally. Thus 'arse over tip' was approved in a play written by the Reverend Clifford Davies—but only because it was to be staged at the Royal Barracks in Portsmouth: 'I suggest that, exceptionally, for a naval audience unlikely to be offended, this should be left.'[52] Perhaps more surprisingly, they passed 'Move your blooming arse' in *My Fair Lady*, even though it was supposedly spoken at Ascot. Troubridge recommended that the playwrights could be permitted an 'equivalent coup de foudre' for the 'bloody' in Shaw's original:

> Respectfully I suggest that this should be allowed as an exception. In this particular case we do not want any invidious comparisons between what the Lord Chamberlain permitted as an exceptional novelty in 1912 and disallowed similarly in 1956. In fact 'bloody' in 1912 is if anything more startling in relation to its date than is 'arse' in 1956. Though generally cut, this is a homely word, well understood by everybody, and is merely what dictionaries term 'low speech', as was 'bloody' once, without being directly disgusting like certain other Anglo-Saxon verbal brevities. This concession need not establish a precedent.[53]

On the other hand, reporting on a *Dick Whittington* in 1957, the Reader noted that 'While I believe "you know what you can do with it" is now generally passed ... "you can shove it up your—", [is] much stronger, and I think too strong'. It was cut.[54] 'Do we leave "a pain in the arse"?' queried Heriot when he read John Osborne's *Epitaph for George Dillon*; 'No we don't,' replied the Assistant Comptroller.[55] And from Arnold Wesker's *Chicken Soup with Barley* ('An impressive, sincere, gloomy play, marred by bad language and a far too intense concentration on natural functions') cuts included 'sod', 'bugger', 'arse', and 'balls'. As Heriot put it: 'We all know that after a severe stroke some elderly people become incontinent. It is hardly necessary to remind us five times that Harry fouls his garments and his sheets.'[56] Reporting on Ronald Duncan's translation of Cocteau's *The Typewriter*, Troubridge noted with approval that 'A volley of "buggers"!'

had 'already been eliminated by the wise submitting management',[57] while even *West Side Story* required a number of deletions, including 'bugging', 'pants open', 'sperm to worm', 'brass arse', and 'pooping around'. There was also some danger that the Romeo and Juliet relationship might be made too physically explicit: 'We don't like people in bed,' observed the Assistant Comptroller. 'This may be alright, as she has a slip,' mused Troubridge; 'It is only Shakespeare's R & J, Act Three, Scene Five, which I have seen done in London with a bed,' he observed, 'though now more usually not.' 'Warn,' directed Scarbrough.[58]

Another contemporary musical which required more forceful intervention was *Expresso Bongo*, which, with Paul Scofield and Victor Spinetti, would run for over 300 performances in the West End. Set in Soho and in and around a nightclub cabaret, Troubridge described the piece as

> a savage and bitter satire upon a number of the aspects of our time, the rise of moron proletarian adolescents like Tommy Steele to wealth through noise-making, skiffle and teenage fans, the rackets of theatrical agency, Soho coffee bars and fashionable night-clubs, and the behaviour of so-called café Society. Its outlook is tough.

He was concerned about a reference to someone as 'The Diana Dors of Hoxton', on the grounds that 'Though Miss Dors is probably not touchy, her origins in Swindon were above Hoxton level, and she might protest with some justification'. There were also issues of blasphemy—'To compare an old charwoman to the Virgin Mary must be near it (especially to Catholics)'—and of a series of tableaux:

> It seems to me that Mary Queen of Scots in nothing but a short kilt and a crown, is more suggestive than the ordinary Windmill nude in a string. The same applies to two girls as Caesar and Brutus, each with one breast exposed; this could be very funny, but it is pure or impure Folies Bergeres.

Overall, the original script for *Expresso Bongo* contained 'some twenty five stains needing vigorous application of the usual St James's Palace detergents'. The final endorsement included the following stipulations:

> Delete 'It was a Saturday night mistake' ... for 'the poor sods' substitute 'poor cows' ... Mary Queen of Scots to be adequately covered by a short kilt ... for 'stroke my fur' substitute 'make me purr' ... delete 'rock my see-saw' and substitute 'rock my cradle' ... for 'spare the rod' substitute 'spare the cane' ... for 'balls up' substitute 'fiasco'.[59]

Given the 'endless opportunities for dirty business' offered by the text, the Reader also suggested that someone should inspect the dress rehearsal.

1958 may have ended with a new policy in place on references to homo-sexuality, but there was no sign that things were going to become generally easier for the Lord Chamberlain as a result. On 30 December 1958, the *Sheffield Star* published a venomous and in part a personal assault:

> The Lord Lieutenant of our county of the West Riding, the Earl of Scarbrough, has always struck me, in his numerous visits to Sheffield and district, as an eminently reasonable man ...
>
> But what sudden transformation overcomes him in his office as Lord Chamberlain?
>
> Or, what is probably nearer the mark, what kind of weird set-up has he been saddled with in this office.
>
> It appears to be run by a handful of relics from the puritanical days when water-closet was a universally-U word for lavatory.

The attack, published under the single word headline 'BULL', had been prompted by John Osborne's outrage at cuts which he said had been demanded in his latest piece, a musical called *The World Of Paul Slickey*. In fact, this was a little unfair on Scarbrough, since Gwatkin had not bothered to consult him about the small number of changes required in the script, and this was the first Scarbrough had heard of the play. Nevertheless, the article concluded: 'It's about time somebody made a stand. Mr Osborne will have plenty of support if he fights, even defies, the ridiculous rulings of the Lord Chamberlain's office.' Other newspapers picked up the story, but when Scarbrough checked the file for the relevant reports and correspond-ence on Osborne's play, he found that the claim and statement attributed to the playwright 'does not seem to bear any resemblance to the cuts required here'. Scarbrough was confused. 'What the author is playing at is not clear to me.' On 31 December he wrote to his Assistant Comptroller:

> The *Sunday Dispatch* and the *Daily Mail* have been ringing me up about a play by this angry young man Mr Osborne. I have maintained a silent attitude towards them. What, though, is it all about? ... I wish you a happy new year.[60]

Scarbrough had tried to usher out some old conflicts through the back door of St James's. But, as 1959 began, new ones were already piling up at the front.

CHAPTER SEVEN

The Tearing Down
of Everything

Class, Politics and
Aunt Edna

While the nation awaits with baited breath the consequences of the publication this week of the notorious pornography-or-art novel *Lolita*, a much bigger problem child has already been left on its London doorstep: Where can I take Aunt Edna?[1]

The Royal Court and their assistants from Stratford are not free from the need for supervision[2]

Speaking at a luncheon in Stratford-upon-Avon in April 1959 to celebrate the 350th anniversary of Shakespeare's birth, Lord Scarbrough told his audience that when reading new playscripts, he frequently 'murmured five words from Shakespeare to himself'. They were: 'It is a bawdy planet.'[3] Tempting though it is to imagine how the crazed and jealous ruler in *A Winter's Tale* might have dealt with some of the plays which landed on the mat at St James's Palace, perhaps a deranged tyrant who ignores both divine and human laws and punishes the innocent for doing and saying things he has himself imagined was not necessarily the most balanced or reliable judge to invoke. Lords Chamberlain were frequently accused of acting as dictators. But in practice (if not in principle) they lacked the absolute power of despotic monarchs. King Leontes never had to worry about public opinion or a free press.

Homosexuality and the Change

Scarbrough's switch in policy over homosexuality may have relieved a little pressure, but his position and authority were not much strengthened. Concessions intended to appease are often read as signs of weakness, inviting further attacks. Though he tried to disguise it, ground had been given, and opponents of theatre censorship had tasted blood. Around him, other battles were being fought and citadels falling. Most notable, perhaps, was the passing in 1959 of the Obscene Publications Act. Though this had no explicit connection with the Lord Chamberlain's control of theatres, it was bound to have an impact upon the culture within which he operated. Demands for greater liberalisation and freedom of expression would surely increase. Yet others were appalled by the shifts and questioned where and when it would all stop. In November 1959, the *Daily Mail* published 'An Inquiry Into The Sordid State Of The British Theatre', in which Cecil Wilson discussed the near-impossibility of finding shows to which Rattigan's famous Aunt Edna could be taken: 'Already the London theatre has a riper crop of plays than the Lord Chamberlain would have dreamed of passing a few years ago,' wrote Wilson, 'and more are on the way to challenge Aunt Edna's prim-ness.' It was not only the Royal Court or Theatre Workshop or Paul Raymond's road shows that Aunt Edna had to be steered away from. As the author delicately put it: 'No pastrycook ever offered a wider variety of tarts than the West End stage offers today.' Even musicals were no longer a safe bet.

> Perhaps Auntie would fancy *Irma La Douce*. Or *would* she when Irma turned out to be a French prostitute and the hero a young man who lived not only with her but on her earnings ...
>   The Soho musical *The Crooked Mile* has a whole chorus of them, as well as a tart for one leading lady and a petty gangster's mistress for the other.
>   Should the title *Lock up Your Daughters*, give Auntie no clue to the nature of the Mermaid Theatre's musical, I might warn her that this is a bedtime story in the bluntest sense, uninhibitedly adapted from the play Henry Fielding called *Rape Upon Rape*.[4]

The change over references to homosexuality meant that some plays which had previously been rejected were now eligible for public perfor-mance. Yet Angus Wilson was probably right to suggest that 'the decision, like so many official decisions in England, has come as an anti-climax', and that general interest in the subject was 'in one of its periodic troughs'.[5] 1959 offered little in the way of new takes on the subject of homosexu-ality, beyond a couple of light and fairly safe comedies which might have been more severely censored previously but which could now be allowed. Troubridge may (surely?) have been exaggerating his shock at the script of William Douglas Home's *Aunt Edwina*: 'I make no doubt that the assistant Comptroller will be transfixed with horror to learn that the subject ... is that of a Colonel in the Coldstream who becomes a woman.' However, the

Reader took the opportunity to try and identify the principles which he believed would now apply in such circumstances:

> Though all these plays on a sex-change theme are in the vilest taste, smacking to me of the freak-show on the fairground, we have now a certain body of precedent, so I had better set out what I conceive to be the position established in general, subject to correction by my superiors. When such plays are purely sensational and catchpenny (as in 'A Girl called Harry', submitted twice), a licence is refused, when they are jocular, even if in very bad taste (as in 'A Resounding Tinkle' and 'The World of Paul Slickey'), they are usually licensed.

The unapologetically snobbish Troubridge actually held Home—brother to the future Conservative prime minister, but himself a liberal—in relatively high regard: 'Mr Douglas Home has the social advantage of having been né invité, he observed with approval; 'he understands the inward arcana of huntin', shootin' and fishin', so his ladies and gentlemen speak and think like ladies and gentlemen, which is rare enough among the many dramatists who still scatter their casts with titles.'[6] Arguably, though, this made his treachery even worse. *Aunt Edwina* centred on Colonel Edward Ryan and his wife, Cecile, who return from a holiday ('Daddy ... said he needed a change') to the country house where their children are waiting for them, with surprising news:

> DAVID: Mummy, there's a woman standing by the gold-fish pond ...
> CECILIA: Yes, I know, dear. That's what I was going to tell you. That's your father ...
> ROSEMARY: Mummy, you don't mean that Daddy's—
> CECILIA: Yes, dear. That's exactly what I do mean ...
> DAVID: I thought it only happened in the *Daily Sketch*.

Edward is dressed in 'a smart Tweed coat' and 'a hat of a bright colour', but much of the humour depends on the incongruity which results from the fact that his/her behaviour remains largely unchanged: 'the lady who comes through the window should have lost nothing of the Guards Colonel, except the black moustache. The voice, even, should be natural and deep.'[7] As Troubridge put it: 'the middle third of the play then becomes a dirtier *Charlie's Aunt*.' At one point, Edward's best friend, Major Reggie Privett, becomes confused and tries to kiss him, and equally concerning was a farcical scene in which Edward/Edwina is pursued by a wealthy, divorced American Senator (male) who 'presses his matrimonial advances' on the 'elderly female who was so recently a guards colonel'. But even this was not the worst: 'Then comes the iniquity,' warned the Reader. Major Privett is the secretary to the local Hunt of which Edward had previously been Master: 'to enable Edwina to continue to hunt the hounds ... Reggie Privett agrees to marry her himself.' This was a step too far:

> to depict a Guards Colonel changed into a woman then proposing a carnal marriage with his former best man, best friend, and second-in-command under any circumstances, above all merely to retain the mastership of a Hunt, is to portray a figure too vile to be permitted on the public stage. The roof of the theatre would probably fall in upon a first night audience witnessing such a scene—or it ought to.

Nor was the final solution necessarily one which Troubridge felt able fully to endorse, when Edward's former wife, Cecilia, herself decides to undergo a sex change, thus allowing them to continue together as Master and Mistress of the Hunt—but with their former roles reversed.

Troubridge thought that at the very least any reference to a possible marriage between Edward/Edwina and Reggie should be omitted: 'while that proposal is included, I cannot recommend the play.' Gwatkin was even less amused: 'I don't think the subject very funny anyhow,' he noted; 'it's normally a tragedy.' But he did not share the Reader's view that removing one particular suggestion would make the play more acceptable: 'I don't see that it is particularly deplorable (as Troubridge thinks) that the changed Colonel should marry his best-man-cum-second-in-command.' Scarbrough agreed that this was not the main issue: 'The main difficulty about the play is the change of sex,' he stated; 'It must be passed or banned on that theme.' However, he was keen to avoid the possibility of finding himself trapped back in the corner from which he had just managed to free himself, and he over-ruled the advice of both the Reader and the Assistant Comptroller: 'I do not find the theme exploited in a beastly ... way. It is made a farce.' A licence was therefore issued, with the only two phrases cut being the words 'the old sod' and 'buggered off'.[8]

Scarbrough also approved *The Birds and the Bees*, another near farce written by Arthur Macrea, whom Troubridge characterised as 'a run of the mill, fairly successful west end light comedy playwright'.[9] The narrative here centred on a fabulously rich French family, whose son and heir, Johnnie, secretly falls in love with a servant girl, Millie, whose father is in prison. In order to avoid Johnnie being married off to Elena, a rich heiress, and with the help of a friend, they concoct a plan to deceive his family:

> MILLIE: What would fool them? Something contemporary. Something—something
> LOUISE: ... Something they've heard about but wouldn't quite understand ...

JOHNNIE: We need to think of something—something a bit beyond them—something that's being talked about—written about ... some irrevocable reason why I can't marry Elena. ...
LOUISE: I know what you could say ... It would be quite irrevocable ... And it is something that's being talked and written about—and it is something they'd know about but wouldn't quite understand ... When the family's assembled, you address us. You say, I have something to tell you. I'd hoped to spare you this—I'd hoped it need never be known, but now you've forced me to speak ... I am not like other boys. I'm strange, I'm odd, I'm peculiar ... I can't marry Elena for the simple reason that I don't like girls.[10]

Although none of the characters in *The Birds and the Bees* is depicted as definitely or actively homosexual, the script could certainly not have been licensed before the change in policy. Even now, as Troubridge recognised, it hardly fitted with the conditions Scarbrough had laid down. For the Reader it was 'a border line case', but probably acceptable:

After considerable cogitation, I consider that, although this is not one of the 'sincere studies' mentioned in the Lord Chamberlain's memorandum, the author just about gets away with it. It is a grimy evening's entertainment, certainly, and contains most of the usual homosexual references and doubles entendres in tolerably wrapped up form, but it is no worse than actual sex change as a comedy theme. And, as a major consideration in my mind, the whole thing is a pretence and Johnnie is not a homosexual.

Gwatkin agreed that while it was 'certainly not a "sincere study of homo-sexuality"', it was 'too feeble to ban', and the script was licensed without difficulty.[11] Yet there were one or two moments in the play which attempted, if not exactly to champion homosexuality, then at least to speak for it as a 'natural' element within existence; the most notable occurs when Charles confronts those members of his family who are arguing that Johnnie's homosexuality is no impediment to marrying a rich heiress:

CHARLES: If you had the faintest knowledge of biology, you'd know it's of no use trying to marry off Johnnie. This sex variation occurs all through Nature—I could produce examples of animals, fish, insects, plants ... Here's another biological truth. To force Johnnie into a marriage he doesn't want and can't physically cope with would unbalance him completely.[12]

Aunt Edna, of course, was the president and founding member of Terence Rattigan's fan club. Sadly, one fears that even his new play in 1959 might have been a little too much for her. Rattigan's account of the life of T.E. Lawrence, *Ross*, was submitted for licence in May. 'If Mr Rattigan has a thesis,' wrote Heriot, 'it is … that Lawrence suffered sexual assault by Turkish soldiers when he was captured and that that indignity broke his spirit and caused his subsequent odd behaviour.' He marked for amendment 'reference to Lawrence's alleged homosexuality'—though quite why changing 'Arab habits' to 'Eastern habits' should have lessened the offence is not completely clear. The Censorship was initially most concerned about the principle of representing real people on stage. Heriot pointed out that, with the exception of one possibly fictional brigadier, they had all been painted 'favourably and with dignity', and that there was 'nothing in the presentation of the real people in this play to which exception could be taken'. Nevertheless, he reminded the Assistant Comptroller that

> in the past we have had plays about celebrities passed by the Lord Chamberlain and remote relations have popped up and made trouble. I suggest, therefore, that if the Lord Chamberlain does issue a licence for this play, it is on the understanding that the management makes every effort to contact any near relatives of Lawrence who are still alive, and get their consent.

After extensive negotiations with the reluctant professor who was Lawrence's surviving brother, the Lord Chamberlain over-ruled his objections and issued a licence

> His brother has been dead 25 years and he is an historical and controversial character. Several books about himself have been written by Lawrence. Many books, innumerable articles and reference have been written about him by other authors, some of whom have been far from kind. The Professor himself apparently agreed to a film life of Lawrence, and two more are in process of being made now, one apparently with his blessing … It is not, therefore, a very cogent argument that he objects to 'any further public discussion' of his brother. The censorship would support a reasonable objection but, in view of the above, I wonder if it is really reasonable. If the play denigrated Lawrence, we should be on a stronger wicket, but it does not … indeed, the reverse.

Two former friends of Lawrence, Robert Graves and Siegfried Sassoon, were among those whose views on the script had been canvassed, and both had vouched for its fairness and sympathetic attitude. Scarbrough decided that the brother's objections were naïve, and that to refuse a licence was bound to create more bad column inches for the Censorship:

> The Professor is, I believe, a Professor of Archaeology and somewhat out of this world. I think he does not realize [sic] that Rattigan's play will be

published and can (and will) go on the television and the radio. Moreover, it can be performed in private theatres in England and anywhere outside the United Kingdom.

Far more publicity and public discussion will be invited if the play carries the notoriety of being banned and clearly the ban cannot be upheld for many more years.

The brother was informed 'that Mr Rattigan would endeavour to meet objections to any particular passage which Professor Lawrence may put forward', and, to be on the safe side, Beaumont, who was to produce the play, was encouraged to include a statement in the programme—as he had done for *The Winslow Boy*—that 'no claims are made that either the events depicted or the characters portrayed are necessarily factual'.[13]

Theatre Workshop Stories

Fings Ain't What They Used To Be

Once again, some of the most bitter censorship battles around the turn of the decade were fought with Theatre Workshop. *Fings Ain't What They Used To Be*, a musical by James Norman and Lionel Bart, was submitted by Gerry Raffles in February 1959. Clearly, there was still blood on the carpet from the recent legal encounter with the company over *You Won't Always Be on Top*, and the Office was keen to avoid another high-profile clash from which it might come off the loser. Troubridge was also disposed to wave it through because he could not imagine it transferring from its natural home. 'The language, made up of every sort of street, prison and rhyming slang and argot, would be incomprehensible to a West End audience,' he confidently asserted; 'and,' he added, 'might have given difficulty to me, had I not served for many years in a Regiment recruited almost entirely from East End cockneys.' Whatever the reasons, Troubridge's response to *Fings* was predominantly positive:

> This is a very tough play with songs for the extreme left-wing theatre at Stratford, East 15. All the characters are attached to a 'spieler', or illicit gambling den, in Soho, or are its patrons ('punters'), or prostitutes and ponces, or corrupt policemen. Yet as such depravity does exist, representing indeed quite a large section of Soho, I see very little to object to in this play, and for once in a way find myself in agreement with Mr Raffles, the Stratford Manager, who opines that 'the moral intent of the play comes through to a reader'. The moral is very clearly that crime does not pay, resulting only in long prison sentences, or in being 'carved up' with razors by a rival gang.

He did not even object to the way in which the forces of law and order were painted:

> As to the wholesale accusations of corruptions against the Police, I do not myself consider that the Lord Chamberlain has any obligation to intervene in the matter: if the accusations are held to be unfounded, it is for the critics to say so.

Only three minor amendments were insisted on before *Fings* received its licence, but complaints soon began to come in. The Public Morality Council quickly voiced disapproval: 'The committee felt that in the light of certain recent murders not far away from Stratford, the general attitude of the play to the police and to general decency, is deplorable.' Moreover, 'The play bristles with bawdy jokes and insinuations'. But the Office had taken its stand, and Gwatkin's reply was one of positive advocacy: 'Such a play, of necessity, must be rough,' and he explained that its heart and its morals were in the right place. 'Unpleasant though the play may be it does not appear to encourage brutality and crime for the principals themselves, far from being heroes, end up with long prison sentences or are subject to retaliatory violence.'[14] In fact, though, Scarbrough had not yet heard the last of *Fings*. Despite Troubridge's doubts about its accessibility to wider audiences, the show would transfer to the Garrick Theatre in February 1960, where it would run for some 800 performances, heaping more embarrassment on the Lord Chamberlain at the start of the next decade.

The Hostage

However, it was the revival of another Theatre Workshop play which haunted and taunted St James's in 1959. As we saw in the previous chapter, Brendan Behan's *The Hostage* had been licensed in the autumn of 1958, with the arguments about one song in particular never fully resolved by the end of its eight week run. In May 1959, Gerry Raffles wrote to the Office again to take up the issue. The production, he said, had been 'a tremendous success' in Paris, and the plan now was to open it at Wyndhams Theatre in the West End. 'The French critics regard it as a most important work,' reported Raffles—a claim annotated at St James's by three blue exclamation marks in the margin. Once again, the Company asked if they could revert to the original version of the song, which had been refused a licence the previous year:

> I met with a Gaelic pawnbroker,
> By Killarney's waterfalls,
> With sobs he cried, I wish I had died,
> The Saxons have stolen my only box of matches.

'I should be extremely grateful if you would reconsider your decision and allow us to sing the song this way.' The response to Raffles's latest request was unequivocal: 'Most certainly not.'

Raffles contacted the producer managing the West End transfer, Donald Albery: 'I will try to get another verse out of Brendan, but if there is anything you can do to get the verse accepted, I shall be most grateful.' Albery's tactic was to take up with Scarbrough the fact that the approved verse had

> proved to be very much more objectionable in practice than the original verse; in fact so objectionable that I understand that one of the performers refused to sing it, and has since substituted the original verse which has caused no offence to anybody at all ... As Brendan Behan is away ill in Dublin, and is also very difficult, could we not on this occasion leave the original version in?

Scarbrough caved in, and on 29 May the Comptroller wrote to Albery: 'In view of the difficult position outlined in your letter, and what you say about this production the Lord Chamberlain is prepared to let you keep the original verse.'

A couple of weeks later the Office made another and perhaps more important concession in relation to the same production when it acceded to a request that an excerpt to be read aloud from a newspaper during Act Two could be varied each night to allow it to remain topical, and need not be specifically approved: 'Any current headline may be read from the paper but they must be read as printed.' Potentially, this was a significant precedent. After all, there were many newspapers, each with many head-lines, which could be inflected and commented upon by an actor without adding to the text. True, they were unlikely to contain swearing, blasphemy or sexual innuendo, or to be critical of the monarchy or of a foreign ally. Nevertheless, permission had been granted for unspecified and unlicensed lines to be spoken within a public performance.

In June, Heriot wrote his official Reader's Report on a revised script of *The Hostage*, noting that it had been 'toned down' for the West End transfer. The fact that the copy sent to the Office was hard to make sense of may not, one suspects, have been entirely accidental: 'There have been so many alterations in the original script that it is difficult, and in some cases impossible, to tell from the correspondence exactly what the Lord Chamberlain has cut,' complained the Reader. He also expressed surprise that it seemed as if Scarbrough had apparently 'allowed himself to be included in the many topical references'. Heriot conceded that the play's 'revolting expression of the worst in the Irish temperament has provoked no response from the public'; but he insisted that, 'In spite of the friendly critics, I adhere to my original opinion that this is a filthy play with nothing to recommend it'. He also proposed three further specific cuts, including 'a genuine extract from the *Daily Express* about Princess Anne joining the Brownies'. Gwatkin also thought that while this particular reference was 'innocuous' in itself, it was vital to 'try and keep Princess Anne out of the limelight'. Scarbrough agreed: 'I will allow no reference to Princess Anne in this beastly play.' He was also adamant that 'The reference to myself was cut in the original and should not creep back again'. The licence was issued only after further detailed negotiations and amendments: ('I'll cock you' became 'I'll kill-cock you', 'little bollix' was changed to 'whore master', and 'steamed before and aft' to 'Everybody laughed'). 'I am sorry that we are the indirect cause of so much trouble,' wrote Albery on 19 June, with his tongue nailed to his cheek; 'Isn't life difficult?' 'Yes!' responded Gwatkin.

Beastly or not, *The Hostage* had hardly opened at Wyndhams when it was awarded first prize for best production at the 1959 Théâtre des Nations Festival in Paris. Moreover, Joan Littlewood had been awarded the 1959 International Olympics Prize for Theatre, and four other members of the Company had received similar honours. Not that this cut much ice with the Lord Chamberlain's Office, or with others who resented the infiltration of Behan's language, politics and morality into the West End. Both St James's Palace and the Home Office received several letters of protest, including one from an MP and another from the very angry Managing Director of The Oil Well Engineering Company ('Manufacturers and suppliers of well drilling machinery and all oil field requirements') in Stockport:

> I am amazed that this play passed your censorship.
> It is anti-English and lying. Perhaps it could not be condemned on that score.
> It depends overwhelmingly on cursing and blasphemy and must disgust any decent minded person.
> If this muck can get past you I am puzzled as to where you would draw the line.
> The author says he is a rebel. Against what? We can do without his plays and without him

Someone else rang up to express incredulity that certain passages had been passed, but was 'too embarrassed to mention the passages concerned'. Others (assuming they were not Ortonesque spoofs) displayed unashamed bigotry:

> As it was written by a drunken Irishman I was expecting something rather surprising. Being no prude I had no objection to the stage portraying the morals, or the lack of them, of men in relation to women, but I did take

the strongest objection to the blatant flaunting of homosexuality, which I am still old enough to look upon as unnatural. It is common knowledge that homosexuality is rampant among actors and actresses and that is probably why they are such a rotten lot.

Clearly, an undercover inspection was called for. 'Damn! I suppose I shall have to go,' grumbled Gwatkin. The Assistant Comptroller found little to enjoy in the performance ('A dreadful afternoon relieved only by the acting of Alfred Lynch') but he had to admit that the audience did not seem to be shocked by what they saw and heard:

> The audience attending a matinee is generally less sophisticated than that attending an evening performance, and so it was at Wyndham's Theatre on Wednesday afternoon. The Theatre was fairly filled with 90% middle aged and elderly women. If these ladies saw them, and some certainly did, they took the cheap little obscenities in their stride, and brought the curtain up three times at the end.

It was not, however, Gwatkin's preferred way of spending an afternoon:

> I was soon tired of the word 'bloody' and of the endless succession of 'whores', 'brothels', etc., in a spate of imitation Irish. The pansy comes over as a half wit and the lines which we objected to in 'Waterfall' (?) [sic] only get over to the few because they are hammered out.

Hill also went to see the show on another occasion, 'As a matter of interest'. However, 'I didn't stay the course I fear and after the second interval I crept away'. His unsolicited account was probably not intended for Scarbrough's eyes:

> did you know that not only is there a coloured pansy called Princess Grace in the show, but another male prostitute 'Tom Collins's runner' who is living in the brothel, who takes clients upstairs like the lady pro, and who leaves the stage on one occasion ... with the words 'I'll go down to the docks and find a sailor'. I suppose that now the Lord Chamberlain allows reference to homo-sexuality it is only logical to allow male prostitutes to be portrayed on the stage, but it is definitely another rubicon crossed.

Hill also noted with distaste the inclusion of 'one or two pretty filthy bits of "business" that the audience seemed to love', and of jibes at the monarchy:

> whatever the actors are allowed to read out of the newspaper it is something to guy the queen that they do read. There is also some thinly

veiled reference to Princess Anne—remarks about tiny teeth on an apple near Virginia Water although I suppose most people would miss them.

He may even have told Gwatkin more than the Assistant Comptroller really wanted to know:

> The actor who is leading the evangelist upstairs to bed, twice puts his hand on her bottom and carefully aligns it so that one finger is pressing on the slit. This was too deliberate for anyone to avoid noticing.

It was, thought Hill, a sad indictment of the modern age that such a play should go down well:

> In 1939 I think the show would have been broken up—in these days it is apparently relished—I believe I was the only one who couldn't take it! I had to leave 4/5 boredom, 1/5 resentment—I should say.

Hill had actually attended the performance in the company of Miss Webster, the typist and secretary in the Lord Chamberlain's Office, whom he then rather ungallantly abandoned. She apparently stayed till the end, and was able to inform him that he had missed a scene of homosexual soliciting.

At the end of September, Hill forwarded to Gwatkin some of the recent complaints about *The Hostage* and asked how he should respond. The secretary despised Theatre Workshop, and had no doubt that they were making a mockery of the Censorship and breaking the rules whenever they chose. Was the Office really just going to give in?

> Dear Brigadier,
> The Theatre Workshop people from my experience in Court where they all lied openly and unashamedly, have no compunction in taking the Censor for a ride and I think they are doing it here. ... The fingering of a woman's bottom is typical of this crowd, who preach intellectuality but introduce as much of the worst carnality as they dare. ...
>
> The fact is that, although not perhaps immediately obvious many of Princess Grace's lines have been given to Mick (and it is he who establishes himself as a pansy, and behaves as a male prostitute throughout the play, acting exactly the same as the female prostitutes. See how the line about picking up a sailor has been altered by omitting the last words ...)
>
> I hope I'm not getting religion, which is an insidious disease, but I am honestly unable to draft a reply to Mr Foster justifying our allowing the actor Mick and to a lesser extent Princess Grace (a coloured gentleman) to portray on the stage male prostitutes plying their trade in a brothel, ogling the soldier Leslie, Mr Mulleady and so on. I don't think we actually

allowed it in the first place, but the hypocritical stinkers who compose the production side of this play have built it into the performance. I need not stress that this represents an important point of policy ie. Serious homo-sexuality the Lord Chamberlain is going to allow, is he going to allow professional homo-sexuality as well?

It was not just *The Hostage* itself that was at issue, but the lessons that would inevitably be taken from it:

Any action against the play will of course rouse interest in it; on the other hand one must also consider its effect on our future policy. In our trade there is no going back, and one male pro today means a flock tomorrow.

Gritting his teeth, Gwatkin donned his most liberal face, and modelled a reply to be sent to complainants:

If a play of this sort is to have any value at all the characters in it must appear to be genuine. Thus, the language and outlook of the inhabitants of a brothel can be expected to be somewhat uninhibited.

When to this is added the fact that the action takes place in Southern Ireland, and that the play is written by an enthusiastically rebellious Irishman, you get a play which has certainly given the censorship some anxiety ...

I must point out that the censorship is not concerned with whether a play is good or bad or whether it is in good taste or otherwise: it is concerned largely with preventing the ultra modern contemporary playwright from going beyond the fairly wide limits of permissible speech and action.

If a play is likely to corrupt it would not be licensed but the Lord Chamberlain feels that he should not use his powers to prevent a play on the grounds that it might upset or annoy certain amongst the audience.

Apart from a little discreet tinkering around the edges (in 1960, for instance, an MP wrote to thank Scarbrough for his effective intervention in removing an offensive joke about the Royal Family) there was little the Censorship felt able to do. It was simply not strong enough, and the production had been too widely acclaimed.[15]

J.P. Donleavy and The Ginger Man

A very different Irish play which also ran into difficulties with the Censorship in the spring of 1959 was *The Ginger Man* by J.P. Donleavy, an adaptation by the writer from his own novel, which was scheduled to open in Hull before transferring to the Royal Court. 'This horrible play resembles an Irish *Look Back in Anger,* crossed with something by James Joyce,' opined Troubridge, identifying in it 'all his inconsequence and sleaziness'. He could detect no point or purpose in it: 'It is all belly-aching (mostly about Ireland), bitching and bad language; it has no story worth mentioning and forty lines to be considered for excision.' And he concluded: 'What they will make of this in Hull, Heaven only knows.' Many of the cuts were focused on language and references to sex or the body:

> Omit 'unnatural acts with farm animals'
> Omit 'she'd do anything but let me in'
> Omit the stage direction 'with a rub of the hand between the legs'
> Omit 'call me a bugger' and 'your father is a sack of excrement, genteel excrement' and 'what was he doing, playing battleships in the tub?' ...
> Omit 'I want nothing between me and flesh the first time' and 'men wagging their things at you from doorways'
> Omit 'She'll piss on my shirt' ...
> Omit 'pompous load of shit' ...
> Omit 'never been partial to threats from the rear' ...
> Omit 'I hope to see you on your arse in the Old Bailey'

Others were to do with religious references:

> Omit 'They're ruining Jesus with publicity'
> Omit 'Oh Lord I forgive thee for all thy faults' ...
> Omit 'The Irish feel that children are brought down upon them by the wrath of God for screwing'

And one or two involved stage business: 'There must be no suggestive business while Dangerfield and Miss Frost are on adjacent mattresses.'[16]

Donleavy's play eventually opened in London in the autumn. The *News Chronicle* called it a 'slice of Dublin low-life', and said it was 'the latest addition to the bawling lusty plays which are making such an impact on the theatre'. The newspaper quoted Donleavy himself as saying 'I expect a couple of rows to walk out every night, angered or shocked or offended', and insisting he was 'not angered' by the eighty or so cuts, made by the Lord Chamberlain: 'I think he has been very liberal about it.'[17] Hill now read the script and concluded that the Reader had failed to spot some of the dangers:

> I see that the action allows a man and woman to drag their mattresses out and to go to bed side by side. The only spoken words thereafter are the man telling the woman to get a glass of water, and she saying 'You

shouldn't have done that'. It is obvious from the remaining dialogue that the lady has been seduced, and this in full view of the audience. Will the stage be plunged in darkness? There is no mention of the action in the synopsis, but it is implicit in the text, and this is such a filthy play that I wonder what will happen.

Don't you think someone had better have a look at it early next week?

Hill himself went to see it, and found the performance less shocking than he had expected:

Oddly enough, in view of the language which had been excised from the piece, and also that which had been allowed to remain, the play did not come over as being really indecent. Much of the dialogue is in the form almost of recitative and the effect which similar language would have in shorter sentences was lost.

As for the action that had made him so anxious:

I am glad to be able to report that the scene with the two mattresses was conducted with the utmost decorum and, given the situation which had been allowed, there was absolutely nothing to which one could object. I was particularly able to see this as I was in a box overlooking the stage.

His assessment was received in the Office with some relief: 'This,' said Gwatkin, 'is a pleasant surprise.'[18]

The World of Paul Slickey

St James's Palace also came off rather well from another of their acrimonious confrontations in 1959, this one involving John Osborne's *The World of Paul Slickey*. As the playwright himself later acknowledged, both script and production would ultimately find themselves, 'permanently labelled with the preface "ill-fated"'.[19] But the history of the play's failure also provides us with a clear example of a West End manager deliberately setting out to destroy a production he was himself promoting, by secretly encouraging the Lord Chamberlain to withdraw a licence he had already given, and cancel a production.

Like *The Hostage*, Osborne's 'bilious musical play' had first been submitted in the autumn of 1958. Heriot dismissed it then as 'a sprawling unfunny personal fling that no West End management would look at if it were not by the celebrity of the month'. It was, he confidently declared, 'broken-backed from the start, being neither a revue, a symbolist satire, nor a musical', and its humour was 'sour and Sixth Form where it is not as tasteless as that of a male chorus dressing-room'. Heriot did not hide his contempt for Osborne: 'The Angry Young Man has become the Envious Young Intellectual, hating all the tradition and wealth he has never had.' On the other hand, from the point of view of actual censorship, only a handful of changes were demanded; these included 'Two homosexual couplets' (the lines 'He's almost definitely queer' and 'He's contrary, he's a fairy') and 'Jack's statement that his wife is as cold as a school lavatory seat in December'. Heriot observed dismissively of the latter that 'Psychologists will be able to use this to explain Mr Osborne'.[20]

An early version of *Slickey* (without music) had, to Osborne's annoyance, been rejected by the management at the Royal Court, 'from whose rib I had sprung'.[21] The musical into which it had been transformed was supposedly to be produced by Donald Albery, and Osborne himself was to direct. However, in early 1959, two further amended texts were submitted to the Lord Chamberlain, neither of which persuaded Heriot of the play's worth. 'It has been slightly revised but remains as tiresome and, curiously, as amateur as ever,' he wrote; 'It still seems to me to be a very shoddy affair and a very ridiculous mouse to emerge from the great White Mountain of English Theatre.' He noted, too, that Osborne was now having trouble finding a management to take the show on; 'It is significant,' he wrote, 'that Donald Albery has washed his hands of this piece.'[22] But in fact Osborne had found a new business partner, David Pelham, who had secured financial backing for a show requiring 24 actors and 10 dancers. There was to be a short regional tour, and the show would then open in April at London's Palace Theatre, where the licensee was Emile Littler.

As we saw at the end of the previous chapter, Osborne knew how to generate column inches and publicity for the show, and was not too much of a gentleman to worry about playing it a little dirty in his dealings with St James's Palace. In the early months of 1959, further arguments and negotiations helped to keep *Slickey* in the public eye: 'Osborne Takes on the Censor Again' announced the *Daily Mail* as the latest version was submitted to the Office in March; the newspaper reported that 'the original Angry Young Man, wasn't at all angry last night', because he believed he was winning his battle with Scarbrough.[23] Anticipation built up to near fever pitch: 'No post-war musical has been awaited in London with such excited speculation as Osborne's *The World of Paul Slickey*', reported the *Daily Sketch*, under the headline 'Will success pacify John Osborne'.[24]

Osborne's play was in part an attack on the popular press and, as the playwright himself put it, 'the disagreeable exploits of a newspaper gossip columnist'. The very name of the central character drew deliberate attention to two contemporary exponents, William Hickey of the *Daily Express* and Paul Tanfield of the *Daily Mail*. But the text also used some vicious mockery and satire to attack a range of other establishment targets and

archaic assumptions. Most original reviewers and later academic critics
tend to agree that one of the principal problems was the play's scatter
gun approach: 'anything and everything comes under the same erratic
fire,' wrote John Russell Taylor; 'mountains and molehills are greeted with
equal fury.'[25]

The World of Paul Slickey opened in Bournemouth on 14 April 1959—a
town described by the *Daily Mail* as the 'last resort of respectability',[26] and
by Osborne himself as 'a disastrous choice', on account of its 'wheelchair
garrison and huge Conservative catchment'. Even though there was a long-
standing agreement between critics and the Society of West End Managers
that a show transferring to London should not be criticised before it got
there, Osborne claimed in his account of the affair that 'Half of Fleet
Street' had descended on the south coast to observe; '"Hello, John," they
trilled, like men bellowing at a badger cornered in its set.'[27] They found
plenty to write about even before the opening:

> Under the discreet cover of Bournemouth's potted palms they stared
> yesterday at John Osborne's purple socks ... So how does he feel about
> trying out his show on the crusty upper crust out of which *Slickey* takes
> the mickey ...
>
> 'It is a bit ironic.' He said ... He spoke in little more than a whisper.
> Retired colonels and rich aunts, nodding in the afternoon sun, looked up
> sharply at the disturbance ...
>
> 'I don't know how these people will react to the show. This class does
> not just dominate Bournemouth. It dominates all England to a great
> extent—where British foreign policy has its roots ... I don't suppose *Slickey*
> will be their idea of a favourite evening in the theatre.[28]

He was not wrong.

'Vulgarity came to the Pavilion Theatre, Bournemouth last night,'
reported one newspaper the following day. It did concede that the opening
performance had received nine curtain calls, and that parts of the audience
had 'roared at many of the targets for Osborne's unerring satire'. But it also
noted that there had been plenty of walk outs and 'protesting cries of "No,
no, no" from the gallery'.[29] It was no surprise that complaints about the
production immediately started to arrive in the Lord Chamberlain's Office;
what was less predictable was that these should have been led by none other
than Emile Littler, the licensee of London's Palace Theatre where *Slickey*
was due shortly to arrive. Having attended a performance in Brighton,
Littler then took himself to St James's Palace, where he informed the Lord
Chamberlain that he 'had never seen anything so suggestive in the way of
business on the stage before', and that 'whole blocks of seats got up and
left and that there were boos and cat calls'. Littler warned the Office that

'He was very afraid that, when the play came on in London next week, there might be a riot', and registered his 'extreme apprehension that trouble and disturbances in the theatre may arise'. Plainly, Littler did not want the production anywhere near the Palace, and he was determined to use the Lord Chamberlain's Office as a way of escaping from his commitment. He said he found it 'difficult to believe that the whole of the business and dialogue has been approved by his Lordship', and he asked that someone from the Office should go to see a performance in Leeds, where the tour had now reached. 'As licensee and owner of the Palace Theatre I am naturally jealous of my reputation and do not wish to be hauled before the Justices at Bow Street should a breach occur.'

The Lord Chamberlain's staff were not mugs, and guessed what Littler was up to:

> He is the licensee of the theatre to which the play is coming and, I may be wrong, but I think that he is backing a loser and would like the Lord Chamberlain to step in and relieve him of the trouble ... He asked that someone from this Office should go to Leeds and see the play in the hope, I believe, that it would be banned. He does not, of course, understand the difficulties over this.

Yorkshire was a long way to go to spy on a performance. 'It would have been more to the point if Littler had raised all this after the disturbances in Brighton and not waited until it was half way through its time at Leeds,' wrote Gwatkin; 'I really don't see why we should send anyone up there.' However, Hill drafted a carefully threatening letter for Gwatkin to send to Osborne's solicitor. 'We are not on a good wicket, and I personally shouldn't like to write anything stronger,' he warned the Assistant Comptroller. Withdrawing a licence once it had been granted was only ever a last resort. On the other hand, if Littler was correct in his judgement that 'the production of the play will be very bad for the Lord Chamberlain's Office', then they needed to try and head it off, perhaps by persuading Osborne and his manager to tone down some of the action. Accordingly, Hill's letter drew attention to two facts:

> The first is that 'business' is an integral and censorable part of a play, and where of a significant nature requires to be described in the MS to become a licensed part of the piece. Action as against an unlicensed interpolation can, therefore, be taken with regard, for example, to indecent posturing that has not been described.
>
> In the second place it remains possible for the Lord Chamberlain to prohibit in toto a play so produced as to offend against 'good manners, decorum or the public peace' ... His Lordship makes no allegation with

regard to the current production of this play, but it has been seriously complained of.

The solicitor—sounding, it must be said, not unlike Osborne himself—was ready to take up the cudgels. He replied immediately to say his clients were 'only too well aware of the powers mentioned in the penultimate paragraph of your letter'. He assured the Lord Chamberlain that they 'would not in any event wish to be parties to a breach of the public peace', but observed that 'what constitutes good manners or decorum is surely a matter of upbringing, environment and religious and political beliefs and disbeliefs'. As he pointed out: 'his Lordship has surely already calmly and dispassionately considered the position and given a decision by issuing a licensed Script.' That, said Osborne's solicitor, should be the end of it:

> I cannot believe that having arrived at that decision (i.e. to license it) his Lordship is now contemplating yielding to persons whose susceptibilities may have been offended by reason of their own particular and often unpredictable views.
>
> With respect, I do not understand why, having licensed the Script, his Lordship should now, by reason of the penultimate paragraph of his letter, hold, as it were, the Sword of Damocles over my Clients' heads.

Meanwhile, Hill was despatched to Leeds to observe a performance of *The World of Paul Slickey*, in the company of a 'bluff North Country audience'. The secretary reported that only a couple of 'elderly and refined people' walked out, and the theatre manager claimed to have received no complaints. As to the on-stage action:

> In general the piece followed the allowed MS, and I record that despite the temptations offered by the theme, the male actors made no attempt to appear as 'pansies'. ... much of the posturing was erotic—but no worse than I have seen elsewhere without a complaint.

But not for the first time, Hill was astonished by some of what Heriot and Gwatkin had allowed to pass:

> When I read the ms before seeing the show I was much surprised that the Examiners had not remarked on the undernoted, and in the Play they were received as I had imagined would be the case. "The honourable Penelope Cumming (referring to orgasm)—well I suppose she's always worth a few inches ... A few lines later Miss Poppy Tupper materialises as that time dishonoured lady "Miss Pop it up her". This is all allowed in the ms.

The banned 'He's almost definitely queer' had been illegally reinstated, but Hill was shocked to find 'that we also allowed a reference to a Nottingham rubber goods factory', not to mention 'Michael's always been in favour of goats', despite its 'strong hint of bestiality'. Nor were these the worst examples: 'Again I must express to surprise that we passed "While his should-be dad fought heathen Turks/His Mum received the Royal Works".' The line resulted in 'a tremendous guffaw' and was, thought the secretary, 'rather too vivid a rendering of the physical sequence involved'. He also disliked 'The Income Tax Song':

> It may be my mind, but I found this whole song, sung mainly by a woman, rather peculiar. The word "screw" which is a euphemism for sexual intercourse is sung with tremendous emphasis and it is odd to use the word "rape" with regard to a man except in one unacceptable context. But it is all in the ms ...

There was 'a very equivocal sex changing theme' and plenty of music-hall innuendo and doubles entendres. 'Even I didn't think John Osborne was so barren a dramatist as to have to stoop to that,' he remarked of one example, and noted with disgust that 'Michael's invitation to Leslie to "take them off" is of course accepted by the audience as a reference to underclothes not spectacles.' He objected to a dance routine in which 'ladies waggled their pudenda', and the gag in which a man who has just been kicked by a horse begins to speak in a high-pitched voice: 'Michael is played by the biggest and most virile looking man on the Stage and he leaves no one in doubt as to what's happened to him.' Overall, this was not the kind of fare Hill expected to see in a respectable theatre: 'I found the piece itself a curious farrago of jokes about the sexual act and appendages that would have fitted very well in a tenth rate road show.' Nevertheless, his final judgement was that Osborne's play, as staged, was in 'horrible bad taste, but not corrupting or immoral', and there were therefore no grounds for endorsing Littler's request to cancel the licence. He did suggest the Lord Chamberlain should tell the management to 'clean up the bed scene' and 'require the omission of the dirty jokes I have mentioned'—even though the Office, 'by design or in innocence', had previously passed most of these. 'Otherwise I should be inclined to leave the public to register disapprobation of the whole of this shoddy piece,' he concluded.

On 4 May, Gwatkin wrote formally to Littler at the Palace Theatre, listing the departures from the licensed manuscript which had been detected and which must be rectified in future preformances:

> 1 Act 1, scene 2, page 9. The stage directions at the commencement of this scene were not observed. Jack is lying on top of Deirdre instead of

sitting on the bed. When he removes himself Jack's shirt is seen to be outside his trousers, and the later dialogue is punctuated by his stuffing it back. Deirdre's slip remains outside the whole time.

Requirement Jack and Deirdre must sit on the bed as allowed: they must not lie. Jack must be fully clothed, not en deshabille, and Deirdre's slip must be inside her breeches.

2 The banned line in the Income Tax Song 'He's almost definitely queer', is reinstated except for the word 'queer'.

Requirement This line must be totally eliminated and no substitute referring to the Income Tax Inspector as a homosexual would be allowed

3 In the next scene, a party of tourists enter including two school girls. A guide paws round the bottom of one of the school girl's skirts before throwing her over his shoulder and running off-stage rubbing his hands in anticipatory fashion.

Requirement This cannot be played until submitted and allowed.

4 Act 2, scene 9, page 8. According to the allowed ms this scene refers only to Father Evilgreene with small requiem chorus and mourning ballet. This scene has been expanded to include a representation of Lord Mortlake's wake as conducted by the 'Daily Racket', and the introduction of his coffin upon the stage. Whilst this scene will not necessarily be prohibited, it is illegal for it to be played until submitted in detail.

Requirement A full subscription and dialogue of this interpolation must be submitted at once.

Much more unusually—and with questionable legality—the letter required that certain lines which had originally been approved were now to be cut, on the grounds that they were being 'produced in such a manner as, in the Lord Chamberlain's opinion, to constitute an offence against decorum.' These were:

5 Act 1, Scene 4 The reference to the Honourable Penelope Cumming, 'well I suppose she's always worth a few inches' must be deleted. An acceptable substitute for 'inches' would be 'lines'.

6 Act 1, Scene 5 page 37 The line in the Income Tax Song "I'm sure he played with little boys" must be deleted.

7 Act 2, Scene 10, page 31 There must be no pause as indicated when Terry sings 'Before I make a pass I'll tell her that the sun shines out of her—face'. If the pause is retained this couplet will be unacceptable.

Osborne's solicitor also received a copy of the letter and the requirements and Littler smugly forwarded them to the show's producer—without mentioning that it was he who had instigated the inspection in the first place—with a demand that he should 'kindly comply with his Lordship's wishes' and confirm in writing 'that his Lordship's instructions have been faithfully carried out'. He also replied to Gwatkin:

> Thank you for sending me his Lordship's requirements regarding *Paul Slickey*.
>
> I have had these duplicated and sent to David Pelham, the producer responsible for presenting the show. I have also written to Mr Pelham as enclosed, and I am endeavouring to get a letter from him to say that all his Lordship's requirements have been observed.
>
> I am sorry that your Department has been put to such trouble regarding this play.

Osborne—presumably quite unaware of Littler's betrayal—was furious. On 5 May he wrote a letter of protest to the Lord Chamberlain, complaining that the list of requirements had arrived in the middle of his final dress rehearsal for the London opening. His passionate attack on the Lord Chamberlain's Office is reminiscent of some of Bernard Shaw's most anguished and affronted letters from half a century earlier

> I feel that in their dealings with myself, the behaviour of your Office has been determinedly frivolous and irresponsible, and because of my past public opposition to the function of your Office, it is difficult not to assume that the treatment I have received at your hands stems from a desire on your part to be wilfully obstructive.
>
> In view of the undoubted policy of liberalisation pursued by the Lord Chamberlain recently, I ask you, Sir Norman, does it not seem outrageous that I should be selected for this treatment? I am one of the few serious artists working in the English Theatre, with a serious reputation in almost every civilised country in the world, countries which have honoured me in various ways. And yet your Office seems intent on treating me as if I were the producer of a third rate nude revue.

In the margin beside this last sentence, someone in the Office added the comment: 'Which he is.' Osborne continued:

> What I find most bewildering is the lack of moral consistency and objectivity which seems to characterise your recent decisions—decisions which seem to be reversed and changed because of the whim of any twisted neurotic who cares to write to you and exploit his own particular weird sexual frustration or moral oddity. Do you honestly believe that the

proportion of those who walked out (not one in Leeds) or who wrote to you ... fairly represents decent and informed opinion? In paying attention to what is without question an infinitesimal and lunatic minority, you are doing a grave injustice, not only to myself, but to the general public and your own Office.

In view of your recent relaxation of policy, I cannot believe that you wish to encourage this appalling situation at the expense of the serious writer and his public.

With a hint of a threat, Osborne claimed to have been 'approached by most of the national newspapers for the right to print the entire text of my correspondence with your office'. But he concluded with an appeal:

I ask you most sincerely and urgently to be helpful and sympathetic ... your license should be a protection to me also. At present, I am not merely unprotected, but I am being exposed to every tide of individual malice, eccentricity and ignorance.

Gwatkin was completely unmoved by Osborne's attack.

I think it was Lord Alfred Douglas who sent a postcard to his father on which was written—'you silly little man'. That is what one would like to write in answer to this. But I suppose the best reply is a short acknowledgement.

For once, the Office held the upper hand and Gwatkin duly wrote to thank the playwright for his letter:

I have shown it to the Lord Chamberlain and he wishes me to say that there is no kind of prejudice against you in this Office, and to ask you to dismiss that from your mind. The Lord Chamberlain was sorry to have to interfere at all with your play but he has duties to perform which he endeavours to carry out with impartiality as well as liberality.[30]

The World of Paul Slickey opened at the Palace Theatre on 5 May. Among the celebrities in attendance were Noel Coward, Cecil Beaton, John Mills, the Profumos, Michael Foot, Aneurin Bevin (who sat next to Hill) and various members of the House of Lords. The performance was a disaster, with even John Gielgud apparently moved to boo during the curtain call. Coward subsequently referred to 'interminable long-winded scenes about nothing', and declared that 'Never in all my theatrical experience have I seen anything so appalling'.[31] Hill observed closely and noted that Osborne and his producer had still not done as they had been told.

Jack, for instance, still lay on top of Deirdre, (though Hill was relieved to see 'there was no motion'), and his shirt was still unbuttoned: 'The Lord Chamberlain's requirement was ignored, although there was no difficulty in complying with it.' Moreover, the performance now opened 'with a modern style National Anthem that was almost a parody, the last bar being almost and I am sure designedly a "razzberry"'. Nor had there been any amendment of the business involving the horse: 'For the record I enclose my opinion ... that it is unfitting for an actor to come on the stage say in a falsetto voice "I can't tell you what that bloody horse has done to me" and then crawl up the stairs clutching his testicles and shouting for "George".' However, observed Hill, 'Mr Heriot tells me emasculation is now allowed'.

Littler's case had been that the play might provoke serious disturbances. If there was ever danger of serious unrest in or outside a theatre, then the Lord Chamberlain had the right—even the responsibility—to close a production down. Accordingly, Hill gave almost as much attention to the audience as he did to the stage. 'The first half of the play was well received', he noted, 'and in the different atmosphere of a first night I found myself rather more impressed with it than I had been.' But the mood changed in the later scenes:

> Until now there had been a hostile element in the gallery, but the stalls had been interested—if not wholly so. From the moment of introduction of the sex-changing theme there was a most perceptible change in the atmosphere; the feeling of lively expectancy changed, heads turned round to look at the theatre instead of concentrating on the stage, and the gallery took up song again, although not too loudly. Jack's remark "This might be a pantomime" was greeted with prolonged and ironical laughter from the Gallery, and even an echo here and there in the stalls ...
>
> The piece drew to its close amidst occasional slight outbursts of misplaced laughter from the gallery, and dead silence from the stalls.

There was even, he suggested, an element of chaos near the end: 'The piece is so ill designed that the penultimate scene appears to be the final one, and at this point dozens of people sprinted for the exit,' he reported. 'The rest of us were very ready to go at the final curtain, although of course the audience was polite enough to give a vigorous round of applause to the actors for a gallant rear-guard action.' Overall, Hill's strong recommendation was that the Lord Chamberlain's Office could safely let well alone, trusting that Osborne's play would sink from its own weaknesses: 'if objectors are not silly enough to give it publicity by going to boo every night, I can't think this farrago of prejudices filing onto the stage by the scruff of the neck will last very long.' His call was to prove an accurate one.

As for the instances where the production was not yet following the Lord Chamberlain's requirements, Emile Littler could be relied on to deal with that. On 7 May, Littler—quite possibly acting on information received—sent a stern letter to the show's producer (which he copied to the Lord Chamberlain):

> We have now played two performances of *The World of Paul Slickey* and the Lord Chamberlain's requirements are not being wholly observed. Will you please give attention to the scene opening on the bed ... the two people are still lying on the bed, although his Lordship requests that they should only be sitting.
>
> It is very irksome for me to have to press for fulfilment for his Lordship's wishes in this manner, but the Licence for the Palace Theatre is in jeopardy and if anything happened to that after these warnings, my Company would have to sue you personally for damages.[32]

For once, the cards had fallen out well for the Lord Chamberlain's Office. With the headline '*Paul Slickey* puts the Establishment under the Knife', the left-wing *Tribune* was almost alone in acclaiming the piece, comparing it favourably to Brecht's *Threepenny Opera*.[33] Most critics slated the production. 'When one throws punches wildly one is sure to miss,' wrote Harold Clurman in the *Observer*, complaining that Osborne 'rides his hobby horse in all directions'.[34] *The Times* criticised 'Its extraordinary dullness', which it blamed on 'the manifest failure of Mr John Osborne to make up his mind what he wanted to do'.[35] As the curtain fell on the opening night 'to the most raucous note of displeasure heard in the West End since the war', Osborne himself fled; 'I must be the only playwright this century to have been pursued up a London street by an angry mob,' he later wrote.[36] The show closed after five weeks. 'I have had the worst notices since Judas Iscariot,' said Osborne in one newspaper interview. There was no question of his backing down publicly: 'not one daily paper critic has the intellectual equipment to assess my work or that of any other intelligent playwright,' he declared.[37] But from the Lord Chamberlain's rather smug perspective, one of the leaders of the rebels had been embarrassed, pushed back firmly in his place, and reminded who was in charge.

The Art of Improvisation

One of the things to emerge from the prosecution of Theatre Workshop for including unlicensed material in their performance of *You Won't Always Be On Top* was that the practice of changing a script was not as unusual as the staff at St James's Palace allowed themselves to think. In the 1940s, Lord Cromer had stirred up a hornet's nest by threatening to impose an absolute ban on comedians reworking their gags or responding to audiences. Technically, such practices were against the requirement of the Theatres Act, since this stipulated that anything said on stage must previously have been approved by the Lord Chamberlain. In 1957, Michael Flanders wrote to the Lord Chamberlain's Office with a query about his show with Donald Swann, *At the Drop of a Hat*: 'We have the opportunity to include topical references or fragments in song ... How do we stand with things like that?' asked Flanders; 'Is it possible for me to give an undertaking to avoid certain subjects and obey certain rules?' In reply, he was simply told that 'His Lordship cannot, of course, agree to waive compliance with an Act of Parliament', and that anything included in the act 'must, therefore, receive prior sanction'.[38] Better, perhaps, not to have asked. The admission under oath in 1958 by someone as eminent as Michael Redgrave that actors did not always stick to the script had caused considerable embarrassment for the Censorship. The alternative strategy to Flanders's commendable honesty was obviously to go ahead and hope no-one noticed.

In January 1959, the innovative young director Stephen Joseph wrote to the Lord Chamberlain's Office to ask whether he could submit 'the synopsis for an improvisation that we want to present during our summer season at the Library Theatre in Scarborough'. He explained the basis of the experiment in more detail:

> Perhaps I should say that the company has been functioning for some time, and that we have been feeling our way towards a more creative form of presentation. The next step we wish to take is this—of improvisation from a synopsis. You will see from the form of the synopsis that we want to keep the play flexible and that there will never be any fixed script. It is our intention to use this synopsis for a full length play. If it succeeds we shall want to do further improvisations ...
>
> I should be grateful for your comments.

When they came, he probably wasn't. 'Logically,' mused Heriot, 'the Lord Chamberlain can hardly license a play that doesn't exist.' He queried whether it might be possible to claim that 'this sort of entertainment' somehow fell outside the Lord Chamberlain's jurisdiction, thus handing over responsibility to the local authority. But Hill, the fount of technical knowledge at St James's Palace, advised that this would be a breach of the legal requirements which the Lord Chamberlain was obliged to observe. Moreover, it would open a door which could never again be closed, since in effect, any control of the stage would be sacrificed:

> The Lord Chamberlain cannot vary the interpretation of the Act to suit his, or anyone else's convenience. If he decides in this case that the

requirement that 'one copy of every new stage play shall be submitted' is met by the provision of a synopsis, and that improvisation is permissible, he will not be able to confine his decision to such plays as he thinks fit.

The opening he provides will be seized with both hands by the producers of all 'advanced' or 'dubious' plays who will submit a synopsis and achieve virtual elimination of the Censorship.

I suggest that the only possible answer to this request is that it is legally impermissible, and I think the letter should be couched in the strongest terms possible, to ensure that the project is abandoned. If it is continued with, I think we should have to prosecute, and I foresee an unpleasant case.

Gwatkin—who happened to be in the middle of discussions with the Windmill over a mysteriously vanishing punctuation mark from the line 'I know you like Revue boys'—confirmed that 'Even the addition of a comma can alter the meaning of a sentence'. He agreed that if the Lord Chamberlain abnegated his responsibility to license or censor every single word of a play, it would become 'legally possible for any amount of unlicensed material to be included' in any performance. As he pointed out, 'the censorship would be virtually dead'.

Yet the Office had also been made aware that improvisation had a long and (at least partly) respectable history, and the regret expressed in Gwatkin's reply to Joseph may well have been (at least partly) sincere. However, the Assistant Comptroller left no room for doubt or argument that it was an art form which could have no place in public theatres in Britain:

Lord Scarbrough has asked me to express to you his thanks for the responsible way in which you have represented to him the project you have for establishing in this country the art of the improvisatore.

The Lord Chamberlain understands that this form of entertainment represents an honourable tradition of the stage stemming at least from the Commedia dell Arte. He is not, therefore, predisposed against it, and in the normal course he would be glad to see if there were any way in which you could be accommodated.

Unfortunately, his Lordship has no doubt that since 1737 ... such entertainment has been illegal in this country. The Theatres Act 1843 ... stipulates that one copy of every new stage play, and of every new act, scene or other part added thereto, must be submitted, before production, to the Lord Chamberlain, if it is to be produced and acted 'for hire'. The Courts have, on many occasions, endorsed the fact that a 'copy' of a stage play comprises the entire dialogue and descriptions of significant action or 'business'. You will understand from this that the substitution of a synopsis for the full MS is not compliance with the Act.

The Lord Chamberlain has no power whatever to dispense with a

Statute, either entirely, or in favour of an individual producer. He is, in consequence, legally bound to demand from you the full dialogue and descriptions of allied action of any play you propose to stage 'for hire'; that is, where the audience pays to come in, either directly or in some indirect manner.

I fear that this will be a big disappointment for you, since I can, in effect, do nothing but confirm that, unless you produce your improvisations in circumstances where the Theatres Act 1843 does not apply, you will be breaking the law.[39]

The issue of improvisation on stage was another challenge which would resurface during the 1960s.

Society at War

How far it was helpful or appropriate to apply the 'angry young man' tag to Osborne and other Royal Court writers is debatable, but there was plenty of anger and protest around in 1959—both on the stage and at St James's Palace. One play which provoked the ire of Readers and other staff was André Davis's *Four Men*, which centred on a (successful) plan by four young men to assassinate the British prime minister, each for a different reason and from contrasting political perspectives. Written in a language which integrates Shakespearean references ('Does your Prime Minister offend you? Then pluck him out!'[40]) with contemporary slang, Davis's play was a runner up in Kenneth Tynan's New Playwriting competition in the *Observer* newspaper. At its best it almost touches on the sort of style which writers such as Howard Brenton would develop nearly a decade later.

> —Was it not a lovely shot? Like the stag at water I caught him. Did you see it? Tick! goes the finger and the gun swells and the bullet spins like this room spins and it drifts across the air like a bee and pitches on his bent head. Then, so sensitive, it touches with its curling tongue and finds its little hole and so crawls in to feed.
> —So much for Buckingham.[41]

It was certainly enough to stir up the knights and brigadiers in the Mall:

> This play, for production by what I take to be a far Left-Wing amateur group in Wolverhampton, represents about the only dramatic phenomenon that I have not before encountered in the nine hundred and forty-nine plays on which I have reported in the past six years. It appears to me to be a direct incitement to murder the prime minister, identified in everything but name as Mr MacMillan on page 7.

Understandably, this was too much for Troubridge:

> inasmuch as the murder of such a Conservative Prime Minister of Britain
> by four young men, in the interests of the prevention of an atomic war,
> by shooting him at night with a dum-dum bullet through the window of
> his country-house dining room, is the central incident of the play, and the
> young men, though at the end about to be arrested, are held up as heroes,
> especially the avowed Communist of the four ... it may be surmised that
> I do not intend to recommend the play.

The play made no attempt to disguise its subject through the kind of
metaphor which sometimes allowed the Censorship to turn a blind eye to
political comment:

> If an unspecified Right-Wing Prime Minister in Ruritania were concerned,
> that would be a different matter, but this is Britain, and in my view the
> mentions of Suez and the like on page 7 clearly indicate Mr MacMillan.

Gwatkin was equally provoked: 'I have read through this and my blood-
pressure has risen several counts.' However, he was uncertain how seriously
to take it. 'To me it is the pretentious hot-air of a lot of inferiority
complexes,' he mused; 'Nevertheless they do go out to bump-off poor
Harold Macmillan.' In the end, he thought it might be better to ignore it
and take the risk: 'I can't believe that anyone listening to this sort of verbal
looseness ... will be encouraged to do so,' he decided; 'and I would doubt
the advisability of paying them the compliment and attendant publicity of
banning this stuff.'

Scarbrough accepted the advice of his Assistant Comptroller

> I have read through this play. I do not think this can be regarded as
> incitement to murder the present Prime Minister: nor do I feel that it
> will lead to a breach of the peace. I would expect it to attract very little
> attention and think it would be a mistake to give it the attention that
> banning would give.

The Office therefore confined itself to a small number of specific cuts.
Macmillan could be murdered in Wolverhampton; one wonders whether
the Lord Chamberlain would have been quite so sanguine if the script had
been submitted by the Royal Court.[42]

If anything, Troubridge was even more incensed by the politics of *Cloud
Over the Morning*:

> This is a horrible little one act play, which I do not think should

be disseminated to unsuspecting Amateurs over the famous imprint of Samuel French. Under cover of a slimy Foreword of the 'We all want Peace don't we?' type, it traduces the British forces in Cyprus, accusing them of torture and murder in the best style of Mrs. Barbara Castle, and glorifying a gang of armed Greek-Cypriot adolescents.

I hold the view that in the Theatre the Services are entitled to look to the Lord Chamberlain for protection, and I remember that a few years since his lordship [sic] accepted this view when a Communist play traduced our forces in Malaya.

Scarbrough remained calm about it. 'The play about Malaya was much worse than this and was presented for a licence at a time when British troops were operating,' he wrote; 'That is not the case with this play and it seems a degree or two less objectionable.'[43] The licence was issued without endorsements.

The view of contemporary British society depicted in John McGrath's *Why the Chicken* was another sign of the times, and almost equally disturbing. 'This is a quite terrifying little play to be given as part of the "fringe" of the Edinburgh Festival,' wrote Troubridge; 'It delineates the "beat" generation of young people in this country, seen at their worst.' Submitted by the Oxford Theatre Company in July 1959, McGrath's play centred on the disaffection and alienation to be found among those attending a youth club at the community centre of a Welsh new town:

Deprived by the transfer of such roots as they had struck in their towns of origin, they are destructive, bored, ungrateful and awaiting in spiritual insecurity the coming of the inevitable H-bomb. They do not know what they want, but they know what they don't want, which is everything offered them.

However, the only intervention the Office felt able to make was in relation to some of the language: 'though doubtless typical of their speech,' wrote Troubridge 'it will not do.' Subject to appropriate amendments, he recommended the script for licence 'with horror'. Gwatkin endorsed his views: 'One can only hope that, by its sheer beastliness, this play can do no harm.' McGrath, meanwhile, objected to the effect and the implication of the changes he had been asked to make. To censor the language and voice was to censor the people who spoke in it:

The author is particularly concerned that when writing dialogue for these characters on the stage that it should appear as natural and realistic as possible and that nothing should be made to sound false as coming from a particular speaker. I am sure you will agree that if we submit paraphrases this quality may be lacking and it would we feel be ruinous to the mood of our play.

But the management had no option other than to submit substitutions:

For 'sod' read 'man'
For 'your face and my backside' substitute 'your face and a cow's rear end'
For 'piss off before you wet yourself' substitute 'widdle off before you wet yourself' ...
Omit 'tease the trousers off him' and 'rubbing herself up against them', substitute 'close like' ...
For 'Now you two that's not allowed in public' substitute 'Now then you two'.[44]

In August, came John Arden's epic anti-war play, *Serjeant Musgrave's Dance*: 'This is another pretty queer affair that the English Stage Company have got hold of,' wrote Troubridge. It was described, he said 'as an "Un-Historical Parable"', and he tried to explain what this might mean:

The 'Un-Historical' part comes from it being set 'in the middle of Queen Victoria's reign' ... as to the Parable, solving the parables of Sloane Square is dodgy work, but I should say the moral is the logical, extreme pacifist one that even conditions so evil as to appear to justify the use of force for their alteration, can never be destroyed satisfactorily by force, which is a self-stultifying remedy.

Again, the Censorship restricted its intervention to such words and phrases as 'pissed', 'dirty turd', 'bare arsed' and 'randy'. Again, the playwright objected to the effect and implications of this: 'Mr Arden feels that these phrases are basically Psychological rather than Physiological,' wrote the Royal Court on his behalf; 'It is very important to him that the spirit of the play is not jaundiced by the deletion of this type of imagery and I can assure you that there will be no pornographic interpretation.' A compromise was reluctantly negotiated on both sides.[45]

The Language of Television

In October, 'Stick your bloody pity' was cut from Willis Hall's *A Glimpse of the Sea* ('I find this expression intolerable from a woman'),[46] which was being staged at the Lyric Hammersmith on a double bill with the same playwright's *Last Day in Dreamland*. The latter had previously been shown on television, creating a new problem for the Office, as the Reader noted:

This is the first time I have seen an actual television script submitted for licence, a novelty in which there are implications, as ten million people have already heard all these words, though not, of course, in the collective juxtaposition of a thousand people in a theatre audience. However, this is not exactly my concern.

Three lines were banned—'stick 'em', 'stick it', and 'got a bird wants laying'—but Hall asked his solicitor, Oscar Beuselinck (who was also John Osborne's solicitor) to pursue the case. He did so, with enthusiasm:

> My Client is deeply disappointed and is at a loss to understand why your Office desires the deletions requested. In this respect he feel fortified by the fact that no less an august body than the British Broadcasting Corporation has allowed the words of which you seek deletion, and apparently no complaints or protests were made thereafter.
>
> In these circumstances if, upon reflection, you would confirm that you are prepared to accept the script as written or, if not, let me have more detailed reasons for your objections.

Gwatkin explained: 'The objection is to "stick", and the accepted place where it is stuck,' while '"Got a bird wants laying" is obvious and offensive.' He also reiterated the old argument that 'what might be said or pictured on the air becomes more personal and embarrassing when it is said by live actors playing to a mixed audience of all ages in a theatre'. But Beuselinck did not give in so easily, and was, at the very least, determined to embarrass the Censors:

> I spent some six years, as did my Client, in the Forces and our understanding of this expression was that one was told to 'stick something on the wall'.
>
> Similar remarks apply to the expressions 'stick 'em' and 'stick it' in *The Last Day In Dreamland*. The author here is drawing on his experiences in real life and he cannot agree and, with respect, I too find it difficult to agree that 'stick 'em' and 'stick it' are other than well-known expressions in common use; and, in ordinary circles, that use does not necessarily mean, except to people of an exceptional turn of mind, that anything is to be stuck in any place in preference to the wall aforementioned. Surely an expression which has a pretty common meaning is not to be banned because people with an exceptionally dirty turn of mind may know of a paraphrase of it.
>
> In these circumstances I am again instructed to ask that the request for the deletion of these words be withdrawn.
>
> With regard to the expression 'Got a bird wants laying', it is conceded that these words are intended to convey that the person in question is

going away for an immoral purpose. The way the matter here has been put appears to be much less offensive than the way it has often been put in other plays which have been approved by your department. Would you prefer the substitution of an expression such as, 'I am going away for an immoral weekend' or 'A dirty weekend?' If not, perhaps you would let me know how your office would suggest that an expression like this be framed.

With regard to the last paragraph of your letter, my Client is surprised that the Lord Chamberlain should appear to be more strict in his censorship than the BBC or should think, as is implicit in your letter, that an audience in a theatre is more varied than the audience of the average television play.

Gwatkin refused to show embarrassment or to concede: 'I don't think that we are very interested in the naïve beliefs of Oscar Beuselinck or his client,' he noted, dismissively; 'they didn't learn much in that line during their war service!' He advised Scarbrough that 'we should stick to our rule', and that any concession should be minimal: 'I think we should be firm about the "laying" but let them have a "dirty weekend".'[47]

An Era Ends

By the autumn of 1959, the Lord Chamberlain's Office seemed almost ready to throw in the towel. 'Don't blame us,' seemed to be the message, 'there's nothing we can do.' Considerable hostility was generated by *The World of Suzie Wong*, a tragic and cynical tale centred on characters who work in and frequent a Hong Kong brothel. Described by the Reader as the latest manifestation of 'that ever popular stage story, the tart with a heart of gold', the play showed a young and impoverished would-be artist from England—the son of a wealthy father—who falls in love with a prostitute, and wants to marry her, even though she already has a child whom she must continue to support in the only way open to her:

SUZY: You want your wife to go upstairs with sailors?
ROBERT: But, Suzy, if we were *married*.
SUZY: Oh, sure! If we were married that changes everything! Like in a fairy story! And happy ever after! You go on become great painter—I give up my job and become good wife!—and my baby? Does the god of Marriage say, 'Good, now I have got them married. Now I will give them all the money they need. I will give them food. And that baby—oh, yes—I will take care of him! I will make him grow up into a fine, healthy man—I will send him to Oxford—make him great movie star. Oh nothing too good for that baby now I have got them married.'—I think not! I think the god of Marriage sit back and laugh and laugh and laugh how he has fooled us![48]

Even the management professed surprise at the ease with which a licence was issued:

> Donald Albery, who is bringing the play over, says: 'A few years ago a script as down to earth as this would have been cut to ribbons. Now it has come back from the censors virtually intact, with an understandable request that we treat the more amorous scenes with discretion.'

Both the Home Office and St James's Palace received some forceful objections: 'How can the British government permit such a play to be produced?' demanded one correspondent. An Officer from the Royal Navy expressed himself

> disgusted and shocked to find that the play was a crude and vulgar portrayal of inebriated sailors and others in an Eastern Brothel, and astonished that your department had passed it for exhibition ... especially at this time when the Government has recently passed a measure to endeavour to curb the exhibition of prostitution in the streets.

It was, said the Officer,

> surprising that a Public Department intended to protect to some extent the mind of the public from immorality and pornography, should pass so degrading a play ... It is scarcely to be wondered at that morality in the Country and in London in particular has dropped to such a low level, when a subject such as this is shown to thousands of people of all ages and treated as entertainment.

'The old sea dog is incensed!' wrote someone at St James's disparagingly in the margin of the above letter, and the Office took comfort in the fact that such voices were few in number: 'two hundred and eighty thousand three hundred and seventy-three people have so far seen the play, and it is fair to mention that we have had only one or two complaints.'

Gwatkin's reply to another objection suggests that the Office was all but ready to wash his hands of the whole business:

> The Lord Chamberlain's control over plays has necessarily to be exercised in the light of contemporary thought, speech and literature. The theatre is a mirror of its period, thus the theatre of Tudor times was very down to earth, that of the Stuarts frankly bawdy and of the early Victorian age sanctimonious.
>
> Things are spoken of in mixed company these days which were

not mentioned when I was a young man. Books leave nothing to the imagination.

He had used the same 'mirror' argument in his defence of Peter Wildeblood's musical, *The Crooked Mile*:

> The milieu of the play is of low life in Soho with coarse language with much prison and gutter slang, but, after all, life is not very elevated in Soho. To have cleaned up the play to any greater extent would have made the performance entirely out of character.

The woman who sent in the *Daily Mail* article lamenting the sorry and vulgar state of British theatre which Wildeblood's script typified insisted that the Lord Chamberlain's brief 'carries a real obligation to elevate public entertainment rather than the reverse'. Gwatkin refuted this. He would act, now, only 'if the production is calculated to conduce to crime or vice or if it is flagrantly indecent'. The problem, explained the Assistant Comptroller, lay with audience taste.

> The unfortunate fact remains that so long as the theatre going public patronises these crude plays they will continue.
> ... One day perhaps the public will revolt against this type of entertainment ... in the mean time all the censorship can do is to keep these productions within reasonable and contemporary bounds.[49]

Any hope, then, lay with the possibility of a return to the values of a different age:

> These things seem to go in cycles and there are signs that the general public is getting tired of plays of an unpleasant type. When the public no longer patronizes very strong plays producers will cease to put them on.[50]

To be fair to the *Daily Mail*, Cecil Wilson's attitude to what he called 'the earthy new trend' in contemporary theatre was by no means wholly negative: 'I welcome this bold new breakaway from tinsel and tea cups,' he concluded; 'Even if it does curb Aunt Edna's playgoing.'[51] However, a letter from a 'Doctor's Wife' published in response in November 1959 suggested it was not so much Aunt Edna that society should be worrying about, but her young nephews and nieces:

> it cannot be good for those just on the threshold of life to have things like prostitution, homosexuality and immoral living rammed down their throats at every turn.

She went on:

> The trend is quite spoiling family theatre-going as we used to know
> it. Where are our old heroes, the Scarlet Pimpernel, Bulldog Drummond,
> Beau Geste, and the like? They are still popular with book-lovers, why
> not in the theatre?
> There is so much that is beautiful and worth while in the world today:
> let us hold on to it and let our children enjoy it, too, not spoil things for
> them by pandering to these perverted playwrights.[52]

The real question, then, as the first decade of the new, golden Elizabethan
age drew to a close, was 'Where Can We Take Our Teenagers'. Not, for
the doctor's wife, at least, into the 1960s.

Sometimes, altogether too much was expected of the Lord Chamberlain
in terms of his power to halt the collapse in moral standards which others
believed to be taking place. In November 1959, the Office received a
distraught letter from 'an ordinary housewife with 3 children to provide
for', complaining that her marriage was in danger, because her husband
had taken to frequenting the strip tease clubs which had become a regular
feature of the entertainment scene: 'I used to be happy, have a good
husband, but since the advent of strip-tease, no more,' she wrote, 'and
I'm sure there must be hundreds of women like myself in the same mind.'
She wanted the Lord Chamberlain take preventative action: 'I don't call
them clubs that operate in Soho, etc. They are just dens of vice which
should be closed.' The Assistant Comptroller expressed sympathy: 'I am
very grieved to hear of your unhappiness,' he told her; 'the more so in that
there is nothing this Office can do in the matter.'[53] As Gwatkin explained,
such clubs—like television and cinema—were completely outside the Lord
Chamberlain's authority.

On 29 December, Troubridge reported on the latest script sent in by the
Royal Court, *The Lily White Boys*. It was not the first time he had read the
play, an earlier version of the text having been licensed in 1958 for production 'in the unlikely setting of a Shrewsbury summer festival'. Troubridge
had disliked its politics and its tone even then, describing it as 'A highly
satirical, "off-beat", Court Theatre type of piece', which appeared to side
with a group of Teddy Boys in a series of confrontations with various
respectable institutions of society, 'all of which are blisteringly attacked'.
The new version, with Brechtian songs by the poet Christopher Logue,
only made things worse. The outcome, said the Reader, was 'a modern
tough British musical of what I may venture to christen the "Got your cosh,
tosh" school'. He half-heartedly recommended that some of the language
might be toned down, but rather doubted whether it was worth it, since

'words like "sod" and "arse" are among the normal flowers of speech in the milieu that is exhibited'. Until recently, there would have been no place on the British stage for savage mockery of the establishment—but the boundaries were no longer secure, and the rules were being torn up. 'Perhaps nowadays it is permissible to suggest widespread corruption of the judicature and magistracy (three times) but at least the Lord Chamberlain should consider it,' suggested the Reader, tentatively. Scarbrough did, and chose not to intervene. Overall, almost in spite of himself, and 'with middle aged horror', Troubridge realised he had no option other than to advocate that the play should be approved. He could hardly take in where society had come to. Or what the Censorship was now resigned to accepting:

> It is a curious reflection upon the intentions of the legislators of 1843 that, under present circumstances, I am about to recommend for licence, with a few verbal alterations, a play that is not only revolutionary, but indeed anarchistic in what it conveys to a Sloane Square audience, since it attacks and propounds by jeers the tearing down of everything, right, left and centre.[54]

The outlook for Aunt Edna was bleak.

Afterword

Did censorship matter during the 1950s? Looking back without anger across a distance of fifty years or so, Arnold Wesker asserted recently that 'The Lord Chamberlain didn't inhibit substance'. As evidence, he cites—almost with surprise that it should have been so—the fact that he was permitted to include among the characters in his 1958 play *Chicken Soup With Barley* 'a sympathetic portrait of a communist mother'. To Wesker, the Lord Chamberlain 'was merely an irritant who forbade swear words and blasphemous expletives'.[1] By contrast, Sir Peter Hall (in a personal interview with the author) suggests that the battle to present plays as their authors intended and to find ways around the ideological prejudices of St James's Palace dominated much of his thinking through the fifties and into the sixties. Beneath the superficially genteel processes of control, he says, the boot of the state remained ready and waiting to be called upon if required.[2] Wesker's experience is largely borne out in the Office's response to Bertolt Brecht; almost without exception, it was Brecht's 'vulgarities' rather than his politics which concerned them. And while the first public performances in English of *Waiting for Godot* and *Endgame* may have been delayed a few months, and the texts suffered a handful of cuts, these probably seem trivial—not to say comic—and can hardly be said to have significantly undermined the power or the meaning of the plays, or hindered their long-term reputation and survival. As we have seen, the action taken by the Watergate Theatre and the Comedy Theatre meant that plays by Tennessee Williams and Arthur Miller could be seen uncut by anybody who really wanted to see them, even in the face of the Lord Chamberlain's opposition. Moreover, while direct reference to homosexuals and homosexuality was forbidden for much of the decade, by the end of it these too could be included with impunity. Well, depending, of course, on what it was that you wanted to say.

Yet the evidence I have put forward in this volume surely suggests that Wesker's claim—while doubtless a fair reflection of his own experience—is overly complacent. Possibly Hall's memory of the iron boot may seem an exaggeration, but it in turn reflects what he perceived. And, as a director,

Hall had considerably more encounters with the Lord Chamberlain than Wesker did. For all that it may have been weakened and evaded and laughed at and undermined, for all that snooks may have been cocked at it, censorship mattered in the 1950s—and it would matter in the 1960s as well.

Early in the new decade, the Lord Chamberlain would receive an anxious letter from two genuine Aunt Ednas, one of them an MBE, who had just returned from living abroad to find themselves shocked by the standards of morality they perceived at home:

> The sights we have seen in London, and the general feeling of obscenity which is observed in every walk of life and shown up in our newspapers would never be tolerated in the so called undeveloped and incivilised [sic] parts of the world. Our literature, films, plays, posters, our talk of legalized abortion, our talk of legalized homosexuality, our lack of modesty are the gifts we hand to our youth, and are their heritage …
>
> There was a period at which the world looked to England for guidance in moral and spiritual fields—I am afraid that now they look in vain.

And theatre, they informed the Earl of Scarbrough, exemplified the problem: 'Sex seems to obsess most of the plays—i.e. one which was recently reviewed in our papers dealing obscenely with sex and homosexuality in a block of flats.' Worst of all, the evils they witnessed seemed to be 'unchecked and without protest from those in authority whose slackness is frightening'.

The Assistant Comptroller sent the ladies a courteous but pointed reply, suggesting that 'if you actually see the plays instead of reading reviews of them', it would become evident that 'most are not so offensive as they are made to appear'. He told them that while 'His Lordship understands your reaction to much of what you see and hear about you', it was simply not practical politics 'to inflict a code of morals upon a nation by law or by force'. The only contribution that St James's Palace could realistically be expected to make was to prevent theatre from becoming a primary instigator of any moral decline: 'So far as stage plays are concerned,' wrote Gwatkin, 'it has been his Lordship's endeavour to ensure that these are not in the van of any movement of the kind to which you refer.' One of the problems the Lord Chamberlain's Office would face over the next few years was that 'in the van'—challenging the political and cultural establishment—was precisely where an increasing number of playwrights and directors would seek to locate themselves. The seeds of his fate as theatre censor had been well and truly sown in the 1950s. But there would be some bloody battles before he could be put out of his misery, and before playwrights and directors would at last find themselves free of his interference.

The two worried ladies had concluded their letter to the Lord Chamberlain by expressing deep concern about what the future might hold, and inviting him to speculate: 'We do say this in all sincerity and with the deepest anxiety,' they wrote, '—WHERE and WHAT NEXT???"[3] The final volume of this history will reveal some answers to their questions.

Biographies

This section offers brief biographies of the principal people working for or on behalf of the Lord Chamberlain's Office, and involved in issues of theatre licensing and censorship during the 1950s:

Lord Chamberlain: Roger Lumley, the 11th Earl of Scarbrough, KG, GCSI, GCIE, GCVO, PC, DL

Scarbrough was born in 1896 and died in 1969. He was Lord Chamberlain from 1952 to 1963.

Son of Brigadier General Osbert Lumley, Roger Lumley was educated at Eton, Sandhurst and Oxford University. He served in the First World War with the eleventh Hussars, and was then elected to Parliament in 1922 as a Conservative MP. In the same year he married Katherine Isobel McEwen. He represented Hull East until 1929, and then York from 1931 to 1937, serving as Parliamentary Private Secretary to William Ormsby-Gore, to Sir Austen Chamberlain and to Anthony Eden (Colonial, Foreign and Home Secretaries). In 1937 he was appointed Governor of Bombay, serving until 1943. According to his obituary in *The Times*, 'He made such an impression there that he was often spoken of as a potential viceroy'. But, as the newspaper notes, 'This high responsibility did not come his way'.[1]

Upon his return from India, Lumley served as an acting Major-General during World War II. Following the war, he continued his connections with the Army, as an honorary colonel. In 1945 he served briefly as Parliamentary Under-Secretary for India and Burma, and in the same year he succeeded to the Earldom of Scarbrough, following the death of his uncle. Scarbrough retained some connections with India; he was President of the East Indian Association of the Royal Asiatic Society and of the Central Asian Society, and from 1951 to 1956 was Chair of the governing body of the School of Oriental and African Studies at London University. In 1956 he went as a special ambassador to the coronation of the King of Nepal.

Scarbrough was made a Knight of the Garter in 1948. He was also Chancellor of the University of Durham from 1958 to 1969. On his retirement in 1963, he became a Permanent Lord in Waiting to the Queen. As a Freemason he was Grand Master of the United Grand Lodge of England, and was also Lord Lieutenant of the West Riding of Yorkshire and the first High Steward of York Minster. He died in June 1969 at his home near Rotherham.

Comptroller of the Lord Chamberlain's Office: Terence Edmund Gascoigne Nugent

Born in August 1895, died in April 1973. Nugent was Comptroller of the Lord Chamberlain's Office from 1936 to 1960.

Nugent was educated at Eton College and Sandhurst. Five generations of his family had served in the Grenadiers, and he joined the Irish Guards in 1914 and fought in the First World War. He was wounded in 1917, and received the Military Cross. He was invested as a member of the Royal Victorian Order (1927), and served as Equerry to The Duke of York from 1927 to 1937, accompanying him on trips overseas. He was also Brigade Major of the Brigade Guards from 1929 to 1933. In 1935 Nugent married Rosalie Heathcote-Drummond-Willoughby, and in 1936 he became a Lieutenant-Colonel. He was invested as a Commander in the Royal Victorian Order in 1937, as a Knight Commander in 1945, and as a Knight Grand Cross in 1952. He held the office of Extra Equerry to King George VI between 1937 and 1952, and to Queen Elizabeth II between 1952 and 1973. In 1960 Nugent received the award of Grand Officer, Legion of Honour, and was created 1st Baron Nugent, of West Harling, Norfolk. From 1960 until his death in 1973, he was Permanent Lord-in-Waiting. Nugent was a lover of cricket and played for the 1st XI at Eton and later for the Duke of Norfolk's XI at Arundel. In 1966 was made President of the MCC. Nugent had no children, and his barony died with him.

There follows part of the obituary for Nugent as published in *The Times* in April 1973 under the headline: 'An Admired Court figure':

> ... He combined the style of an Ouida Guards officer with a spontaneous kindliness and infectious sense of humour that made him welcome in all the many and varied circles in which he moved. 'Tim' Nugent's tall, elegant figure passed easily from attendance at Court to the company of music-hall artists, from the Long Room at Lords to the Turf Club, and wherever he found himself he was among friends. His wide knowledge of the world, capacity for hard work, common sense and tact enabled him to succeed in several difficult roles ...

His letters were models of resourcefulness and tact. He would handle an awkward subject with honesty and candour and his sincerity was so transparent that it never gave offence. His conversation always added to the gaiety of a company, large or small. The love of cricket he had never lost since his Eton days was rewarded when, to his great delight, he was made President of the MCC.

Nugent is also praised for efficient organisation of Buckingham Palace Garden Parties and other court events during his time as Comptroller in the Lord Chamberlain's Office: 'The ordering of all official functions fell to him and the silken ease for which they were renowned owed much to his cool judgment and the affection in which he was held.' Turning to his duties in relation to theatre, the obituary declares that Nugent

> managed the delicate and controversial conduct of stage censorship with consummate skill. Harbingers of the permissive society railed against the anomaly of a retired officer of Foot Guards seated in St James's Palace, blue-pencilling theatrical scripts. But the theatre people liked and trusted him and the BBC, over which he had no jurisdiction, often unofficially consulted him. A keen amateur both of straight plays and musical shows, he cut only with reluctance what he knew would be regarded as over the odds by public opinion of the day. Tolerant he was, but hard to fool. When he had passed a script so blameless that it might have been read aloud at a church assembly, he was liable to check on the performance after some weeks when it was being played on a Saturday night in the provinces, remote from St James's Palace.[2]

A couple of weeks later, *The Times* published another remarkably fulsome accolade, written by Richard Attenborough and Laurence Olivier. They drew attention to Nugent's 'immense contribution to the welfare of the members of our profession', citing his involvement as 'the longest serving council member of the London Academy of Music and Dramatic Art' and on the council of the Royal Academy of Dramatic Art, as well as his tenure as chair of the Combined Theatrical Charities Appeal Council since its establishment in 1965. 'Closest to his heart,' they suggested, had been his role held since 1955 as President of the King George's Pension Fund for Actors and Actresses—'a position which brought him into very personal contact with so many people in the theatre for whom he had such a very deep and lasting affection.' According to Attenborough and Olivier, 'mere statistics could never do justice to Tim Nugent's endeavours' and 'the debt of gratitude owed to him by so many' was 'quite simply, incalculable'. Indeed, they claim that Nugent was widely regarded 'as the most beloved man of the theatre who was not actually a part of the theatre'. Their tribute concludes:

> It is with a feeling of profound joy that we who experienced the inspiration generated by his love of his fellow men and women are able to recall his limitless enthusiasm, warmth and humour and, above all, his humanity. In short, Tim Nugent was, for so many of us, the epitome of the term, a gentle man: one whose like it is difficult to contemplate ever encountering again.[3]

It is safe to say that not all playwrights, actors and directors working in the fifties and sixties would have fully subscribed to the tone or sentiments of such compliments.

Assistant Comptroller of the Lord Chamberlain's Office: Brigadier Sir Norman Wilmshurst Gwatkin

Born August 1899, died July 1971. Gwatkin was Assistant Comptroller in the Lord Chamberlain's Office from 1936 to 1960, and then Comptroller from 1960 until 1964.

Gwatkin was educated at Clifton College, Bristol and the Royal Military College at Sandhurst, and was then commissioned in 1918, in the service of the Coldstream Guards. He was invested as a Member of the Royal Victorian Order in 1937, as a Commander in 1946, and as a Knight Grand Cross in 1963, and received the award of Companion, Distinguished Service Order in 1944. He began the war as a Major and ended it commanding a brigade in the Guards Armoured Division. He was awarded a DSO for his services here. After the war, he held the office of Extra Equerry to King George VI between 1950 and 1952, and to Queen Elizabeth II between 1952 and 1971. He was Secretary and Registrar of the Order of Merit between 1963 and 1971, and was invested as a Knight Commander in 1964. He married in 1957, and had one adopted daughter.

The Times published two obituaries of Gwatkin, both written by people who had worked with him, one in the army and the other in the Lord Chamberlain's office. The first is headlined 'Soldier of High Standards', and focuses on the experience of serving under Gwatkin as Adjutant at Sandhurst in the thirties. It describes him as 'smart beyond belief, and a formidable figure with his fierce moustache, his impeccable turn-out and his clanking spurs'. Those who served

> will remember him as the epitome of a smart soldier with superb standards, tempered with a bubbling and irrepressible sense of humour: who helped

them to grow up, to assume responsibility, and to realize that soldiering
was fun as well as a vocation.

The writer also refers to Gwatkin's 'distinction as a fighting soldier in the
war' and 'his indomitable spirit as a sick man during these last few years'.[4]
According to the memoirs of another General who encountered him
during the war,

> Norman Gwatkin was a man of enormous character. A Coldstreamer,
> with a high colour, a choleric expression, a loud and infectious laugh,
> he was loved by our Grenadiers and known as were few senior officers.
> 'There's the Brigadier!' they would say, chuckling, and I remember one
> Sergeant adding, and he's an inspiration to the men! ... He cheered all
> men, wherever they were and whatever the circumstances.[5]

The other *Times* obituary, headlined 'Administrative Skill', was written
by Sir Terence Nugent, who worked above him as Comptroller:

> In Norman Gwatkin kindness, courage and gaiety were personified and
> for a great many people nothing will be quite the same again without
> him.
>
> I had the privilege of working with him in the Lord Chamberlain's
> Office for more than twenty years and I could not have wished for a more
> delightful, easy and loyal colleague. Extremely efficient he had a lightness
> of touch which made it fun to work with him and which seemed to smooth
> away all problems and difficulties. His training as a guardsman fitted
> him to tackle the big ceremonial occasions which the Lord Chamberlain's
> Office was called upon to organize. A quick and decisive worker he was
> never rattled and he dealt with any unforeseen snags that might arise
> calmly and with dispatch.

Nugent goes on to talk specifically about Gwatkin's role in relation to
censorship:

> In the Lord Chamberlain's absence Norman often had to interview authors
> or producers and discuss with them the cuts and alterations that were
> required. However disgruntled or even angry the author or producer may
> have been on arrival at Norman's office he almost invariably left convinced
> that his case would be carefully and sympathetically considered and very
> likely roaring with laughter at some remark, probably ribald, that Norman
> had made.

Nugent also tells us that:

His last years were dogged by bad health and he had to give up his shooting and his other active interests which he loved so well, a grievous blow to so energetic a man: but his courage never failed him and he retained his good spirits and splendid sense of humour to the end.

Nugent concludes:

'He was a man, take him for all in all
I shall not look upon his like again'.[6]

Secretary to the Lord Chamberlain: Ronald John Hill.

Born in December 1911.

Hill became a Clerk to the Prince of Wales in 1934, and transferred to the same role in the Lord Chamberlain's Office in 1936. He married in 1942. In 1955, Hill was promoted to the position of assistant secretary to the Lord Chamberlain, and in 1958 he became Secretary in the same Office, a position he retained until his retirement in 1976. Hill was also a Serjeant-at-Arms to the Queen, and was received by her on his retirement at a ceremony at Buckingham Palace. Officially, Hill had very limited powers and authority by comparison with the senior staff at St James's Palace; yet he wrote many internal documents—some of them very lengthy—about the history and practices of theatre censorship, as well as making recommendations and proposals. His contributions were often crucial to the debates and decisions which took place in the Office. Unfortunately, almost no biographical details of his life seem to be documented.

Senior Examiner of Plays (Reader): Charles Heriot

Born in Glasgow in 1905, Heriot attended Glasgow Academy, Glasgow University and Glasgow School of Art—where he studied Art of the Theatre. He worked in London with Louis Casson on a production of *Macbeth*, spent 3 years in professional theatre, including repertory work, touring and the West End, and a year with the Lena Ashwell players. He then worked in advertising and journalism, and was a general editor in the book department of Odham Press Ltd before he joined the Lord Chamberlain's office as assistant examiner of plays in 1937. Heriot served in the Royal Air Force during the War, and became Senior Examiner in 1947. He remained in this post until the 1968 Theatres Act was passed. Heriot was married to Adelaide Binnie Murgatroyd, a writer and publisher, who died in 1964.

Heriot retained an involvement in amateur drama as a producer and director. A review of his 1949 production of a historical drama called *The Queen Who Kept Her Head* described him as 'a professional stage and costume designer'. It also reported that 'Not the least of Mr. Heriot's achievements was the contriving of magnificent Tudor costumes from the only cheap material at hand, old army blankets'.[7]

On his retirement, a presentation was made to him in the Lord Chamberlain's Office in November 1968. He received a cigarette case, engraved with the message:

Charles Heriot
Examiner of Plays
1937–1968
From his friends in the Lord Chamberlain's office.

They also gave him 50 Woodbines tipped cigarettes.

Heriot died in 1972.

Assistant Examiner of Plays: Lieutenant-Colonel Sir Thomas St Vincent Wallace Troubridge, 5th Baronet, M.B.E., *Croce di Guerra*, Order of the Crown of Italy.

Born in 1895, son of Sir Thomas Troubridge, and educated at Wellington College and Sandhurst, Vincent Troubridge was commissioned in 1914 into the King's Royal Rifle Corps, and served in the First World War, where he was wounded at Salonika. He returned to England in 1917 and worked with Army Intelligence, receiving an MBE in 1919 and retiring with the rank of Captain. In 1938 he succeeded his father as fifth baronet. Troubridge was a fluent German speaker, and served on the army's General Staff during the Second World War. He was promoted to the rank of Lieutenant-Colonel. Troubridge had married Pamela Clough in 1939, but there was no issue, and on his death his title passed to his cousin.

Troubridge was deeply committed to theatre throughout his life, in a range of different ways. According to one obituary, his interest was first stimulated by a visit to see the German version of the *Everyman* Morality Play in 1913, while studying at a military academy in Baden. After the First World War, Troubridge joined the Stage Society and was involved with its Sunday night productions. In 1930 he was the co-author of a 'trenchant letter to *The Times* ... which was instrumental in bringing new life into the Society'. He also contributed articles to *The Stage*, became front of house manager at the Strand Theatre, and translated several German plays into English, including *The Unguarded Hour*, which opened at Daly's Theatre in 1935. Troubridge became chairman of the library committee of the Garrick

Club, and a founder member of the Society for Theatre Research in 1948. He also 'kept up a continuous output of theatrical articles in the national and world press'. He wrote frequently for *Theatre Notebook*, including a series on Early 19th Century Plays which featured in eight issues between 1948 and 1950, and which contributed new information. 'Many of the plays were noted as "not in Nicholl"—a fact which Professor Allardyce Nicoll freely acknowledged in the revised edition of his *History of English Drama*.' A 1951 lecture on Theatre Riots in history—'delivered with tremendous panache'—was also published by the STR in 1951 as one of its *Studies in English Theatre History*, and his full length book *The Benefit System in the British Theatre* was published posthumously by the Society in 1967.

Troubridge was an adviser for *Theatre Notebook* from 1954 until his death, and remained a very active committee member for the Society for Theatre Research until 1961: 'He livened our deliberations in committee with his forthright, occasionally Rabelasian yet always pertinent observations,' and 'was always generous in putting at the disposal of the society his vast fund of information'; indeed he 'would take endless trouble in searching out answers to inquiries ... from scholars and students.' In a short obituary in *The Times*, Sybil Rosenfeld wrote that 'theatre research has sustained a severe loss', and that 'No one was more knowledgeable in the highways and by-ways of the nineteenth-century stage'. She noted that 'His reading in this field was wide and his memory prodigious', and that he would 'be much missed from among us'.

In March 1949, Troubridge was the author of an article in the *Stage* about the history of theatre censorship ('Censorship Under Fire'). A few months later he wrote a letter from his Club (White's of St James's) to Tim Nugent, the Comptroller of the Lord Chamberlain's Office, to say that having left his post with a literary agency he now had time on his hands, and to offer himself as an additional Reader. Nugent invited him to come in and discuss the matter. In August 1951, a letter from Gwatkin offered him the position, to run for ten years from April 1952: 'I accept with extreme satisfaction the invitation,' he replied; 'it will be a great pleasure to undertake such congenial work under the direction of yourself and my old friend Tim Nugent.' According to his obituary in *Theatre Notebook*, Troubridge—who traced his own ancestry back to Lord Nelson—'was well fitted to the onerous task of censorship', because 'there was in him an odd Puritanical streak'. While he was apparently 'the last person to regard himself as keeper of the public conscience', Troubridge was nonetheless 'vehement in denunciation of the lowering moral standards of his day'. He continued in his role until his death in December 1963, frequently recommending far more draconian cuts and less compromising responses and stances than his superiors were prepared to allow.[8]

Notes

Notes on Archive Referencing

There are two separate archives in the British Library Manuscript Collections on which I have drawn substantially; both come under the general heading: 'The Play Collections':

The texts of unpublished plays submitted for licensing between 1900 and 1968 are referenced here as 'LCP' (Lord Chamberlain's Plays) followed by a year, an oblique stroke, and a box number. This is the referencing system used within the archive and its index.

The material from the Lord Chamberlain's Correspondence Files 1900–1968 is also referenced here as in the archive, using the abbreviation 'LCP CORR' to indicate the archive. Material relating to plays which were licensed is filed separately from that related to plays which were refused licences.

In the case of a *licensed play*, LCP CORR' is followed by the title of the play, the year under which it is filed, and a file number.

For an *unlicensed play*, 'LCP CORR' is followed by the title of the play, then 'LR' (indicating 'Licence Refused') and a year.

There is also correspondence relating to plays which were neither licensed nor refused. These are known as 'Waiting Box Plays'. To reference these, 'LCP CORR' is followed by the title of the play, then 'WB' (indicating 'Waiting Box') and a year.

The other archive on which I have drawn extensively is the Lord Chamberlain's Office Files, part of the Royal Archive, and currently held at Windsor Castle. These files contain further general and extensive papers—letters, minutes, memoranda, cuttings etc.—from the Lord Chamberlain's Office relating to theatre licensing and censorship. This material was evidently kept separate from the material related directly to specific plays submitted for licence, which is held in the British Library collections.

All material cited from the Royal Archive is referenced as in the archive itself; namely: 'RA LC/GEN', followed by an oblique line and one of several numbers under which the material is categorised: 310, 344, 440 or 512. Although the logic for the division and location of files is not always obvious, those labelled 310 were intended to indicate that the focus was the Advisory Board; 344, the Examiners of Plays; 440, the Theatres Act; and 512 apparently indicated Censorship. (The impossibility of maintaining these as discrete categories is evidenced by the fact that 440 and 512 were effectively amalgamated after 1958.) The above number is in each case followed by another oblique line and another figure which indicates the appropriate year of the file, and then the individual title which the Lord Chamberlain's Office assigned to it.

It should be noted that individual files sometimes contain relevant materials drawn from years other than the one indicated by the file reference number.

I am grateful to Her Majesty Queen Elizabeth II for allowing me access to the relevant sections of the Royal Archive, and for permitting me to make use of and quote from the files.

References are correct to the best of my knowledge. However, many of the plays cited are obscure, and often there is no satisfactory way of checking whether details as recorded in the Lord Chamberlain's Correspondence archives (places and dates of performances, names of authors etc.) are always correct. Some correspondence (and most of the titles and names as they appear on index cards) are handwritten, and I may have sometimes mis-read. I have tried to indicate with a '[?]' those references over which I am particularly doubtful. There are also some discrepancies between information about licences issued for productions as indicated in the Lord Chamberlain's files, and the details about productions listed in J.P. Wearing's invaluable *Calendars of the London Stage for the 1950s*. Where there are differences which I have been unable to resolve, I have given precedence to the evidence of the Lord Chamberlain's archive as reliably indicating *intended* production details.

Introduction

1   See RA LC/GEN/440/59: 'Mr Stephen Aris Assisted with his Article on Censorship And The Law In "Granta"'.
2   Report from the Joint Select Committee of the House of Lords and the House of Commons on the Stage Plays (Censorship) together with the Proceedings of the Committee, Minutes and Appendices (London: Government Publication, 1909), p. 190.
3   RA LC/GEN/440/59: 'Mr Stephen Aris Assisted with his Article'.
4   David Thomas, David Carlton, and Anne Etienne, *Theatre Censorship: From Walpole to Wilson* (Oxford: Oxford University Press, 2007).
5   RA LC/GEN/440/67: 'Joint Committee on Stage Censorship Appreciation by Lord Chamberlain (Earl of Scarbrough) on Desirability of Continuing Censorship of Stage Plays'.
6   *Ibid.*
7   See RA LC/GEN/440/59: 'Mr Stephen Joseph of Studio Theatre Ltd Informed that the Art of Improvisatore would be Illegal if Performed for Hire'.
8   See RA LC/GEN/440/53: 'Complaint Against Ice Parade of 1953 Blackpool Pleasure Beach and a Note on Status of Ice Shows Generally'.
9   See RA LC/GEN/440/54: 'A Definitive Statement on Puppet Shows for the Variety Artistes Federation'.
10 RA LC/GEN/440/57: 'Town Clerk of Derby given Advice as to Dealing with Indecent Performances by Road Shows'.
11 RA LC/GEN/440/57: 'Mr Billy Kaye asks if Kilts may be Worn on Stage Without Underpants'.
12 For a copy of this article see RA LC/GEN/512/56: 'Lord Chamberlain Refuses to Take Part in a Debate on Censorship in the Arts Theatre'.
13 See RA LC/GEN/440/58: 'Theatres Act, 1843 Theatre Managers Association in Defence of'.

Chapter 1

1 RA LC/GEN/440/53: 'Complaints Against Posters Used to Advertise "One Way Traffic" with Notes on Methods of Evading the Lord Chamberlain's Ruling Against a Change of Name'.

2 See 'The Form and Order of Service that is to be performed and the Ceremonies that are to be observed in The Coronation of Her Majesty Queen Elizabeth II in the Abbey Church of St. Peter, Westminster, on Tuesday, the second day of June, 1953' at http://www.oremus.org/liturgy/coronation/cor1953b.html

3 Dominic Sandbrook, *Never Had It So Good: A History of Britain from Suez to the Beatles* (London: Abacus, 2006), p. 66.

4 RA LC/GEN/440/53: 'Mr Hossain Complains of Nudity on the Stage'.

5 *Daily Express*, 23 May 1953, p. 4.

6 Unpublished manuscript of *High Spirits*, LCP 1953/5284. The Revue was licensed for The King's Theatre, Edinburgh, in March 1953. Written by Peter Myers, Alec Grahame and David Climie; Music by John Pritchett and Ronald Cass; Additional Lyrics by Richard Vosbrugh; Additional Music by Norman Dannatt. It opened at the London Hippodrome on 13 May 1953 with a cast including Leslie Crowther, Ian Carmichael, Patrick Cargill and Joan Sims, and design by Osbert Lancaster. It ran for 125 performances till the end of August.

7 See LCP CORR: 1953/5284: *High Spirits*. Reader's Report by Charles Heriot, 27 February 1953.

8 *Ibid*. Memorandum dated 22 May 1953.

9 *Ibid*. Memorandum by Scarbrough, 26 May 1953.

10 As reported in *Manchester Guardian*, 15 November 1956, p. 10. The public debate, entitled 'Do We Need a Censor', took place in the Arts Theatre Club on 12 November, with Sherek supporting theatre censorship and Richard Findlater opposing.

11 Reader's Report by Charles Heriot, 29 May 1953. See LCP CORR: 1953/5620: *Gloriana*. It was licensed for the Royal Opera House in Covent Garden for 5 June 1953.

12 Letter to the Lord Chamberlain from a Mr Grahame in Twickenham, dated 21 July 1953, and Scarbrough's reply, dated 24 July. The proposed script was to be entitled 'Comrades in Arms'. See RA LC/GEN/512/53: 'Mr. Grahame Submits Synopsis of a Play the Heroine Being a Princess of Great Britain—Discouraged from Proceeding'.

13 Letter from Norman Gwatkin to Guthrie of June 1952, quoted in a memorandum from Nugent to Scarbrough dated 14 September 1953. See RA LC/GEN/512/53: 'Mr Lipscom Told Not Possible to Allow Play about King Edward VII'.

14 Nugent's comments are from the memorandum quoted above. His letter to Lipscom is dated 16 September 1953.

15 The revue was originally called *At the Lyric*, and later changed to *Going to Town*. Reader's Report by Heriot dated 19 November 1953, Scarbrough's note undated. See LCP CORR: 1953/6045: *At the Lyric*. This was a Tennent production, licensed for Cambridge Arts Theatre, on 24 November 1953.

16 Letter from the Home Office dated 17 April 1953, and Nugent's advice of three days later. See RA LC/GEN/440/53: 'As to Mr Rowland's Pageant Using The Regalia and the Queen's Speech'.

17 Gerard Fay, 'THE BRITISH THEATRE I: The Decay of the Music-Hall'. *Manchester Guardian*, 19 April 1954, p. 5.

18   See RA LC/GEN/440/53: 'Complaint Against Ice Parade of 1953 Blackpool Pleasure Beach and a Note on Status of Ice Shows Generally'.

19   Reader's Report by Troubridge, 15 January 1953. See LCP CORR: 1953/5053: *Wide Boy*. Ian Stuart's play was licensed for the Regal Theatre, Southend, on 23 January. In October, the title was changed to *Vice in the Streets*.

20   Reader's Report by Troubridge, 22 January 1953. See LCP CORR: 1953/5075: *Squatter*. Written by Gordon Oliver, licensed for Community Theatre, Slough, 5 February 1953.

21   LCP CORR: 1953/5053: *Wide Boy*.

22   Reader's Report by Troubridge, 10 January 1953, Scarbrough's comments undated. See LCP CORR: 1953/5030: *Lady for Hire*. Written by Dudley Harcourt, the script was licensed for performance at Q Theatre, Brentford, on 6 February 1953.

23   Reader's Report by Troubridge, 18 February 1953. See LCP CORR: 1953/5240: *Lady of the House*. An adaptation by Bruce Walker from a play by Mary Preston, it was licensed for the Palace Court, Bournemouth, on 25 February 1953. The title was changed in September 1955 to *House of Shame*, then in February 1956 to *Women of Sin*, and in March 1956 first to *The Call Girl Racket*, and then to *Women of the Streets*.

24   Reader's Report by Troubridge, 18 March 1953. See LCP CORR: 1953/5381: *Women are My Business*. Written by John Sherwood and licensed for St George's Theatre, Kendal, 24 March 1953.

25   Hill's memorandum is dated 30 June 1954, and Scarbrough's letter to the MP is 6/7/54. See LCP CORR: 1954/6235: *Ladies for Hire*. This revised version of Dudley Harcourt's play was licensed for Sheerness Hippodrome on 14 January 1954.

26   Reader's Report by Troubridge, 14 February 1953. See LCP CORR: 1953/5206: *The Good Woman of Setzuan*. Eric Bentley's translation was licensed for the Progress Theatre, Reading, on 18 February 1953.

27   Reader's Report by Charles Heriot, 23 November 1954. See LCP CORR: 1954/7264: *The Good Soldier Schweik*. MacColl's adaptation of Hasek's novel was licensed for Theatre Workshop at the Theatre Royal, Stratford East, on 26 November 1954.

28   Reader's Report by Troubridge, 21 June 1955. See LCP CORR: 1955/8138: *Mother Courage*. The script for Theatre Workshop's production was licensed for the Queens Hall, Barnstaple, on 28 June 1955.

29   Reader's Report by Troubridge, 16 October 1955. See LCP CORR: 1955/8308: *The Threepenny Opera*. Submitted by 'Peachum Productions', licensed for the Theatre Royal, Brighton, 31 December 1955.

30   Reader's Report by Troubridge, 6 June 1953. See LCP CORR: 1953/5647: *To Sup with the Devil*. Licensed for Northampton Repertory Theatre, July 1953.

31   Reader's Report by Heriot, 7 May 1953. See LCP CORR: 1953/5545: *To See the Queen Pass By*. Licensed for Botleys Park Concert Hall, Chertsey, 11 May 1953.

32   See LCP CORR: 1953/4995: *Stalag Seventeen*. Reader's Report by Heriot, 5 January 1953. Written by Donald Bevan and Edmund Trizcinski, and licensed for Edinburgh Lyceum on 10 February 1953.

33   Reader's Report by Troubridge, 7 February 1953. See LCP CORR: 1953/5149: *Here Comes April*. Written by Dudley Lester and Audrey Erskine, licensed for the Connaught Theatre, Worthing, 20 February 1953.

34   Reader's Report by Troubridge, 26 July 1954. See LCP CORR: 1954/6944:

Thirty Pieces of Silver. Licensed for the Little Theatre, Gateshead on Tyne, 5 August 1954.

35 Reader's Report by Troubridge, 27 January 1953. See LCP CORR: 1953/5293: *What The Stars Foretell.* Written by Robert Kemp and licensed for Royal Princess' Theatre, Glasgow, 9 March 1953.

36 Reader's Report by Troubridge, 24 February 1953. See LCP CORR: 1953/5267: *The Woman's Way.* Written by Arthur Everitt and licensed for the Everyman Theatre, Reading, 27 February 1953.

37 Reader's Report by Troubridge, 2 November 1954. See LCP CORR: 1954/7191: *The Real News.* Written by Peter Howard and licensed for the Westminster Theatre, 12 November 1954.

38 See unpublished manuscript of *Murder Story,* LCP 1954/4.

39 See LCP CORR: 1954/6284: *Murder Story.* Kennedy's play was licensed for the Cambridge Arts Theatre on 22 January 1954. The Reader's Report by Heriot was dated 18 January 1954.

40 Reader's Report by Troubridge, 7 October 1953. See LCP CORR: 1953/5896: *Guilty and Proud of it.* Martin's play was licensed for Poplar Civic Theatre on 14 October 1953.

41 Letter from Troubridge to Heriot, 31 December 1952, and note from Gwatkin, 2 January 1953. See RA LC/GEN/512/53: 'Sir St Vincent Troubridge Points out Danger of Arts Council Patronage of Unlicensed Plays'.

42 LCP CORR: 1953/5896: *Guilty and Proud of it.*

43 See LCP CORR: 1953/ 5211: *Five Philadelphia Physicians,* Reader's Report by Troubridge, 13 February 1953, and Scarbrough's comment, 17 February. Licensed for the Embassy Theatre, 25 February 1953.

44 See LCP CORR: 1953/5408: *Les Gueux au Paradis.* Reader's Report by Troubridge, 27 March 1953 and Scarbrough's comment, 31 March. Written by G.M. Martens and Andre Obey, licensed for Toynbee Hall, 10 April 1953.

45 See unpublished manuscript of *Straight from Heaven,* LCP 1954/60.

46 See LCP CORR: 1954/7190: *Straight from Heaven.* Reader's Report by Troubridge, 20 October 1954, and subsequent correspondence. Letter from Scarbrough to the Dean of Windsor, 1 November 1954, and the Dean's reply the following day. Written by Royce Ryton and Robert Simoman, licensed for the New Theatre, Bromley, 5 November 1954.

47 See Fay, 'The Decay of the Music-Hall', p. 5.

48 Internal memorandum written by Ronald Hill, 23 November 1953. See RA LC/GEN/512/53: 'Letter to Certain Licensees on the Subject of Nudes'.

49 Letter to the Lord Chamberlain, 18 February 1953. See RA LC/GEN/440/53: 'Anonymous Complaint about Empire Theatre Woolwich and Barry Piddock'.

50 See RA LC/GEN/512/53: 'Letter to Certain Licensees on the Subject of Nudes'. Letter from Gwatkin to theatre managements, 1 December 1953'.

51 Fay, 'The Decay of the Music-Hall'.

52 See LCP CORR: 1955/7818: *Paris by Night.* Reader's Report by Heriot, 4 April 1955. The revue was licensed for the Prince of Wales's Theatre on 6 April 1955.

53 Reader's Report by Heriot, 8 March 1955. See LCP CORR: 1955/7711: *Bon Soir Cocks.* Licensed for Woolwich Empire, 10 March.

54 Paper by Hill, 21 January 1955. See RA LC/GEN/512/55: 'Paper on the History of Nudity—Deputation from the Public Morality Council'.

55 Reply by Gwatkin, 11 March 1954, to a complaint about nudity at the Windmill. See RA LC/GEN/440/54: 'Mr. Wellman Complains of the Windmill and Nudes in General'.

56 See 1954 Annual Report of the Public Morality Council, p. 9.

57 See 1956 Annual Report of the Public Morality Council, p. 13.

58 F.L. Haigh at the Home Office contacted Hill on 17 March 1954. Hill's letter of reply was sent on the following day. See RA LC/GEN/440/54: 'A Statement On Nudity for the Home Office'.

59 Letter from Gwatkin, 12 February 1954. See LCP CORR: 1954/6276: *Revudeville no. 263.*

60 Report by LCC Inspector, 16 March 1955. See LCP CORR: 1955/7711: *Bon Soir Cocks.*

61 Reader's Report by Heriot, 27 February 1953. See LCP CORR: 1953/5282: *Revudeville no. 256.*

62 See LCP CORR: 1953/5916: *Revudeville no. 261.*

63 Reader's Report by Heriot, 26 February 1954. See LCP CORR: 1954/6472: *Revudeville no. 264.*

64 Letter to the Lord Chamberlain from the Public Morality Council, 5 October 1954, and note from Titman, 2 October. See LCP CORR: 1954/7021: *Revudeville no. 268.*

65 Report by Hill, 14 October 1954. See LCP CORR: 1953/5640: *Folies Parisiennes.* Licence originally issued to Paul Raymond for performance at Theatre Royal, Margate, 11 June 1953.

66 Correspondence between Gwatkin, Raymond and the Chief Constable of Oldham, November and December 1954. See LCP CORR: 1953/5640: *Folies Parisiennes.*

67 Correspondence between the Colonial Office and the Lord Chamberlain's Office, December 1952–January 1953. See RA LC/GEN/512/53: 'Government of Kenya Advised Re Application of Theatres Act to "Business" and Stage Decorations'.

68 See LCP CORR: 1947/7906: *The Respectable Prostitute.* Report by Superintendent Hegg of C Division, 3 November 1953. Script originally licensed for County Theatre, Bangor, 21 May 1947.

69 See LCP CORR: 1954/6235: *Ladies for Hire.* Written by Dudley Harcourt, licensed for Sheerness Hippodrome, 14 January 1954. There were frequent complaints made both about the performance itself and the posters used to advertise it. The *Daily Mail* campaigned against it, as did several MPs. It was inspected by the Lord Chamberlain's Office in August 1955, at which point Gwatkin was able to put pressure on the management to amend it.

70 See LCP CORR: 1953/5693 and 1954/6307: *Wish You Were Here.* Correspondence and report by Hill, January 1954. The original script by Arthur Kober and Joshua Logan was licensed for the Casino Theatre on 5 January 1953, and a revised version was licensed for the same theatre on 26 January 1954.

71 See LCP CORR: 1954/7069: *La Venexiana.* Frederick May's translation of the original script of Girolamo Fracastoro was licensed for the Ridley Smith Theatre at Leeds University on 27 October 1954.

72 Reader's Report by Troubridge, 26 January 1955, and subsequent correspondence. See LCP CORR: 1955/7552: *Uncertain Destiny.* Licensed for Cambridge Arts Theatre, 7 February 1955.

73 Reader's Report by Troubridge, 26 January 1955, and subsequent correspondence. See LCP CORR: 1947/8553 and 1955/7553: *Legacy.* Originally licensed for Theatre Royal, Stratford East; revised version licensed for Cambridge Arts Theatre, 7 February 1955.

74 See LCP CORR: 1955/7847: *Vile Inheritance.* Written by Howard Arundel, and

licensed for Cleethorpes Empire on 18 April 1955. In June, the title was changed to *Call of the Flesh*.

75   Reader's Report by Heriot, 9 January 1953. See LCP CORR: 1953/5018: *Wonderful Time*. Revue licensed for London Hippodrome, 15 January 1953.

76   See LCP CORR: 1955/8674: *Aladdin*. The performance by Waterlow Amateur Dramatic Society was licensed for Cripplegate Theatre in December 1955/January 1956. Script by P.H. Adams and Conrad Carter.

77   See LCP CORR: 1955/7737: *Turn on the Heat*. The revue was licensed for the County Theatre, Bedford, on 17 March 1955.

78   See LCP CORR: 1953/5031: *The Naughtiest Night of Your Life*. Licensed to Barry Piddock of D.J. Piddock Productions, for the Queen's Theatre, Poplar, 19 January 1953.

79   See LCP CORR: 1954/6817: *The Crucible*. Licensed for Bristol Theatre Royal, 11 August 1954.

80   See LCP CORR: 1953/6126: *Babes in the Wood*. Licensed for Rutherglen Repertory Theatre, 21 December 1953.

81   See LCP CORR: 1955/7633: *Fanny Get Your Gun*. Written by Davy Kaye, this revue was licensed for the Plaza, West Bromwich, 18 February 1955.

82   See LCP CORR: 1954/6505: *Facts of Life*. Written by Roger Macdougal and licensed to Henry Sherek for Blackpool Grand on 18 March 1954.

83   A 'U' was issued for a film judged suitable for anyone, while the 'X' category restricted admission to adults only.

84   Scarbrough's comment is undated; he is commenting on a letter written by Sherek on 5 September 1954. See RA LC/GEN/440/54: 'Certain Managers Propound Question of Having "X" Certificates for Plays'.

85   See LCP CORR: 1952/4831: *Guys and Dolls*. The show had been licensed and had opened over a year earlier.

86   See LCP CORR: 1954/6249: *I am a Camera*. Originally submitted by Laurence Olivier productions in March 1952, Van Druten's play was licensed for Wyndhams Theatre on 8 January 1954. The Public Morality Council wrote a letter of complaint on 6 May 1954, and another on 29 June, following Gwatkin's response. Scarbrough's final reply to them was written on 29 September.

87   See 1956 Annual Report of the Public Morality Council, p. 13.

88   See LCP CORR: 1955/8266: *Anniversary Waltz*. Written by Jerome Chodorov and Joseph Fields, and licensed for the Globe Theatre, 24 August 1955.

89   Reader's Report by Troubridge, 28 May 1951. See LCP CORR: *Lady Chatterley's Lover*, WB 11 (1951). In fact, the licence was never formally issued and no public performance could have taken place.

90   See LCP CORR: *Hinkemann* LR (1935) and LR (1947).

91   Reader's Reports by Troubridge, 11 February 1953 and 25 July 1955. See LCP CORR: 1958/1479: *Rose Tattoo*. There were private productions, but the script was not publicly performed until Williams accepted the cuts. It was licensed for the New Shakespeare Theatre, Liverpool, on 26 January 1958.

92   See LCP CORR: 1954/6597: *Waiting for Godot*. The script was licensed for the Criterion Theatre on 1 July 1954. The correspondence with Lady Howitt took place in November and December 1955.

93   'The Form and Order of Service ...', http://www.oremus.org/liturgy/coronation/cor1953b.html

Chapter 2

1 Letter from Norman Gwatkin to the Home Office, 12 May 1955. See RA LC/GEN/512/55: 'Fresh Consideration of Plays with Unpleasant Themes'.

2 See LCP CORR: 1953/5250: *The Maids*. The script was originally refused a licence on 14 January 1953, and the revised version was licensed for the Royal Court on 24 February.

3 Nicholas de Jongh, *Not in Front of the Audience: Homosexuality on Stage* (London: Routledge, 1992), pp. 49–52.

4 Dominic Shellard, *Kenneth Tynan: A Life* (London: Yale University Press, 2003), p. 218.

5 Dominic Sandbrook, *Never Had it So Good* (London: Abacus, 2006), pp. 599–600.

6 Shellard, *Kenneth Tynan*, p. 220

7 Reported, for example, in the *Daily Telegraph*, 29 October, 1953, p. 7.

8 Shellard, *Kenneth Tynan*, pp. 218–19.

9 Sandbrook, *Never Had it So Good*, p. 600.

10 For all this correspondence between Gwatkin and W.C. Roberts at the Home Office see RA LC/GEN/512/55: 'Fresh Consideration of Plays with Unpleasant Themes'.

11 See LCP CORR: 1955/7450: *Encore*. Written by John Sims, the revue was licensed for Leicester Co-operative Hall on 10 January 1955. For script see unpublished manuscript of *Encore*, LCP 1955/11.

12 Instruction from Gwatkin to theatre manager, 4 February 1954. See LCP CORR: 1954/6369: *Here Comes Yesterday*. Written by Ralph Reader, licensed for Harrow Coliseum, 12 February 1954.

13 *Ibid.*

14 See LCP CORR: 1954/7238: *World of Women*. Written by Jack Taylor and licensed for the Grand Theatre, Southampton, on 19 November 1954.

15 *Ibid.*

16 See LCP CORR: 1954/7248: *Mind your Manors*. Written by Michael Finn and E. Wilson-Hyde, and licensed for the Everyman Theatre, Reading, 20 December 1954.

17 See LCP CORR: 1955/7901: *The Reluctant Debutante*. Licensed for the Theatre Royal, Brighton, May 1955.

18 See LCP CORR: 1956/9346: *Something about a Sailor*. Written by Earle Couttie and licensed for Shanklin, Isle of Wight, August 1956.

19 *Randle's Scandals* was licensed for Central Pier, Blackpool, 23 October 1952. A lengthy report following an inspection by the London County Council of a performance at the Chelsea Palace in November 1953 led to this letter from the Lord Chamberlain's Office, dated 5 December 1953. See LCP CORR: 1952/4644: *Randle's Scandals*.

20 See LCP CORR: 1954/7263: *Jokers Wild*. Jack Hylton's revue had been licensed for the New Theatre, Oxford, on 27 November 1954.

21 See LCP CORR: 1955/7657: *Foreign Bodies*. Revue licensed for the G.C. Theatre Group at Cheltenham Civic Playhouse, 7 February 1954.

22 Written by Marjorie Squires, a licence had been refused in October 1952. A revised version was licensed for the Grand Theatre, Llandudno, on 6 December 1953. See LCP CORR: 1953/5113: *The White Terror*.

23 Written by André Roussin, licence refused on 17 April 1953. See LCP CORR: *Les Oeufs de L'autruche*.

24 See RA LC/GEN/440/53: 'Miss De Crespigny Informed a Translation of an Old Play Subject to the Censor'.

25 See LCP CORR: 1953/5960: *Little Idiot.* Bagnold's play, with changes, was licensed for the Q Theatre, Brentford, on 4 November 1953.

26 Dan Rebellato, *1956 and All That: The Making of Modern British Drama* (London: Routledge, 1999), p. 178.

27 *South* was originally to have been produced in 1953 by Tennent and Beaumont productions, but was not licensed until March 1959, for the People's Theatre in Newcastle. For all correspondence and debate see LCP CORR: 1959/1791: *South*.

28 Reader's Report by Heriot, 16 March 1953. See LCP CORR: 1953/5355: *Serious Charge.* Licensed for the Apollo Theatre, 22 September 1953.

29 John Johnston, *The Lord Chamberlain's Blue Pencil* (London: Hodder and Stoughton, 1990), p. 176.

30 LCP CORR: 1953/5355: *Serious Charge.*

31 The *Observer,* 20 February 1955, cited in Dominic Shellard, Steve Nicholson and Miriam Handley, *The Lord Chamberlain Regrets: A History of British Theatre Censorship* (London: The British Library, 2004), pp. 146–7.

32 Nicholas de Jongh, *Not in Front of the Audience: Homosexuality on Stage* (London: Routledge, 1992), p. 66.

33 Philip King, *Serious Charge* (London: Samuel French Ltd), p. 51.

34 *Ibid.,* p. 35.

35 LCP CORR: 1953/5355: *Serious Charge.*

36 Rebellato, *1956 and All That,* p. 211.

37 Alan Sinfield, *Out on Stage: Lesbian and Gay Theatre in the Twentieth Century* (London: Yale University Press, 1999), p. 242.

38 In the event, it was 1959 before a film version was finally made (starring Cliff Richard among the cast), with the homosexual accusation restored, and as Aldgate and Robertson show, more concern among the film censors about the violence of youth culture depicted than about the original issue. For detailed discussion of the stage and especially the film version in relation to censorship, see Anthony Aldgate and James C. Robertson, *Censorship in Theatre and Cinema* (Edinburgh: Edinburgh University Press, 2005), pp. 86–100. Their work is crucially informed by citations from archive files of the British Board of Film Censorship.

39 Opened at the Adelphi Theatre in November 1953, and received a full professional production at the Garrick shortly afterwards,

40 See Beverley Baxter, 'Why Ban This Problem Play?', *Evening Standard,* 24 November 1950, p. 9; 'Censor Holds Back This Adult Play', *Daily Mail,* 22 November 1950, p. 5; and the *Observer* (Ivor Brown), 26 November 1950, p. 6.

41 Report on meeting in the Lord Chamberlain's Office, dated 14 May 1953. See LCP CORR: 1964/4458: *The Children's Hour.*

42 See RA LC/GEN/512/53: 'Report on *Serious Charge*—First Play Licensed with any Association with a Perversion Theme'. (NB possible dating error in title of original file; '53' should perhaps read '55'.)

43 Written by J. Joseph-Renaud and Guillot de Saix, translated by Ronald Adam. Licence refused 17 February 1954. See LCP CORR: *King of Life* LR.

44 See LCP CORR: *The Trial of Oscar Wilde* LR. The script was translated by Hugh Ross Williamson. Licence refused on 12 April 1954.

45 Unpublished manuscript of *The Trial of Oscar Wilde.* See Unlicensed LCP List 1: Box 33 (dated 12 April 1954).

46   Reader's Report by Troubridge, 23 February 1954. See LCP CORR: *The Wicked and the Weak* LR. The script was by Philip Chappel.

47   See Shellard, *British Theatre Since the War* (London: Yale University Press, 1999), p. 58.

48   See Dominic Shellard, Steve Nicholson and Miriam Handley, *The Lord Chamberlain Regrets: A History of British Theatre Censorship* (London: The British Library, 2004), pp. 148–9, and p. 182, n. 36.

49   Memorandum by Scarbrough, 25 November 1958. The play was licensed for the Scala Theatre on 26 November 1958. See LCP CORR: 1958/1494: *The Immoralist*.

50   Reader's Report by Troubridge, 13 January 1955. See LCP CORR: *The Golden Mask* LR. The licence was refused on 19 January.

51   Unpublished manuscript of *The Golden Mask*. See Unlicensed LCP List 1: Box 33 (dated 19 January 1955).

52   LCP CORR: *The Golden Mask*.

53   Unpublished manuscript of *The Golden Mask*.

54   LCP CORR: *The Golden Mask*.

55   Unpublished manuscript of *The Golden Mask*.

56   For full record of correspondence on Sartre's play see LCP CORR: *Huis Clos*. LR 1945/160. Also: 1959/522. Also: 1960/52. It was eventually licensed for Goldsmiths College, London, on 31 December 1959.

57   See unpublished manuscript of *Personal Enemy*, LCP 1955/14.

58   See LCP CORR: 1955/7672: *Personal Enemy*. Licensed for the Grand Opera House, Harrogate, on 2 March 1955.

59   See LCP CORR: 1958/1494: *The Immoralist*.

60   See LCP CORR: 1958/1459: *Tea and Sympathy*. The script was eventually licensed for the Comedy Theatre, on 10 December 1958. The interview with Anderson referred to here appeared in the *Sunday Graphic*, 22 May 1955, p. 6.

61   The play was eventually licensed for the Ilford Little Theatre, on 21 October 1964. For all correspondence see LCP CORR: 1964/4496: *Cat on a Hot Tin Roof*.

62   See LCP CORR: 1958/1463: *View from the Bridge*. It was eventually licensed for Wimbledon Theatre on 20 November 1958.

Chapter 3

1   Memorandum from Gwatkin to Scarbrough, 23 May 1957. See 'RA LC/ GEN/440/67: Joint Committee on Stage Censorship Appreciation by Lord Chamberlain (Earl of Scarbrough) on Desirability of Continuing Censorship of Stage Plays'.

2   Robert Muller, 'The Play You May Never See', *Picture Post*, 14 April 1956, p. 30.

3   Anthony Field, interviewed on 14 March 2007 as part of the British Library and Sheffield University Theatre Archive Project. See http://www.bl.uk/projects/ theatrearchive/field.html

4   Memorandum by Gwatkin, 30 August 1956. See RA LC/GEN/440/58: 'Consideration by Home Office of Proposal to Amend the Theatres Act 1843 to Allow the Lord Chamberlain to Attach Conditions to his Stage Plays Licence—not Adopted. Subsequent Decision to License Certain Plays Dealing with Homosexuality'.

5   Paper by Hill entitled 'Private Theatres', 31 August 1956. RA LC/GEN/440/58: 'Consideration by Home Office'.

6 Letter from Hill to Nugent, 31 August 1956. RA LC/GEN/440/58: 'Consideration by Home Office'.

7 Undated memorandum. RA LC/GEN/440/58: 'Consideration by Home Office'.

8 The Watergate directors present were Lieutenant-Colonel the Honourable James Smith, described by the *Evening News* as 'the 50 year old bachelor uncle of Viscount Hambleden' and Mr Ian Hunter.

9 For all correspondence and memoranda cited here, see RA LC/GEN/440/58: 'Consideration by Home Office', n. 4.

10 *The Children's Hour* opened at the Arts Theatre on 19 September, running for just under six weeks and fifty performances.

11 *Daily Mail*, 20 September 1956, p. 3.

12 *Observer*, 16 September 1956, p. 15.

13 Memorandum written by Nugent, 14 September 1956, reporting phone call from the British Board of Film Censorship. See RA LC/GEN/512/56: '*Tea and Sympathy* Granted an X Certificate by British Board of Film Censors'.

14 Memorandum written by Gwatkin, 25 October 1956. See LCP CORR: 1958/1459: *Tea and Sympathy*.

15 See LCP CORR: 1958/1459: *Tea and Sympathy*.

16 See RA LC/GEN/440/58: 'Consideration by Home Office', n. 4.

17 'First-Night Crowds Pull at Marilyns's Mink', *Evening Standard*, 12 October 1956, p. 30.

18 *Daily Express*, 12 October 1956, p. 1 and p. 5.

19 *Daily Mail*, 12 October 1956, p. 14.

20 *Daily Telegraph*, 12 October 1956, p. 9.

21 *Illustrated London News*, 22 October 1956, p. 30.

22 For all correspondence see RA LC/GEN/440/60: 'Question in the House as to Abolition of Censorship and Possible Action Viz a Viz the Comedy Theatre Scheme'.

23 *Ibid*.

24 Annual report by the Stage Plays, Radio and Television Sub-Committee, published in the Public Morality Council Annual Report 1957, p. 11. See also RA LC/GEN/440/58: 'Public Morality Council Report 1957'.

25 Letter from Nugent to Scarbrough, 22 August 1958. RA LC/GEN/440/60: 'Question in the House as to Abolition of Censorship'.

26 *Daily Mail*, 5 March 1957, p. 4.

27 *Daily Telegraph*, 29 April 1957, p. 11.

28 *Daily Telegraph*, 2 May 1957, p. 8.

29 Letter from Stephen Mitchell, headlined 'Censorship Helps Dramatists'. See *Daily Telegraph*, 6 May 1957, p. 8.

30 *Daily Telegraph*, 9 May 1957, p. 8.

31 Letter dated 30 April 1957. See LCP CORR: 1959/1721: *The Entertainer*.

32 Ronald Duncan, 'CENSORSHIP!', *Daily Mail*, 5 March 1957, p. 4.

33 See RA LC/GEN/440/67: 'Joint Committee on Stage Censorship Appreciation by Lord Chamberlain (Earl of Scarbrough) on Desirability of Continuing Censorship of Stage Plays'.

34 RA LC/GEN/440/67: 'Joint Committee on Stage Censorship'.

35 Memorandum by Scarbrough marked 'Most Secret'. See RA LC/GEN/440/67: 'Joint Committee on Stage Censorship'.

36 Hill's proposed amendment and justification for it were sent to Scarbrough on 30 May. RA LC/GEN/440/67: 'Joint Committee on Stage Censorship'.

37 Scarbrough's report of his meeting was dated 4 June 1957. See RA LC/ GEN/440/58: 'Consideration by Home Office', n. 4.
38 For all correspondence and memoranda cited here, see RA LC/GEN/440/58: 'Consideration by Home Office'.
39 See RA LC/GEN/440/58: 'Notes on Lord Chamberlain's Conference with West End Theatre Managers Assn.'.
40 See RA LC/GEN/440/58: 'Consideration by Home Office', n. 4.

Chapter 4

1   Internal minute circulated in the Lord Chamberlain's Office for comments. See RA LC/GEN/440/58: 'Consideration by Home Office of Proposal to Amend the Theatres Act 1843 to Allow the Lord Chamberlain to Attach Conditions to his Stage Plays Licence—not Adopted. Subsequent Decision to License Certain Plays Dealing with Homosexuality'. A comment in the margin suggests as an answer to the question cited here: 'By the context'.
2   *Ibid.*, internal minute.
3   *Ibid.*, internal minute.
4   Angus Wilson, 'Morality', *International Theatre Annual*, Number 4. London, John Calder, 1959, pp. 184–9.
5   See LCP CORR: 1956/8872: *Hot and Cold in All Rooms*. Licensed for Theatre Royal, Leicester, 17 February 1956.
6   From the unpublished manuscript of *Hot and Cold in All Rooms*. See LCP 1956/11.
7   See LCP CORR: 1956/8872: *Hot and Cold in All Rooms*.
8   Unfortunately, since the original script is missing we shall probably never know the nature of Cecil's defence.
9   From the unpublished manuscript of *Hot and Cold in All Rooms*.
10 See LCP CORR: 1958/1463: *A View from the Bridge*.
11 Philip King and Robin Maugham, *The Lonesome Road* (London: Samuel French Ltd, 1959), p. 71.
12 *Ibid.*, pp. 64–5.
13 *Ibid.*, p. 71.
14 See LCP CORR: 1959/1831: *Lonesome Road*. Written by Philip King and Robin Maugham, *Lonesome Road* was staged privately at the Arts Theatre in August 1957, but not licensed for public performance until March 1959 for production at Cripplegate on 11 March 1959.
15 Reader's Report by Troubridge, 6 April 1957. See LCP CORR: *Foolish Attachment* LR, 16 April 1957.
16 From the unpublished manuscript of *Foolish Attachment*. See Unlicensed LCP List 1: Box 34 (dated 16 April 1957).
17 See LCP CORR: *Foolish Attachment* LR.
18 Reader's Report by Heriot, 15 May 1957. See LCP CORR: *No Retreat* LR, 28 May 1957.
19 From the unpublished manuscript of *No Retreat*. See Unlicensed LCP List 1: Box 34 (dated 28 May 1957).
20 See LCP CORR: *No Retreat*.
21 Reader's Report by Troubridge, 14 May 1957. See LCP CORR: 1958/1452: *The Catalyst*. A licence was refused in May 1957, and the script was licensed for the Royal Court, 13 November 1958.
22 Ronald Duncan, *The Catalyst* (London: The Rebel Press, 1964), pp. 77–8.

23 See LCP CORR: 1958/1452: *The Catalyst*.
24 The play was presented privately at the Arts Theatre Club in March 1958.
25 *Daily Mirror*, 5 September 1957, p. 1.
26 *Daily Mirror*, 10 September 1957, p. 1. The results of the poll showed readers overwhelmingly supporting the recommendations on prostitution, but more than half opposed the decriminalisation of homosexual behaviour.
27 See, for example, *Daily Telegraph*, 9 September 1957, p. 9 and 10 September 1957, p. 8; *Daily Mail*, 7 September 1957, p. 1.
28 *Daily Telegraph*, 9 September 1957, p. 8.
29 *Daily Mail*, 5 September 1957, p. 1.
30 *The Times*, 18 March 1957, p. 9.
31 'Sex and Punishment', *The Times*, 5 September 1957, p. 11.
32 Reported in *The Times*, 27 September 1957, p. 7.
33 Reported in *The Times*, 12 September 1957, p. 7.
34 Reported in *The Times*, 25 September 1957, p. 5.
35 See report on the Chester Diocesan Conference, *The Times*, 9 October 1957, p. 5.
36 *The Times*, 8 November 1957, p. 7.
37 Reader's Report by Troubridge, 12 December 1957. See LCP CORR: 1960/1069: *Compulsion*. Written by Meyer Levin, the play was eventually licensed for Croydon's Pembroke Theatre in September 1960.
38 All extracts taken from unpublished manuscript of *Compulsion*. See LCP 1960/30.
39 See LCP CORR: 1960/1069: *Compulsion*.
40 See LCP CORR: 1958/667: *We're No Ladies*; Licensed for 20th Century Theatre, 22 January 1958. See also 1961/1660: *We're No Ladies*.
41 Hill's report dated 7 February 1958. LCP CORR: 1958/667: *We're No Ladies* and LCP CORR: 1961/1660: *We're No Ladies*.
42 LCP CORR: 1958/667: *We're No Ladies* and LCP CORR: 1961/1660: *We're No Ladies*.
43 See LCP CORR: 1964/4496: *Cat on a Hot Tin Roof*.
44 Alan Sinfield, *Out on Stage: Lesbian and Gay Theatre in the Twentieth Century* (London: Yale University Press, 1999), pp. 192–3.
45 See LCP CORR: 1958/1120: *Suddenly Last Summer*. Licensed for the Globe Theatre, 11 June 1958.
46 Quotations taken from the version of *Something Unspoken* published in Tennessee Williams, *'Baby Doll' and Other Plays* (London: Penguin Books, 1968), p. 97.
47 *Ibid.*, p. 108.
48 Readers' Report by Troubridge, 29 May 1958. See LCP CORR: 1958/1097: *Something Unspoken*. Licensed for the Globe Theatre, 11 June 1958.
49 Dominic Shellard, *British Theatre Since the War* (London: Yale University Press, 1999), p. 58.
50 Reader's Report by Heriot, 5 May 1958. See LCP CORR: 1958/1017: *A Taste of Honey*. Licensed for Theatre Royal, Stratford East, 15 May 1958. Revised version licensed for Wyndhams Theatre (1959/1714: *A Taste of Honey*) on 9 February 1959.
51 Undated comment—probably written by Gwatkin. See LCP CORR: 1958/1017: *A Taste of Honey*.
52 Letter from Nugent to Scarbrough, 22 August 1958, and undated newspaper article. See RA LC/GEN/440/60: 'Question in the House as to Abolition of Censorship and Possible Action Viz a Viz the Comedy Theatre Scheme'.

53   All quotations taken from text of play as published: Joan Henry, 'Look on Tempests', *Plays and Players*, July 1960.
54   Sonnet CXVI, 'Let me not to the marriage of true minds admit impediment ...'
55   Sinfield, *Out on Stage*, p. 249, n. 4.
56   For all discussion here see LCP CORR: 1959/256: *Look on Tempests*, and also 1959/515. Originally licence approved for the Globe Theatre, 6 October 1959. Revised version licensed for Theatre Royal, Brighton, 22 December 1959.
57   For all correspondence and minutes see RA LC/GEN/440/58: 'Consideration by Home Office', n. 1.
58   *The Times*, 21 November 1958, p. 9.
59   Mrs Jean Mann (Coatbridge and Airdrie); see House of Commons Parliamentary Debates 1958–1959, volume 596, 24 November to 5 December, columns 454–57.
60   F.J. Bellenger, MP for Bassetlaw. See House of Commons Parliamentary Debates 1958–1959, volume 596, 24 November to 5 December, column 419.
61   *Daily Mail*, 7 November 1958, p. 3
62   Wilson, 'Morality', n. 4.

Chapter 5

1   Reader's Report by Troubridge, 6 March 1958. See LCP CORR: 1958/867: *A Resounding Tinkle*.
2   Letter to Scarbrough from his secretary Hill, September 1959. See LCP CORR: 1959/55: *The Hostage*.
3   Reader's Report by Dearmer, 21 December 1957: 1957/603: *Beth*.
4   From the unpublished manuscript of *You Won't Always Be on Top*. See LCP 1957/43.
5   For all correspondence and reports see LCP CORR: 1957/351: *You Won't Always Be on Top*.
6   Unidentified review. See LCP CORR: 1957/351: *You Won't Always Be on Top*.
7   Letter dated 4 December 1957. See LCP CORR: 1957/271: *Flowering Cherry*.
8   LCP CORR: 1957/351: *You Won't Always Be on Top*.
9   In a letter to the Lord Chamberlain of 26 September 1959, discussing complaints about Theatre Workshop's production of *The Hostage*. See LCP CORR: 1958/1359: *The Hostage*.
10   See LCP CORR: 1957/351: *You Won't Always Be on Top*.
11   *Daily Mail*, 17 April 1958, p. 5.
12   Speech as reported in, for example, *News Chronicle*, 17 April 1958, p. 5 ('Theatre Men Fined for Altering Play').
13   See, for example, *Daily Worker*, 17 April 1958, p. 3 ('Theatre is Fined for Imitating Churchill').
14   *Daily Herald*, 17 April 1958, p. 2.
15   *Glasgow Herald*, 17 April 1958, p. 6 ('From London: The Censor's Critics').
16   *Daily Mirror*, 18 April 1958, p. 4 ('The St James's Eavesdroppers').
17   LCP CORR: 1957/351: *You Won't Always Be on Top*.
18   See LCP CORR: 1956/8932: *Look Back in Anger*. Licensed for the Royal Court, 28 March 1956.
19   Reader's Report by Troubridge, 10 March 1957. See LCP CORR: 1957/10041: *The Entertainer*. Licensed for the Royal Court, 5 April 1957.
20   Letter from Assistant Comptroller to the Town Clerk of Sutton, 17 May 1965,

detailing the required endorsements and cuts. See LCP CORR: 1959/1721: *The Entertainer.*

21   LCP CORR: 1957/10041: *The Entertainer.*

22   Reader's Report by Troubridge, 2 March 1957. See LCP CORR: 1957/9996: *Fin de Partie.*

23   Letter confirming a licence would be issued, 13 March 1957. See LCP CORR: 1957/9996. *Fin de Partie.*

24   See LCP CORR: 1957/578: *Endgame.*

25   Harold Hobson, 'Annus Mirabilis', *Sunday Times*, 9 February 1958, p. 23.

26   For all correspondence and discussion see LCP CORR: 1957/578: *Endgame.* The licence was offered in early August 1958, but not issued as required until October.

27   See LCP CORR: 1958/1309: *Krapp's Last Tape.* Submitted on 17 September 1958 and licensed for the Royal Court on 15 October.

28   Reader's Report by Troubridge, 2 March 1957. See LCP CORR: 1957/9996: *Fin de Partie.*

29   See LCP CORR: 1956/9633: *The Bald Primadonna.* Translated and adapted by Donald Watson, and licensed for the Cambridge Arts Theatre on 28 November 1956.

30   See LCP CORR: 1957/9795: *The Lesson.* Licensed for Oxford Playhouse, 14 January 1957.

31   See LCP CORR: 1957/32: *The Chairs.* Translated by Donald Watson, licensed for the Royal Court, 17 April 1957.

32   See LCP CORR: 1957/105: *Amédée.* Licensed for Cambridge Arts Theatre, 15 May 1957.

33   See LCP CORR: 1958/654: *Victims of Duty.* Licensed for Cambridge Arts Theatre, 20 January 1958.

34   Reader's Report by Heriot, 8 May 1957. See LCP CORR: *The Balcony.* WB (1960).

35   For all correspondence, discussions and endorsements see LCP CORR: *The Balcony.* WB (1960) and 1965/469: *The Balcony.* A licence was eventually issued to Cambridge's ADC theatre at the end of 1965.

36   Reader's Report by Troubridge, 1 October 1958. See LCP CORR: 1958/1359: *The Hostage.*

37   See LCP CORR: 1958/1359: *The Hostage.* Licensed for Theatre Royal, Stratford East, October 1958.

38   See the *Guardian*, 15 October 1958, p. 7; *Daily Telegraph*, 15 October 1958, p. 10; *Observer*, 19 October 1958, p. 19.

39   Harold Hobson, 'Triumph at Stratford East', *Sunday Times*, 19 October 1958, p. 21.

40   For all correspondence see LCP CORR: 1958/1359: *The Hostage.*

Chapter 6

1   Parliamentary debate 8 May 1958, responding to a question from Michael Foot asking whether there were plans to abolish censorship. See RA LC/GEN/440/58: 'Consideration by Home Office of Proposal to Amend the Theatres Act 1843 to Allow the Lord Chamberlain to Attach Conditions to his Stage Plays Licence not Adopted'.

2   Richard Findlater, 'Does Victoria STILL need the censor?', *Evening Standard*, 19 October 1956, p. 14.

3   See report on debate in *Manchester Guardian*, 15 November 1956, p. 10.

4   See LCP CORR: 1956/8760: *Rory Pavlova*. Written by J.A. Swanson, licensed for the Town Hall, Dingwall, 27 January.

5   See LCP CORR: 1957/9825: *Iron Duchess*. Licensed for Brighton Theatre Royal, 19/1/57. Originally submitted under the title *Cook General*.

6   See LCP CORR: 1956/9664: *Johnny Johnson*. Licensed for Woodford Youth Centre, 3 December 1956.

7   Reader's Report by Troubridge, 9 March 1958. See LCP CORR: 1958/843: *Shadow of Heroes*.

8   See, for example, the *Guardian*, 8 October 1958, p. 5; the *Observer*, 12 October 1958, p. 19; and the *Guardian*, 30 September 1958, p. 6.

9   See LCP CORR: 1958/843: *Shadow of Heroes*. Licensed for the Scala Theatre, 2 April 1958. In July, the title was changed to *Murder in Budapest*.

10 London Letter: New History Play', *Guardian*, 30 September 1958, p. 6.

11 See LCP CORR: 1958/843: *Shadow of Heroes*.

12 *Observer*, 12 October 1958, p. 19.

13 *Guardian*, 30 September 1958, p. 6.

14 Letter from Gwatkin to Professor H. Street, Faculty of Law Manchester University, 5 February 1962. See RA LC/GEN/440/62: 'Professor H. Street's Draft on Censorship for his Book on Civil Liberties Checked and Commented Upon'. Street devoted a section (pp. 53–68) to theatre censorship in Britain in his seminal book *Freedom, the Individual and the Law* (London: Penguin Books, 1963).

15 Dominic Shellard, Steve Nicholson and Miriam Handley, *The Lord Chamberlain Regrets: A History of British Theatre Censorship*. (London: British Library Publications, 2004), pp. 152–3.

16 Reader's Report by Geoffrey Dearmer, 15 May 1956. See LCP CORR: *Life of Christ* LR 18 May 1956. The script, by J.W. Branigan, was for a pageant to have been performed in Bradford's Odsal Stadium.

17 See LCP CORR: 1957/218: *The Road to Emmaus*. A licence was refused for the original version of James Forsyth's script in early June, and the revised version was licensed for Queen's Hall, Cuckfield, in late July.

18 See LCP CORR: 1958/1310: *Pobun*. Adapted by Olwyn Mears and licensed for the Town Hall, Langefni, 14 October 1958 'on the understanding that there is no physical representation of the Deity'.

19 See LCP CORR: 1959/1642: *Follow Me*. Troubridge was reporting on a revised version of this script by Tyrone Guthrie, a play originally licensed in 1932.

20 See LCP CORR: 1956/8797: *The Friend of God*. Written by Reverend G.A. Williams, licensed for Habergham School, Burnley, in February 1956.

21 See LCP CORR: 1957/9920: *The Leader*. Written by David Shellan, licensed for Beckenham Grand Hall in February 1957.

22 See LCP CORR: 1958/867: *A Resounding Tinkle*. Licensed for the Royal Court, 18 March 1958.

23 See LCP CORR: 1957/59: *The Making of Moo*. Licensed for the ESC at the Theatre Royal, Brighton, 9 May 1957.

24 See LCP CORR: 1956/9033: *The Rock*. A 'sincere and reverent' play by A.E. Green, licensed for South Benfleet Church Hall, in April 1956. And LCP CORR: 1956/8988: *The Power and the Glory*, licensed for the Phoenix Theatre in March 1956.

25 See LCP CORR: 1958/690: *Valmouth*. Licensed for the Royal Court on 23 August 1958.

26 See LCP CORR: 1959/1642: *Follow Me*. Licensed for Gateway Theatre, Edinburgh, 20 January 1959.

27 See LCP CORR: *Green Pastures* LR 13 June 1930.

28 See RA LC/GEN/512/56: 'Miss Walker Informed her Act can Only be Censored if Incorporated in a Stage Play'.

29 See LCP CORR: 1956/9329: *La Cirque De Paris*. Licensed for the Palace Theatre, Hull, 9 August 1956. The original title was *Les Nues de Paris*.

30 See LCP CORR: 1957/9803: *The Nude*. The script was submitted as a translation by Frank Goldstein and Edward J. Warne, from the French of Charles du Chastelet. It was licensed for the Norwich Hippodrome in January 1957.

31 See RA LC/GEN/440/57 'Town Clerk of Derby Given Advice as to Dealing with Indecent Performances by Road Shows'.

32 See LCP CORR: 1957/57: *Showgirls*. Submitted by R. Howard Arundel. and Jack Gilham Entertainments Ltd, licensed for the Royal Court in Warrington, May 1957.

33 Unidentified newspaper cutting. See RA LC/GEN/512/56: 'A Nude at Camberwell Palace Moves when a Mouse Runs Over the Stage'.

34 See LCP CORR: 1956/8903: *A Girl Called Sadie*. Written by David Kirk (i.e. Eugene Hamilton), licensed for Preston Hippodrome, March 1956.

35 See LCP CORR: 1956/9319: *Free Love*. Written by Jack Bradley, licensed for the Palace Theatre in Reading, July 1956.

36 See LCP CORR: 1957/104: *Odd Man In*. Written by Claude Magnier, adapted by Robin Maugham. Licensed for the Theatre Royal, Brighton, May 1957.

37 See LCP CORR: 1956/8861: *Vampires from Venus*. Written by Dominic Roche, licensed for Manchester Hippodrome, 24 February 1956.

38 See LCP CORR: 1957/454: *Crime on Goat Island*. Translated by Henry Reed, licensed for Oxford Playhouse, 28 November 1957.

39 See LCP CORR: 1958/1429: *Judith*. Licensed for the Clarendon Press Institute, Oxford, 10 November 1958.

40 See LCP CORR: 1957/606: *Man Beast and Virtue*. Translated by E. Eager, licensed for the Theatre Royal, Stratford East, January 1958.

41 See LCP CORR 1957/9926: *Camino Real*. Licensed for the Phoenix Theatre, London, March 1957.

42 Letter to the Lord Chamberlain's Office. See LCP CORR 1957/9926: *Camino Real*.

43 See LCP CORR: 1956/9372: *Lysistrata*. Licensed for Oxford Playhouse Theatre, August 1956.

44 Quotation from the *Sunday Dispatch*, used in the programme for the production.

45 *Illustrated London News*, 1 March 1958; *Sunday Times*, 23 February 1958.

46 See LCP CORR: 1956/9372: *Lysistrata*.

47 *Daily Telegraph*, 5 March 1958, p. 1. and *Daily Mail*, 5 March 1958, p. 1.

48 See LCP CORR: 1956/9372: *Lysistrata*.

49 Letter from the Assistant Comptroller to the English Stage Company, 9 April 1958. See RA LC/GEN/440/58: 'Lord Chamberlain Declines to be Represented at Debate on Censorship Organised by English Stage Society at Royal Court Theatre'.

50 See RA LC/GEN/440/58: 'Proposed Visit of a Deputation Led by the Earl of Harewood to Discuss Censorship Problems with the Lord Chamberlain'.

51 Reader's Report by Troubridge, 2 May 1956. See LCP CORR: 1956/9158: *The Quare Fellow*. Licensed for the Theatre Royal, Stratford East, 1 June 1956.

52 See LCP CORR: 1958/1289: *Who Done Hugh Dunnett*. Licensed for Royal Naval Barracks, Portsmouth, 14 October 1958.
53 See LCP CORR: 1956/9245: *My Fair Lady*. Script by Alan J. Lerner, submitted by H.M. Tennent Ltd, licensed for the Globe Theatre, 27 May 1956.
54 See LCP CORR: 1957/479: *Dick Whittington*. Written by David Poulson, licensed for the New Theatre, Bromley, 26 December 1957.
55 See LCP CORR: 1958/629: *Epitaph for George Dillon*. Licensed for the Royal Court, 21 January 1958.
56 See LCP CORR: 1958/1084: *Chicken Soup with Barley*. Licensed for the Coventry Belgrade Theatre, 6 June 1958.
57 See LCP CORR: 1956/9764: *The Typewriter*. Licensed for the Green Room Theatre, Manchester, 31 December 1956.
58 See LCP CORR: 1958/1397: *West Side Story*. Licensed for Manchester Opera House, 13 November 1958.
59 See LCP CORR: 1957/489: *Expresso Bongo*. Written by Wolf Mankowitz and Julian More, and licensed for the Savoy Theatre, 31 December 1957.
60 See LCP CORR: 1959/1836: *The World of Paul Slickey*.

Chapter 7

1 'Where Can I Take Aunt Edna?: Cecil Wilson Conducts An Inquiry Into The Sordid State of the British Theatre', *Daily Mail*, 2 November 1959, p. 6
2 Letter from Gwatkin to Troubridge, 6 February 1960. See LCP CORR: 1960/535: *The Lily White Boys*.
3 *Guardian*, 24 April 1959, p. 3.
4 'Where Can I Take Aunt Edna?', *Daily Mail*, 2 November 1959.
5 Angus Wilson, 'Morality', *International Theatre Annual*, Number 4 (London, John Calder, 1959), p. 184.
6 See LCP CORR: 1959/132: *Aunt Edwina*. Licensed for Devonshire Park, Eastbourne, 11 August 1959.
7 From the unpublished manuscript of *Aunt Edwina*. See LCP 1959/34.
8 See LCP CORR: 1959/132: *Aunt Edwina*.
9 See LCP CORR: 1959/458: *The Birds and the Bees*. Licensed for the Lyric Theatre, 21 December 1959.
10 From the unpublished manuscript of *The Birds and the Bees*. See LCP 1959/55.
11 See LCP CORR: 1959/458: *The Birds and the Bees*.
12 Unpublished manuscript of *The Birds and the Bees*.
13 See LCP CORR: 1959/30: *Ross*. Licensed to H.M. Tennent for the Globe Theatre, 3 November 1959.
14 See LCP CORR: 1959/1733: *Fings Ain't What They Used To Be*. Licensed for the Theatre Royal, Stratford East, 17 February 1959.
15 For all details here see LCP CORR: 1958/1359: *The Hostage*; and 1959/55: *The Hostage*. The original script was licensed for the Theatre Royal, Stratford East, on 21 October 1958, and the revised version for Wyndhams Theatre on 24 June 1959.
16 See LCP CORR: 1959/1939: *The Ginger Man*. Licensed for the New Theatre, Hull, 14 September 1959.
17 See *News Chronicle*, 11 September 1959, p. 3.
18 See LCP CORR: 1959/1939: *The Ginger Man*.
19 John Osborne, *Almost a Gentleman* (London, Faber and Faber, 1991), p. 116.

20   See LCP CORR: 1959/1836: *The World of Paul Slickey*. Licensed for the Palace Theatre, Bournemouth, 10 April 1959.

21   Osborne, *Almost a Gentleman*, p. 118.

22   See LCP CORR: 1959/1836: *The World of Paul Slickey*.

23   *Daily Mail*, 29 December 1958, p. 3.

24   *Daily Sketch*, 8 April 1959, p. 15; quoted in Osborne, *Almost a Gentleman*, p. 122.

25   John Russell Taylor, *Anger and After* (London: Methuen, 1962), p. 49.

26   *Daily Mail*, 14 April 1959, p. 3.

27   Osborne, *Almost a Gentleman*, p. 123.

28   *Daily Mail*, 14 April 1959, p. 3 (Edward Goring, 'Slickey Takes the Mickey Among the Upper Crust').

29   *Daily Mail*, 15 April 1959, p. 1 ('Nine Curtains but Some Snub Slickey') and p. 16. (Paul Tanfield, 'My World Was Never Like This').

30   For all details here see LCP CORR: 1959/1836: *The World of Paul Slickey*.

31   See Osborne, *Almost a Gentleman*, p. 127.

32   See LCP CORR: 1959/1836: *The World of Paul Slickey*.

33   Mervyn Jones, '*Paul Slickey* puts the Establishment under the Knife', *Tribune*, 17 April 1959, p. 5. Cited in Malcolm Page, *File on Osborne* (London, Methuen, 1988), p. 26. The article was published before the London opening.

34   *Observer*, 10 May 1959, p. 16.

35   *The Times*, 6 May 1959, p. 15.

36   Osborne, *Almost a Gentleman*, p. 126.

37   *Evening Standard*, 6 May 1959.

38   See LCP CORR: 1957/9814: *At the Drop of a Hat*. Licensed for the Fortune Theatre, 17 January 1957.

39   For all details here see RA LC/GEN/440/59: 'Mr Stephen Joseph of Studio Theatre Ltd Informed that the Art of Improvisatore Would be Illegal if Performed for Hire'.

40   Extracts taken from the text of André Davis's *Four Men* published in Kenneth Tynan (ed.), *The Observer Plays* (London: Faber and Faber, n.d.), p. 437.

41   *Ibid.*, p. 466.

42   See LCP CORR: 1959/1927: *Four Men*. Licensed for the Century Theatre, Wolverhampton, 13 April 1959.

43   See LCP CORR: 1959/469: *Cloud Over the Morning*. Written by T.B. Morris. Licensed for Cripplegate Theatre, 10 December 1959.

44   See LCP CORR: 1959/115: *Why the Chicken*. Licensed for Cranston Street Hall, Edinburgh, 17 August 1959.

45   See LCP CORR: 1959/171: *Serjeant Musgrave's Dance*. Licensed for the Royal Court, 25 September 1959.

46   See LCP CORR: 1959/300: *A Glimpse of the Sea*. Licensed for the Lyric Theatre, Hammersmith, 9 November 1959.

47   See LCP CORR: 1959/299: *Last Day in Dreamland*. Licensed for the Lyric Theatre, Hammersmith, 9 November 1959.

48   From the unpublished manuscript of *The World of Suzie Wong*. See LCP 1959/42.

49   See LCP CORR: 1959/38: *The Crooked Mile*. Licensed for Manchester Opera House, 26 June 1959.

50   See LCP CORR: 1959/248: *The World of Suzie Wong*. Licensed for the Prince of Wales's Theatre, 27 October 1959.

51   'Where Can I Take Aunt Edna?', *Daily Mail*, 2 November 1959.

52 Where Can We Take Our Teenagers', *Daily Mail*, 5 November 1959, p. 6.
53 See: RA LC/GEN/440/59: 'Mrs Bellamy Complains that her Husband Frequents Strip Tease Clubs in Soho'.
54 See LCP CORR: 1960/535: *The Lily White Boys*.

Afterword

1 Arnold Wesker, 'Living-room Revolt', *Guardian*, 26 January 2008, p. 14 ('Review Section').
2 Peter Hall in a personal interview with the author about theatre censorship, October 2007.
3 See RA LC/GEN/440/60: 'Mrs Fitz-Henry and Other Ladies Deplore the Falling Standards of Morality'.

Biographies

1 Obituary of Lord Scarbrough, *The Times*, 30 June 1969, p. 16.
2 Obituary of Lord Nugent, *The Times*, 30 April 1973, p. 16. See also a further obituary in *The Times*, 11 May 1973, p. 22.
3 Further obituary of Nugent published in *The Times*, 19 May 1973, p. 16.
4 Obituary of Gwatkin, *The Times*, 4 August 1971, p. 12.
5 See General Sir David Fraser, *Wars and Shadows: Memoirs of General Sir David Fraser* (London: Allen Lane, 2002). Also http://members.chello.nl/~h.w.a.schutte2/operation.htm
6 Obituary of Gwatkin, *The Times*, 4 August 1971, p. 12.
7 See the History of the Settlement Players, a group based in Letchworth: http://www.settlement-players.org.uk/html/golden_jubilee.html
8 For obituaries of Troubridge see *The Times*, 18 December 1963, p. 12, and 27 December 1963, p. 10, and especially Basil Francis, 'St Vincent Troubridge, Soldier and Scholar, 1895–1964, *Theatre Notebook*, Volume 9, no. 2, Winter 1964/65, pp. 66–8.

Select Bibliography

Archival Material

The Lord Chamberlain's Correspondence Files (Manuscript Room, British Library)
Lord Chamberlain's Office Files (Royal Archive, Windsor)
The Lord Chamberlain's Collection of Licensed Plays 1900–1968 (Manuscript Room, British Library)
Annual Reports of the Public Morality Council
Production Files (V&A Theatre and Performance Collections Archives)
Hansard's Parliamentary Debates

Books, Articles and Unpublished Dissertations

NB   Not including playscripts.

Aldgate, Anthony and Robertson, James C., *Censorship in Theatre and Cinema* (Edinburgh: Edinburgh University Press, 2005)

Billington, Michael. *State of the Nation: British Theatre Since 1945* (London: Faber and Faber, 2007)

Brown, Ivor (ed.), *Theatre, 1954–55* (London: Max Reinhardt, 1955)

Brown, Ivor (ed.), *Theatre, 1955–56* (London: Max Reinhardt, 1956)

Chandos, John, pseud. [i.e. John Lithgow Chandos MacConnell], *To Deprave and Corrupt: Original studies in the Nature and Definition of Obscenity* (London: Souvenir Press, 1962)

Childs, David, *Britain Since 1945: A Political History* (London: Routledge, 1997)

Chothia, Jean, *English Drama of the Early Modern Period, 1890–1940* (London: Longman, 1996)

Conolly, L.W., *The Censorship of English Drama, 1737–1824* (San Marino, California: Huntington Library, 1976)

Curtin, Kaier, *'We Can Always Call them Bulgarians': The Emergence of Lesbians and Gay Men on the American Stage* (Boston: Alyson Publications, 1987)

de Jongh, Nicholas, *Not in Front of the Audience: Homosexuality on Stage* (London: Routledge, 1992)

de Jongh, Nicholas, *Politics, Prudery and Perversions: The Censoring of the English Stage 1901–1968* (London: Methuen, 2000)

Etienne, Anne, 'Les Coulisses de Lord Chamberlain: La Censure Théâtrale de 1900 à 1968'. Ph.D. dissertation, L'Université d'Orleans, 1999

Findlater, Richard, *Banned!: A Review of Theatrical Censorship in Britain* (London: MacGibbon & Kee, 1967)

Findlater, Richard (ed.), *The Twentieth Century*, Volume 169, No. 1008, February 1961

Florance, John Allan, 'Theatrical Censorship in Britain 1901–1968'. Ph.D. dissertation, University of Wales, 1980

Freshwater, Helen, *Theatre Censorship in Britain: Silencing, Censure and Suppression* (Basingstoke: Palgrave Macmillan, 2009)

Hennessy, Peter, *Having it So Good: Britain in the Fifties* (London: Allen Lane, 2006)

Hobson, Harold (ed.), *International Theatre Annual No. 1* (London: John Calder, 1956)

Hobson, Harold (ed.), *International Theatre Annual No. 2* (London: John Calder, 1957)

Hobson, Harold (ed.), *International Theatre Annual No. 3* (London: John Calder, 1958)

Hobson, Harold (ed.), *International Theatre Annual No. 4* (London: John Calder, 1959)

Houchin, John, *Censorship of the American Theatre in the Twentieth Century* (Cambridge: Cambridge University Press, 2003)

Johnston, John, *The Lord Chamberlain's Blue Pencil* (London: Hodder & Stoughton, 1990)

Lawrence, D.H., *Sex, Literature and Censorship*, edited by Harry T. Moore (London: Heinemann, 1955)

Marowitz, Charles, *et al.*, *New Theatre Voices of the Fifties and Sixties* (London: Methuen, 1981)

Marowitz, Charles, *et al.*, *Encore Reader: A Chronicle of the New Drama* (London: Methuen, 1965)

Marr, Andrew, *A History of Modern Britain* (London: Macmillan, 2007)

Morgan, Kenneth O., *The People's Peace: British History, 1945–1990* (London: Oxford University Press, 1990)

Nicholson, Steve, *The Censorship of British Drama, 1900–1968: Volume One: 1900–1932* (Exeter: University of Exeter Press, 2003)

Nicholson, Steve, *The Censorship of British Drama, 1900–1968: Volume Two: 1933–1952* (Exeter: University of Exeter Press, 2005)

Norman, Frank, *Why Fings Went West: A Time Remembered* (London: Lemon Tree Press, 1975)

O'Higgins, Paul, *Censorship in Britain* (London: Nelson, 1972)

Osborne, John, *Almost a Gentleman: An Autobiography* (London: Faber and Faber, 1991)

Osborne, John, *Damn You, England* (London: Faber and Faber, 1994)

Rebellato, Dan, *1956 And All That: The Making of Modern British Drama* (London: Routledge, 1999)

Roberts, Philip, *The Royal Court and the Modern Stage* (London: Cambridge University Press, 1999)

Sandbrook, Dominic, *Never Had It So Good: A History of Britain from Suez to the Beatles* (London: Abacus, 2006)

Shellard, Dominic (ed.), *British Theatre in the 1950s* (Sheffield: Sheffield Academic Press, 2000)

Shellard, Dominic, *British Theatre Since the War* (New Haven: Yale University Press, 2000)

Shellard, Dominic, Nicholson, Steve, and Handley, Miriam, *The Lord Chamberlain Regrets* (London: British Library Publications, 2004)

Shellard, Dominic, *Kenneth Tynan: A Life* (London: Yale University Press, 2003)

Sinfield, Alan, *Out on Stage: Lesbian and Gay Theatre in the Twentieth Century.* (London: Yale University Press, 1999)

Sked, Alan, and Cook, Chris, *Post-War Britain: A Political History* (Harmondsworth: Penguin, 1979)

Smith, Malcolm, *Britain and 1940: History, myth and popular memory* (London: Routledge, 2000)

Stephens, John Russell, *The Censorship of English Drama, 1824–1901* (Cambridge: Cambridge University Press, 1980)

Street, Henry, *Freedom, the Individual and the Law* (Harmondsworth: Penguin, 1963)

Thomas, David, Carlton, David and Etienne, Anne, *Theatre Censorship: from Walpole to Wilson* (Oxford: Oxford University Press, 2007)

Travis, Allen, *Bound and Gagged: A Secret History of Obscenity in Britain* (London: Profile Books Ltd, 2000)

Tribe, David, *Questions of Censorship* (London: George Allen and Unwin, 1973)

Tynan, Kenneth, *Theatre Writings* [selected and edited by Dominic Shellard] (London: Nick Hern Books, 2007)

Wearing, J.P., *The London Stage, 1950–1959: A Calendar of Plays and Players*, 2 volumes (London: Scarecrow Press, 1993)

Wolfenden, Sir John, Report of the Committee on Homosexual Offences and Prostitution (London: HMSO, 1957)

Index